From Crisis to Austerity

Neoliberalism, Organized Labour, and the Canadian State

Edited by: Tim Fowler

QUILL BOOKS

© Red Quill Books Ltd. 2013
Ottawa

www.redquillbooks.com
ISBN 978-1-926958-23-1

∞ ✪

Printed on acid-free paper. The paper used in this book incorporates post-consumer waste and has not been sourced from endangered old growth forests, forests of exceptional conservation value or the Amazon Basin. Red Quill Books subscribes to a one-book-at-a-time manufacturing process that substantially lessens supply chain waste, reduces greenhouse emissions, and conserves valuable natural resources.

Library and Archives Canada Cataloguing in Publication

From crisis to austerity : neoliberalism, organized labour, and the Canadian state / edited by Tim Fowler.

Includes bibliographical references.
ISBN 978-1-926958-23-1

1. Recessions—Canada—History—21st century. 2. Financial crises—Canada—History—21st century. 3. Canada—Economic conditions—21st century. 4. Canada—Economic policy—1991-. 5. Canada—Politics and government—2006-. 6. Labor unions—Canada—History—21st century. 7. Working class—Canada—History—21st century. 8. Neoliberalism—Canada. I. Fowler, Tim, 1983-

HC115.F756 2012   330.971'073   C2012-907636-8

QUILL BOOKS

RQB is a radical publishing house.
Part of the proceeds from the sale of this book will support student scholarships.

TABLE OF CONTENTS

Section III:
Long Term Responses and Solutions to Crisis

FROM CRISIS TO AUSTERITY: AN INTRODUCTION

Tim Fowler[1]

Neoliberal capitalism came into crisis in late 2007. The most recent crisis of capitalism, dubbed 'The Great Recession,' was experienced to various degrees in different countries. Many analysts have noted that while Canada did, of course, experience the Great Recession, the recession was not as deep in Canada as in other countries. They have pointed to large, concentrated banks, tighter bank regulations, and government financial support for capital in the form of stimulus spending, among other policy instruments. While Canada may not have been hit as hard as other countries, the Canadian state did engage in austerity measures targeted at trade unions and the broader working class during the recession, ostensibly to help speed along Canada's recovery. This book sits at the intersection of the crisis of capitalism, the state's response to the crisis, and the Canadian labour movement. It seeks to investigate the root causes of the crisis in Canada, and to understand the Canadian state's response to the crisis. It also provides a discussion of how the labour movement has experienced the crisis, responded to the crisis, and responded to the Canadian state's response. The purpose of this introduction is to provide a brief overview of the themes and arguments in the book. As such, the crisis tendencies of capitalism, the role the state plays in a capitalist society, the political economy of neoliberalism, and union renewal efforts will all briefly be discussed.

---

[1]   I would like to thank the George Rigakos at Red Quill, as well as the two anonymous reviewers, for their comments on this chapter.

A good deal of critical-left literature has already been generated on the most recent crisis of capitalism.[2] This literature, however, has tended to provide theoretical overviews of the crisis, detailing how capitalism is prone to crisis of over-accumulation and falling rates of profit. Much of the literature has also been centred around the United States, where the crisis first occurred. The literature on the Great Recession has convincingly shown that capitalism is a system prone to crisis. The neoliberal era emerged out of the crisis of the Keynesian era, and as McNally demonstrates, helped to restore profitability rates for capital after 1982. This restoration of profitability was accomplished almost exclusively on the backs of the working class as wages stagnated, hours of work increased, job security eroded, and unions fell into defensive and concessionary positions. That recovery for capital, itself prone to regular regionalized crises (notably in finance), was not, and could not be permanent. In the relentless drive for expanding profits, capital increased productivity, displacing workers from manufacturing jobs, and created vast surplus capacity. As rates of profit in manufacturing declined, capital gorged on financial speculation ultimately leading to the bursting of speculative bubbles that crashed the system in 2007/08. As is usual under conditions of general crisis, the response by the ruling class and their apologists has been to attempt to reassert profitability by increasing the rate of exploitation of workers.

State response to the crisis has been varied between nations, but virtually all state responses have had the theme of austerity. Part of the general response by states to the Great Recession has been to introduce austerity measures which the working class has

---

[2]   The following is a very limited overview of some of the critical-left literature produced about the Great Recession. It is certainly not an exhaustive list, but it does provide some of the best writing on the crisis: Greg Albo, Sam Gindin, and Leo Panitch, *In and Out of Crisis: The Global Financial Meltdown and Left Alternatives* (Oakland: PM Press, 2010); John Bellamy Foster and Fred Magdoff, *The Great Financial Crisis: Causes and Consequences* (New York: Monthly Review Press, 2009); David Harvey, *The Enigma of Capital and the Crises of Capitalism* (Oxford: Oxford University Press, 2010); David McNally, *Global Slump: The Economics and Politics of Crisis and Resistance* (Oakland: PM Press, 2011); Leo Panitch, Greg Albo, and Vivek Chibber, eds., *The Crisis This Time: Socialist Register 2011*; and Murray E. G. Smith, *Global Capitalism in Crisis: Karl Marx and the Decay of the Profit System* (Halifax: Fernwood, 2010).

felt the brunt of. States have further rolled back welfare state provisions, attacked the freedoms of trade unions, and have done so while cutting corporate tax rates and providing "bailout" money to manufacturing and financial capital. The working classes have directly felt the impact of these austerity measures, as welfare state spending, changes to (un)employment insurance, and restrictions on trade union freedoms dramatically affect the material conditions of these classes. If the Great Recession can be interpreted as a crisis of neoliberal capitalism, the response has been lock step with neoliberal theory - supply side economics and restrictions on collective economic action have been the guiding principles of state responses to crisis.[3]

Capitalist Crisis & The State

A general understanding of the nature of the capitalist state can be found in Marx and Engels' *Communist Manifesto*. The earliest Marxist theory of the state can be found in this oft-cited passage from *Manifesto*: 'the executive of the modern state is but a committee for managing the common affairs of the whole bourgeoisie.'[4] The capitalist state has an essential class character: it is an institution of the capitalist class, and is but one tool used by the bourgeoisie to maintain the capitalist mode of production. Marxist theories of the state have since evolved, but the general understanding by Marxists is that the state retains its essential class character.[5] While

---

[3]   While Marx himself never developed a full theory of the functioning of the state in capitalist society (the closest to a full theory, perhaps, can be found in his essay *The Eighteenth Brumaire of Louis Bonaparte*), the functioning of the state in the capitalist mode of production has nonetheless been a topic of interest to Marxist theory. Debates about the function of the state, as well as arguments about the relative autonomy of the state, have been fleshed out by many scholars, including the discussions between Poulantzas and Miliband. Of particular interest are Ralph Miliband, *The State in Capitalist Society* (Halifax: Fernwood Publishing, 2009 [1969]); Nicos Poulantzas, "The Problem of the Capitalist State," *New Left Review* 58 (November - December 1969): 67 – 78; and Ralph Miliband, "The Capitalist State: A Reply to Nicos Poulantzas," *New Left Review* 59 (January - February 1970): 53 – 60.

[4]   Karl Marx and Friedrich Engels, *The Communist Manifesto* (New York: Washington Square Press, 1964), 61.

[5]   For a good overview of the development of critical theories of the state see Martin Carnoy, *The State and Political Theory* (Princeton: Princeton University Press, 1984).

the current state is a capitalist state, and inherently works for the interests of the capitalist class, the functionality of the state is not as cut and dry as Marx and Engels suggested.

Leo Panitch, writing on the role and nature of the Canadian state, has noted that capitalist states retain a degree of relative autonomy from the capitalist class. Simply, the state must maintain a certain degree of autonomy from the capitalist class: the state acts on *behalf* of the capitalist class, not at their *behest*.[6] The capitalist state cannot simply act at the behest of the capitalist class, for if it did, the state would become 'dysfunctional to it managing the common affairs of that class.'[7] The degree of autonomy that the capitalist state has from the capitalist class allows the state to act in the *long term* interests of the capitalist class, rather than dealing with short term demands from the capitalist class. For example, measures that may increase capitalist profitability in the short term could lead to long term decline of profits. We can point to bare-bones environmental regulations, for example, of the tension between short term and long term goals of the capitalist class. In the short term, environmental regulations are a barrier to capitalist accumulation; in the long term they serve to maintain an adequate supply of natural resources which, in turn, maintains the long term profitability of capitalism. Further, should the state lay bare its essential class character, this may have the unintended consequence of sharpening class consciousness among the working class.

The state must navigate these contradictions. Panitch, drawing on James O'Connor, has outlined main functions of the capitalist state: accumulation, legitimization, and coercion.[8] The primary roles of the capitalistic state are to 'maintain or create the conditions in which profitable capital accumulation is possible. However, the state also must try to maintain or create the conditions for social harmony. A capitalist state that openly uses its coercive forces to help one class accumulate capital at the expense of other classes loses its legitimacy.'[9] The primary function of the state is to create and maintain the conditions for

---

6   Leo Panitch, "The Role and Nature of the Canadian State," in *The Canadian State: Political Economy and Political Power*, ed. Leo Panitch (Toronto: University of Toronto Press, 1977), 4.
7   Ibid.
8   Ibid.,8; James O'Connor, *The Fiscal Crisis of the State* (New York: St. Martin's Press, 1973).
9   Panitch, "The Role and Nature of the Canadian State," 8.

high levels of profitable accumulation. However, in pursuit of these conditions, the state cannot appear to be acting within the interests of one class alone, and thus must appear legitimate.

The legitimation function plays out in a number of different ways, but it does so primarily through legislative advancements that benefit the working class: socialized health care, unemployment insurance, retirement security, a minimum wage, and health and safety legislation are all examples of the legitimation function at work. Indeed, the functions of welfare state programming have a dual role in capitalism. First, these programs play into the legitimation function; but, secondly, they also ensure the long term survival and reproduction of the working class. This implies that the legitimation function also ensures long term accumulation for the capitalist class.

The final function of the capitalist state is that of coercion. The state can use its monopoly over the use of force to maintain social order and capitalist accumulation. The coercion function is, perhaps, the easiest to identify. The capitalist state uses this function to quell social unrest which may challenge legitimation: the police force is used, at times, to escort replacement workers across picket lines, to break up protests, and to provide physical protection to private property. The state must use the coercion function sparingly, however, lest it risk undermining its own legitimacy.

The Canadian state has always been active in encouraging trade and economic activity within Canada, promoting the growth of national markets.[10] In an era of neoliberal globalization the accumulation function of the Canadian state has taken a different form. While internal trade and economic growth are still important fiscal policies, the Canadian state has shifted away from primarily promoting national markets, instead pursuing the 'elimination of borders between the Canadian economy and the rest of the world.'[11] This echoes Bob Jessop's more general theory of states

---

[10]   See Gregory Albo and Jane Jenson, "A Contested Concept: The Relative Autonomy of the State" in *The New Canadian Political Economy*, eds. Wallace Clement and Glen Williams (Kingston: McGill-Queens University Press, 1989) for an overview of the developments in and theories of the political-economy of the Canadian state.

[11]   Gregory Albo and Jane Jenson, "Remapping Canada: The State in an Era of Globalization" in *Understanding Canada: Building on the New Canadian Political Economy*, ed. Wallace Clement (Kingston: McGill-Queens University Press, 1997), 215.

under globalization which argues that one of the key functions of the capitalist state in globalization is to manage the 'insertion of the national economy into the global economy in hope of securing some net benefit from internationalization.'[12]

During the Great Recession, the three functions of the Canadian state were laid bare. The primary role of the Canadian state during this time was to ensure capitalist profitability. This was done, primarily, through the use of short term infrastructure spending by the federal government - the Canada Action Plan. The Action Plan involved spending stimulus dollars on 'shovel ready' infrastructure projects, in the hopes of kick-starting the economy. This stimulus spending was coupled with neoliberal fiscal policies, namely corporate tax cuts, which were introduced at both the federal and various provincial levels. The Canadian government, and various provincial governments, also engaged in austerity measures aimed at curbing government spending, also in the name of sound economic management. The austerity measures ranged from cutbacks to social spending to government mandated wage freezes on public sector employees. At the same time that governments were engaged in public sector austerity, these same governments ensured the viability of many private sector firms. For example, the faltering automotive sector received millions in government loans from the Canadian and Ontario governments. During the height of the Great Recession, the Canadian government ensured the necessary conditions were in place for both the short and long term profitability of capital. In doing so, it introduced austerity measures which were largely felt by the Canadian working class.

One of the main features of the Canadian legitimation function, the welfare state, has slowly been eroded since the onset of neoliberal policies in Canada. It would be very difficult for the Canadian state to completely do away with welfare state provisions in one fell swoop, as this would severely undermine the legitimacy of the Canadian state. Besides slowly dismantling the welfare state, the Canadian state has acted to *delegitimize* those forces that act as a barrier to capitalist accumulation. In this case, the target of the Canadian state has been the Canadian labour movement. The

---

[12]   Bob Jessop, "Towards a Schumpeterian Workfare State? Preliminary Remarks on Post-Fordist Political Economy," *Studies in Political Economy* 40 (Spring 1993):14.

neoliberal era in Canada has been characterized, in part, by an assault on trade union freedoms. Panitch and Swartz argue that the Canadian state has been increasingly willing to use coercive measures to restrict the rights of unions, and in doing so have painted these coercive measures as 'temporary' exceptions to otherwise free collective bargaining.[13] During the Great Recession, the Canadian state has delegitimized trade unions, 'portraying them as obsolete islands of inefficiency in the market, and portraying union members as overpaid, underproductive, and, in the case of public sector unions, as a drain on the tax base.'[14] This has allowed the coercive activities of the state - interfering in collective bargaining, restricting trade union freedoms, and ordering striking workers back-to-work - to appear perfectly legitimate.[15]

Neoliberalism, The Assault on Unions, and The Politics of Inequality

Neoliberalism can be understood as a form of class warfare; as a political and economic theory, neoliberalism 'proposes that human well-being can be best advanced by liberating individual entrepreneurial freedoms and skills within an institutional framework characterized by strong private property rights, free markets and free trade.'[16] In practice, neoliberalism has been 'a project to achieve the restoration of class power'[17] by the capitalist class, an attempt to restore whatever power was lost during the era of Fordist Keynesianism. In order to restore class power, neoliberal policies have involved a sustained assault on trade unions, and a

---

[13]   Leo Panitch and Donald Swartz, *From Consent to Coercion: The Assault on Trade Union Freedoms, third edition* (Aurora: Garamond Press, 2003).

[14]   Tim Fowler, "Working for the Clampdown: How the Canadian State Exploits Economic Crises to Restrict Labour Freedoms," *Studies in Political Economy* 88 (Autumn 2011): 81.

[15]   During the Great Recession, the Canadian state took the virtually unprecedented move of interfering in free *private sector* collective bargaining, between the Canadian Autoworkers union and the 'big three' auto manufacturers. This was followed, in the wake of the newly elected Conservative majority at the federal level, of the federal government ending or threatening to end three legal labour disputes in a row with back-to-work legislation in the name of maintaining economic stability.

[16]   David Harvey, *A Brief History of Neoliberalism* (Oxford: Oxford University Press, 2005), 2.

[17]   Ibid., 16.

broader political-economic project designed to redistribute wealth *upwards,* away from the working class. One of the key achievements of neoliberalism has been the maximization of high incomes for the upper classes in society.[18]

Part of neoliberalism has involved a shift in the role of government to more blatantly support the accumulation function on behalf of capital. Besides enacting policies to help capital accumulation, neoliberal governments have enacted legislation, often surrounding tax policies, to shift income distribution towards the top income brackets. This has involved lowering the tax rate for the highest tax bracket, deregulation of the market, and tax breaks on investment. As Harvey argues, these policies 'began the momentous shift towards greater social inequality and the restoration of economic power to the upper class.'[19] Since the onset of neoliberal policies, the shift of income distribution towards the top has been sustained, and the share of income at the top has steadily increased. This has been done, in some cases, by the deliberate failure by governments to adapt public policies to the changing economy.[20] In other cases, this has been done by purposeful government policies designed to increase accumulation. When public policy changes to redistribute income upwards have occurred, these changes are frequently couched in the language of "trickle down" economic, so as to not upset the legitimacy of the state.[21]

A key component of neoliberal public policies has been a reorientation of government policy away from unions.[22] Neoliberals see unions as a barrier to flexibility and capitalist accumulation, so neoliberal policies seek to remove this barrier. Hence, the policies of neoliberalism have invariably involved attacks on trade union freedoms. The liberalism of neoliberalism has highlighted 'individual rather than collective approaches to economic and social

---

[18]   Gérard Duménil and Dominique Lévy, *The Crisis of Neoliberalism* (Cambridge: Harvard University Press, 2011), 18.

[19]   Harvey, *A Brief History of Neoliberalism,* 26.

[20]   Jacob S. Hacker and Paul Pierson, *Winner-Take-All Politics* (New York: Simon & Schuster, 2010), 43.

[21]   For an account of upward redistributive policies in Canada, see Stephen McBride and Heather Whiteside, *Private Affluence, Public Austerity: Economic Crisis & Democratic Malaise in Canada* (Halifax: Fernwood Publishing, 2011), Chapter 4.

[22]   Ibid., 59.

problems.'[23] This shift to individualism has cast unions as outdated and anachronistic at best, and at worst as a barrier to the ability for individuals to advance in the market. Besides this ideological assault, a very real legislative assault has taken place on trade unions: 'weakening, bypassing, or violently destroying the powers of organized labour is a necessary precondition for neoliberalization.'[24]

Neoliberal orthodoxy holds that 'unions operate to distort the natural price flexibility of the marketplace, resulting in higher levels of unemployment and wage-based inflationary pressures. Consequently, government policy should be directed towards eliminating these sources of inflexibility.'[25] Hence, neoliberal governments have introduced wide ranging policies to restrict trade union rights and freedoms, and to narrow the scope of the activities of unions. Restrictions on union organizing and union security arrangements are a cornerstone of neoliberal trade union legislation.[26] Neoliberal policies have made it much harder for workers to join trade unions, they have restricted the right-to-strike through the use of back-to-work legislation and essential service designation, and there have been ever increasing penalties for so-called "illegal" strikes. Besides dealing with the political, social, and economic realities of neoliberalism - which are inherently hostile towards trade unionism - Canadian unions have had to deal with heightened attacks against them during the crisis.

Union Responses to Crisis

Labour in Canada currently faces a number of challenges. More than three decades of neoliberalism has amounted to class warfare from above, with capital re-asserting itself as the dominant policy actor and using neoliberal public policy to restore whatever

---

[23]   Stephen McBride and John Shields, *Dismantling a Nation: The Transition to Corporate Rule in Canada* (Halifax: Fernwood Publishing, 1997), 18.

[24]   Harvey, *A Brief History of Neoliberalism*, 116.

[25]   McBride and Shields, *Dismantling a Nation*, 26.

[26]   Jim Stanford and Leah F. Vosko, "Challenging The Market: The Struggle to Regulate Work and Income" in *Challenging the Market: The Struggle to Regulate Work and Income*, eds. Jim Stanford & Leah F. Vosko (Montreal & Kingston: McGill-Queen's University Press, 2004), 13; Gary Teeple, *Globalization and the Decline of Social Reform: Into the Twenty-First Century* (Aurora: Garamond Press, 2000), 118.

political clout and economic power may have been lost during the Keynesian era in Canada. The Canadian union movement has seen tumbling union density in Canada (from 37% in the 1980s to 31% in 2009);[27] a reduction in the number of strikes per year - an indication, perhaps, of declining militancy;[28] intensifying legal restrictions on organizing new members and on the right to bargain and strike;[29] and an overall decline in the political and economic power of unions, stemming from the aforementioned challenges.

Much of the North American literature on union renewal and responses to the neoliberal challenge places unions into two over-arching categories: business unions and social movement unions (SMUs). Business unions are essentially built around the model of servicing members - the union's activity is limited to the workplace through collective bargaining, shop steward activities, and grievances. SMUs generally take a role in electoral politics; they build international solidarity and solidarity with other unions, are engaged in projects of building internal union democracy and develop links with their local communities. Perhaps more importantly SMUs see themselves as part of a larger social movement with the active desire to change society; SMUs see the labour movement of having a broad sense of solidarity with the greater working class and see labour as a leader for the working class.

Business unions often enter into partnerships with capital to ensure production for employers, and also to ensure that employers remain competitive within their industry. In this sense, business unions are concerned with generating high levels of capitalist profit. Business unionism is a fundamentally flawed project - the high levels of capitalist profits they seek to generate can only be created through the exploitation of their members. While business unionism is a dead-end endeavour, many unions have adopted this response to the challenges facing them as they see cooperation as

---

[27]   HRSDC (2011) Work – Unionization rates. Available at: http://www4.hrsdc. gc.ca/.3ndic.1t.4r@- eng.jsp?iid=17. Union density is the percentage of non-agricultural workers covered by a collective agreement. See p. 657, 14.5, 14.6.

[28]   "Chronological Perspective on Work Stoppages," Labour Program (HRSDC), http://srv131.services.gc.ca/dimt-wid/pcat-cpws/recherche-search. aspx?lang=eng; "Number of strikes and lockouts, employers and workers involved and time loss, Canada, 1901 to 1975" (Statistics Canada data). The same website has access to data from 1976 - 2012.

[29]   See Panitch and Swartz, *From Consent to Coercion.*

the only way to ensure continued production, and thus continued jobs, for their members.

Social Movement Unionism has been heralded, by its proponents, as the only way forward for trade unions. The key tenets to SMU include revitalizing internal union democracy, organizing the unorganized, rank-and-file involvement in organizing, militant collective bargaining, alliances with community organizations, and international solidarity. SMU is a more holistic approach to trade unionism which, on some level, does not see the membership in a union ending at the workplace. SMUs are, at least in theory, interested in their members as both workers on the job and members of a broader society, and thus seek to change that broader society for the better. There are some very clear limitations to SMUs. Much like business unions, SMUs seek to exist within neoliberalism. Both business unions and SMUs recognize that neoliberalism is hostile to trade unions, and both types of unions seek to exist within neoliberalism; business unions do this by reforming the workplace, SMUs by attempting to reform society at large. This is, perhaps, best shown by the success stories of SMUs which mostly deal with how SMUs have engaged with new organizing tactics to grow union density within neoliberalism. Neither business unionism nor SMU encourages alternate thinking which could lead to ideas of how to replace neoliberal capitalism with another set of political-economic arrangements.

The key to true union renewal must be to treat trade unions as political organizations based in the working class and seeking a clear working class alternative to neoliberal capitalism. Unions are currently the only way the working class can organize itself into a cohesive political unit to challenge capital. While the literature on SMUs champions organizing, 'the implications of union organizing for class are seldom deliberated and the relevance of class for union organised is seldom contemplated.'[30] The neoliberal era has been an era of regression in working class consciousness.[31]

---

[30]   Gregor Gall and Jack Fiorito, "The backward march of labour halted? Or, what is to be done with 'union organizing'? The cases of Britain and the USA," *Capital and Class* 35, no. 2 (2011): 24.

[31]   Jonah Butovsky and Murray E. G. Smith, "Beyond Social Unionism: Farm Workers in Ontario and Some Lessons from Labour History," *Labour/Le Travail* 59 (Spring 2007): 72.

Individualism, as one of the ideological underpinnings of neo-liberalism, has severely dulled class consciousness. True attempts at union renewal must work to rebuild and revitalize an internal culture of working class solidarity within unions, and within the broader working class in order to build the strength of the labour movement.

Union renewal needs a class based strategy to go forward. With a class-based strategy, the unions can 'renew themselves by becoming social movements in order to move away from the economistic orientations of the past.'[32] Here Gall and Fiorito are concisely stating what many other critical-left trade unionists and academics have previously argued: trade union renewal must expand beyond simple workplace issues, and stop the myopic march forward of simply organizing new members and then defending the narrow economic interests of these members. The labour movement, by becoming a social movement, can re-take up the position as the vanguard of the working class.[33] Through a transition to a social movement with a class base, the labour movement can *then* seek to shape the exogenous political and economic environments it finds itself in, in order to replace neoliberalism with a new political economy. The first step, however, in doing this, is revitalizing trade unions as working class organizations.

Outline of the Book

The book is organized into three main sections. The first section, *Putting the Great Recession in Context*, provides an overview of the Great Recession in Canada. In the first chapter, McBride & Whiteside provide an overview of the historical and theoretical contexts of the crisis in terms of the state. The authors use Panitch's conceptualizations of the roles and functions of the capitalist state to partially explain the political orientation of the

---

[32]   Gall and Fiorito, "The backward march of labour halted?," 238.
[33]   An excellent overview of the role of union's within the Marxist frame-work can be found in Richard Hyman's classic work *Marxism and the Sociology of Trade Unionism* (London: Pluto Pamphlets, 1971). Volume 36, no. 1 (2012) of *Capital & Class* was dedicated to the work of Hyman, and includes a 'celebration and critical reassessment' of Hyman's work, which updates the literature on the position of union's within Marxist theory.

state during this crisis, but they greatly expand on the framework Panitch employs. McBride & Whiteside convincingly argue that at different historical junctures, there have been different balances between the functions of the state: at some points, coercion becomes more prominent than legitimation, and vice versa. The chapter also discusses how the crisis has led, broadly, to the democratic malaise in Canada, arguing that with the crisis the state has been able to engage in an 'erosion of civil liberties and lack of adherence to constitutional norms.'

Faroque & MacLean discuss the links between social and economic inequality and the Great Recession. In their chapter, "From the Great Recession of 2008-2009 to Fiscal Austerity: The Role of Inequality," the authors convincingly show that the state response to the Great Recession had an essential class character to it. Canada's recessionary experience was mild, compared to the United States and other advanced industrial economies; yet, the Canadian state introduced extensive austerity measures, in the name of recovering from the crisis. Indeed, Faroque & MacLean argue that the austerity measures came about *in spite* of a milder Canadian recession and the exceptionally low Canadian government debt-to-GDP ratio. These authors conclude by suggesting that the austerity measures the Canadian state have introduced are reflective of general orientation of the state to introduce public policy that reflects on the power of the wealthy. From there, they highlight a need to shift the balance of power in society away from corporate interests.

This section of the book concludes with a chapter by Fowler, who outlines the response by the Ontario government to the Great Recession. The Ontario government introduced extensive austerity measures, aimed at public sector workers - who had no hand in creating the crisis. The government attempted to force a zero percent wage freeze on all public sector employees for two years, but was unable to unilaterally implement this wage freeze due to legal developments. The government then turned to a 'consultation' process, where unions were asked to sit down with the government to negotiate the wage freeze. Fowler argues that the unions which participated in the 'consultation' process showed signs of business unionism in the face of coercive tactics by the state.

The second section of the book looks specifically at how unions have experienced and responded to the crisis. Chapter four, by

Nelson & Meades, provides a case study of collective bargaining in a time of austerity. Nelson & Meades, the co-presidents of CUPE local 4600, detail the difficulties of negotiating a collective agreement in the public sector in a time of austerity. CUPE 4600 represents part-time instructors and teaching assistants and at Carleton University, and was in a round of collective negotiations immediately following the provincially mandated wage freeze in Ontario. The authors also note that the struggles to reach a new collective agreement highlighted the need for 'broad based student, community, and worker resistance' to austerity measures, and the greater neoliberal project. The article shows how rising tuition costs, linked with declining university services and job opportunities present a reason for students to work with workers on a common front. The chapter provides insights into how public sector workers have felt and dealt with austerity measures.

Conversely, in the concluding chapter of this section, by Murnighan & Stanford, shows how the Canadian Autoworkers, a private sector union, has been impacted by the crisis. Murninghan & Stanford outline the effects the Great Recession had on the automotive sector in North America - a crisis in auto occurred alongside a crisis in capitalism. This resulted in virtually unprecedented action by the American and Canadian states to "prop up" the Big Three domestic auto producers. The loans these companies secured came along with governmental demands for concessions in the collective agreements that the CAW had previously negotiated. The authors show how the most severe concessions were warded off, but that the labour movement has been reduced to winning partial, incremental victories. The case of the CAW shows that one of the weaknesses that trade unions have faced during the great recession was the failure for the broader political-economic fight-back against the governmentally demanded concessions to resonate more with both the members of the union and the broader public.

The third, and final, section of the book looks at various long term responses and fight-backs to crisis. They highlight the need for union renewal, and for the need of a working-class political program. These chapters diverge slightly from earlier chapters in the book, as they are more theoretical in nature, and sketch out potential paths for organized labour to take out of the crisis and beyond.

Smith & Butovsky's chapter takes a different focus than the other chapters in this book, in that they do not analyse unions as simply entities unto themselves. The authors suggest that unions must play a greater role in organizing the Canadian working class in a struggle against capitalism. Through this lens, Smith & Butovsky critique the current direction of the Canadian labour movement, noting that Canadian labour can be described as 'social-democratic, nationalistic, and class-collaborationist.' These authors criticize the Canadian labour movement for its tendencies to business unionism, and its support of the social-democratic NDP. They also rightfully criticize the use of economic crisis to further entrench neoliberalism in Canada, noting that while the recession may not have been as severe in Canada as elsewhere, the Canadian government still engaged in a stimulus package aimed at capital, corporate tax cuts, a 'miserly' approach to social programs, and a focus on deficit reduction. The authors conclude by arguing that the only way the Canadian labour movement can reinvent itself is for a broad labour counter offensive which sheds the links to social democracy, Canadian nationalism, and cooperation with capital.

The book concludes with a chapter by Camfield, who also calls for a broad left-wing renewal effort in Canadian labour. He has also noted the social-democratic and class-collaborationist tendencies in Canadian labour, recalling, for example, that the CAW has repeatedly granted concessions to auto manufacturers to ensure short term profitability; and has also noted that top union officials remain supportive of the NDP. The response to the Great Recession, according to Camfield, has been 'small-scale, low-key, and timid.' Camfield outlines how labour has found itself in the position it is currently in, through neoliberal restructuring, a weak infrastructure of dissent, and demobilized bureaucratic 'responsible' unionism. Camfield also calls for a revitalization of the union movement, based on socialist policies. He suggests that a new anti-capitalist movement committed to working class politics within and outside unions is necessary.

THE CANADIAN STATE AND THE CRISIS: THEORETICAL AND HISTORICAL CONTEXT

Stephen McBride and Heather Whiteside[1]

Introduction

Since the onset of a financial and economic crisis in late 2007 the dominant policy practice of the Canadian state, following a brief, shallow, and reluctant exercise in stimulus spending, has been overtly geared toward the rescue of capital at the expense of labour. This is achieved through large, publicly-funded bail-outs of leading capitalist sectors (auto and banking) followed by a planned return to draconian fiscal austerity, a reinvigoration of regressive forms of taxation, and the enthusiastic promotion of further trade liberalization (CETA and 'Buy American') which opens up to foreign competition areas of the state that were hitherto protected (e.g., provincial government procurement). Rather than the crisis having produced a shift in the dominant neoliberal policy paradigm, the Great Recession has thus far been followed by even greater state retrenchment for labour and the public sector, while support for capital (particularly finance capital and other internationally-oriented fractions) is enhanced.

The current crisis is, of course, only the latest in a series of crises that seem endemic to the capitalist system. The neoliberal period of capitalist development in particular, from the mid-1970s to the present, has been extremely crisis-prone. This period has

---

[1]   The authors would like to thank Tim Fowler and two anonymous reviewers for helpful comments on an earlier draft.

witnessed three major recessions and numerous financial break-downs, with the most recent crisis being by far the most serious to date. Our focus ultimately will be on the way the Canadian state has responded to this latest crisis, but this cannot be understood in isolation. Instead it ought to be seen as but the latest expression of state support for capital accumulation in the face of recurrent systemic crises.

We begin by reviewing a number of theories of crisis, and link this to theorizations of how the state helps to promote recovery through its support for capital accumulation, social legitimation, and resort to coercive measures. By connecting various hetero-dox theoretical perspectives to the actual unfolding of policy over the Keynesian and neoliberal eras it becomes obvious that these underlying roles remain the same though they manifest in very different ways. In particular the benefits experienced by labour through neoliberal variants of state support for capital have grown exceptionally thin and systemic instability persists. These features have been only further aggravated by reactions to the most recent crisis. This is detailed in the second half of the chapter where we argue that the bailouts, fiscal austerity, regressive taxation, and deeper trade liberalization further extend these neoliberal trends. Despite providing an opportunity to re-think the policies partially responsible for the crisis, policy makers instead chose a route of denial, minimalism, bilateralism, and business as usual. Thus the Canadian state has consolidated and extended its com-mitment to neoliberalism, a decision that is likely to deepen an already existing legitimacy deficit.

Capitalist crises, the state in capitalist society and crisis recovery promotion

Theorists have identified various cycles of accumulation, in which crises, that vary in duration and frequency, play a central role. Long wave theorists (which includes Regulation theory and Social Structure of Accumulation analyses) emphasize cycles of long term development – lasting from several years to hundreds of years, and most commonly those that run for forty to sixty years (named

'Kondratieff cycles').[2] Given the frequency of crises, these perspectives place an importance on the extra-economic institutions
which offset tendencies towards crisis by providing stability for
the system and facilitating long term growth.[3] State policy directly
influences many of these institutions by, for example, establishing
the monetary and fiscal/financial regime, the wage-labour nexus,
and methods of insertion into the international regime.[4] Similarly,
Keynesian theory recognizes the inherent boom and bust nature of
capitalism and attempts to address these ups and downs through
state policies aimed at manipulating aggregate demand.

A nother radical approach to understanding crises and the role of the
state is the Marxist overaccumulation perspective. Overaccumulation is
a condition of surplus capital and takes the form of a glut of commodities on the market, idle productive capacity, and surplus money capital
that cannot find outlets for profitable investment.[5] For David Harvey,
a leading overaccumulation theorist, the fairly regular nature of crises

---

[2] Kondratieff cycles, or 'waves', capture the fairly regular pattern of upswings
     and downswings that characterize developments in the capitalist system over
     the long run. Roughly 40 to 60 years in length, periods of economic boom
     tend to followed by recession, which in turn develops into greater instability.
     Long wave theorists often emphasize the institutional and technological inno-
     vations which underpin the upswing, and point to how these same features
     eventually produce contradictions which lead to the downswing. See Phillip
     Anthony O'Hara, *Growth and Development in the Global Political Economy
     (London: Routledge, 2006), Chapter 1.*

[3] For example, with the Social Structure of Accumulation approach extra-eco-
     nomic institutions are said to help temporarily offset the inherent contradictions
     and conflicts within the capitalist mode of production by producing the stabil-
     ity, predictability, coordination, and compromise that is needed to facilitate long
     term investment, demand and growth within a capitalist economy. Some of the
     key institutions that supported growth during the postwar upswing in the US
     and other Western states were: Pax Americana (US international hegemony), a
     capital-labour accord (e.g., relatively stable and cooperative collective bargaining),
     a moderation of competition, and the Keynesian welfare state (which enhanced
     stability, provided for conflict resolution, enhanced effective demand, etc.), and a
     system of regulated finance (the Bretton Woods agreement). See Phillip Anthony
     O'Hara, *Growth and Development in the Global Political Economy (London:
     Routledge, 2006); Stephen McBride and Heather Whiteside, Private Affluence,
     Public Austerity: Economic Crisis and Democratic Malaise in Canada (Winnipeg:
     Fernwood Publishing, 2011), Chapter 2.*

[4] See Michael Aglietta, "Capitalism at the Turn of the Century: Regulation
     Theory and the Challenge of Social Change," *New Left Review* 232 (1998);
     Robert Boyer and Yves Saillard, eds., *Regulation Theory* (New York: Routledge,
     1995); Phillip Anthony O'Hara, *Growth and Development in the Global
     Political Economy* (London: Routledge, 2006).

[5] David Harvey, *Limits to Capital (London: Verso, 2006), 195.*

is the result of contradictions within the capitalist system, and cannot be located in the failure of extra-economic institutions. Three central contradictions relate to competition and antagonisms that exist within the capitalist class, between labour and capital, and between capitalist production and non- or pre- capitalist sectors.[6] Short of moving to another mode of production, these contradictions cannot be eliminated, but fixes to crises can be established by capital and the state. Harvey calls these 'spatio-temporal fixes' and for our purposes here suffice it to say that this involves, amongst other things, opening up new markets and creating new wants and needs, and avoiding crises or defraying costs through the use of credit and long term investments in physical or social infrastructure.[7] The state plays an important role in each new fix by articulating, implementing, and managing these strategies.

Together these theories point to different ways of examining the three important roles commonly ascribed to the state in capitalist society. These relate to activities that influence accumulation (ensuring profitability of the system as a whole[8]), legitimation (ensuring social harmony), and coercion (repressing subordinate classes).[9] That said, the balance between the state's roles can be expected to change under different historical conditions. Other things being equal, for example, under conditions of austerity, when material concessions are being reduced or withdrawn and when ideological appeals may be ineffective, a greater reliance on coercion might be expected. In Canada, we can note a worrying trend to aggressive policing of political demonstrations, an erosion of civil liberties, increased use of repressive labour legislation, and lack of adherence to constitutional norms over the neoliberal period.[10]

---

6   David Harvey, *Spaces of Capital (Edinburgh: Edinburgh University, 2001),*
     79-80.
7   See David Harvey, *Spaces of Capital; David Harvey, The New Imperialism*
     (Oxford: Oxford University Press, 2003).
8   Notwithstanding our emphasis here on the support played for the system as a
     whole, instances of instrumentalism can often be found. Further, support for
     accumulation is not always or even often directed toward national capital. In
     Canada there is a long history of foreign ownership of natural resources and in
     other sectors, including manufacturing. Targeted corporate welfare has also
     been common in Canada throughout its development.
9   Leo Panitch, ed., *The Canadian State: Political Economy and Political Power*
     (Toronto: University of Toronto Press, 1977); James O'Connor, *The Fiscal
     Crisis of the State* (New York: St. Martin's Press, 1978).
10   See Stephen McBride and Heather Whiteside, *Private Affluence, Public
     Austerity, Chapter 6.*

The crisis policy responses of the state whether in the form of creating new extra-economic institutions as long wave theorists emphasize, or helping to design new spatio-temporal fixes as over-accumulation theorists suggest, relate primarily to role of providing support for future capital accumulation. Keynesianism and associated postwar policies helped resolve the problems of the Great Depression by encouraging strategies like Fordism which linked rising labour productivity to rising wages, and thus economic growth to mass consumption and effective demand. Internationally, embedded liberalism[11] served to provide a stable framework for trade and investment, encouraging economic growth and profit making for productive capital at the expense of global finance (which faced relatively tight controls at the time).

In Canada, as is the case elsewhere, the state also assisted capital accumulation and national development by building up internal linkages or filling in vacuums through the creation of state owned enterprises (Crown corporations) in areas where capital was unable or unwilling to participate. This was also used as a mechanism to support accumulation following significant private sector bankruptcies in the early decades of the twentieth century.[12] Crown corporations have also in the past been created, at least in part, to enter into joint ventures with domestic firms. However, other incentives were frequently used to encourage accumulation without the creation of public corporations, such as subsidies, tax breaks, and various regulatory protections. Often in the postwar era Canadian capital and labour were also supported through the development of a "branch plant" status in the manufacturing sector.[13]

Social cohesion and legitimacy during the Keynesian era were promoted through corporatism, tripartite negotiations, elements of Fordism, and other Keynesian policies (such as demand management and facets of the welfare state) which promoted a relatively generous social wage and aimed for full employment. These institutions and fixes, developed initially as a reaction to the Great

---

[11]   John G. Ruggie, "International Regimes, Transactions, and Change: Embedded Liberalism in the Postwar Economic Order," *International Organization* 36:2 (1982).

[12]   See Heather Whiteside, "Crises of Capital and the Logic of Dispossession and Repossession," *Studies in Political Economy* 89 (2012).

[13]   Leo Panitch, "Dependency and Class in Canadian Political Economy," *Studies in Political Economy* 6: (Autumn 1981): 284.

Depression of the 1930s and later matured over the post war era, produced a high level of growth, economic stability, and gains for both labour and capital. As a result, legitimation activities of this sort can be labeled 'concrete legitimation'[14] given that they conferred substantial legal and material benefits for labour in addition to providing for the relative social harmony that was ultimately beneficial for capital accumulation. Of course, even in the Keynesian era coercion was far from absent. There was repression of communists and other radicals during the McCarthy-ite period in particular, and state-assisted efforts to rid Canadian trade unions of communist leaders, where these had been elected, can be seen in unions such as Mine-Mill and the Canadian Seamen's Union.[15] Similarly the structure of the postwar industrial relations system contained elements of both coercion and consent[16] and state interventions on picket lines were common throughout the period.

Given that each crisis resolution also contains the seeds of its own destruction, for a host of reasons (such as overproduction, the growing multinational nature of capital, the rise of global finance capital, and a profit-squeeze induced by labour), arrangements that had at one time proven to be extremely successful began to unravel in the 1970s. These changes fundamentally altered the terrain of capital accumulation, making a return to the policy arrangements of the postwar era impractical. Furthermore, the looming environmental crisis today is a clear indicator of the contradictions inherent in a system that promotes ever-increasing mass consumption and production, making a return to this model undesirable as well.

The rise of global neoliberalism in the 1980s therefore can be viewed as an attempt by the state and capital to fix the problems of

---

14   Stephen McBride, *Not Working: State, Unemployment and Neo-Conservatism in Canada* (Toronto: University of Toronto Press, 1992), 23.

15   See Irving Abella, *Nationalism, Communism and Canadian Labour* (Toronto: University of Toronto Press, 1973), 302-311; Stuart Jamieson, *Times of Trouble: Labour Unrest and Industrial Conflict in Canada, 1900-1966* (Ottawa: Study Number 22 for the Task Force on Labour Relations, Queen's Printer, 1968), 321-23; and H.C. Pentland, *A Study of the Changing Social, Economic and Political Background of the Canadian System of Industrial Relations* (Ottawa: Draft Study prepared for the Task Force on Labour Relations, 1968), 321.

16   Stephen McBride, "Coercion and Consent: The Recurring Temptation of Corporatism in Canadian Labour Relations," in *Labour Gains, Labour Pains — 50 Years of PC 1003*, eds. Cy Gonick, Paul Phillips and Jesse Vorst (Halifax: Fernwood, 1995), 79-96.

the 1970s: global overaccumulation and the growing problems that this created for the extra-economic institutions of the Keynesian era[17]. This then led to significant changes in how the state attempted to support capital accumulation. All too often this support has conflicted with the role of legitimation, and in its place coercion has come to assume a more prominent role in state policy.[18] Support for capital accumulation over the neoliberal period has been often associated with policies that encourage accumulation by dispossession. This includes privatization and state-backed financialization (which relies on taxpayer funds to bailout capital when crises hit). Dispossession refers to profit-making "based on predation, fraud, and violence" and its features include commodification and privatization (of land, labour power, state owned assets, etc.); asset appropriation through imperialism; and the use of national debt and the credit system as a new and radical form of Marx's primitive accumulation.[19] This process "open[s] up vast fields for overaccumulated capital to seize upon" and releases assets at low cost to be turned into profitable use by overaccumulated capital.[20] Jamie Peck and Adam Tickell also provide a useful distinction between roll-back and roll-out phases of the neoliberal project,[21] which highlights the activism of the state in pursuit of neoliberal objectives and also the extent to which constant change and response to recurrent crises serves an underlying continuity of goals.

Through the enactment of privatization policies in the 1980s and beyond, the state helped to dampen economic problems experienced in the 1970s by creating the opportunity for greater capital accumulation through the invention of markets within what was

---

[17]   Although it could equally be said that the Keynesian welfare state was as much undermined by the rise of neoliberalism at the time as it was proving problematic on its own terms.

[18]   See, for example Leo Panitch and Donald Swartz, *From Consent to Coercion: The Assault on Trade Union Freedoms,* 3rd ed. (Toronto: University of Toronto Press, 2008) regarding trade unions; Stephen McBride and Heather Whiteside, *Private Affluence, Public Austerity,* 98-101, on the erosion of civil liberties.

[19]   David Harvey, *The New Imperialism, 144-145.*

[20]   Ibid., 149.

[21]   The roll-back phase refers to the initial destruction of the key institutions and programs of the Keynesian era. Roll-out, on the other hand, identifies a phase of constructing new institutions and programs that embed the neoliberal approach to governance. See Jamie Peck and Adam Tickell, "Neoliberalizing Space," *Antipode, 34:3 (July 2002).*

previously the realm of the state. This strategy does not guarantee profitability, however, as it could be argued that the global capitalist system remains entrenched in a long downturn[22] and furthermore dispossession can lead to greater problems in the long run.[23] However crises are at least potentially resolved through accumulation by dispossession. This fits within the overall tenor of the neoliberal era (roughly 1980 to present) given its emphasis on market-led economic and social restructuring.[24]

Financialization, another prime expression of accumulation by dispossession during the neoliberal era, is a process whereby financial markets, institutions and actors gain influence over economic policy and economic outcomes at the expense of participants in the real economy of production and distribution of real products. As Harvey suggests, financialization has a strong predatory component as it has been associated with Ponzi schemes and other forms of corporate fraud, and promotes high levels of personal and national indebtedness which create conditions of servitude for debtors.[25] Regulatory changes at the level of state policy along with changes in production and technology have encouraged this process and it for some time supported capital accumulation (or at least masked underlying problems) by allowing for consumption to occur even if real growth did not. Stability, however, was never a feature of these arrangements as extreme systemic instability and volatility has been a persistent feature of the past three decades. Spectacular and largely unpredicted financial crises occurred in Mexico in 1994-95, East Asia in 1997-98, Russia 1998, Turkey 2000, and Argentina 2001-3.[26] Prior to 2007, the neoliberal period was also marked by two major recessions, in the early 1980s and early 1990s, and by periodic stock-market crashes, from Black Monday

---

[22]   Robert Brenner, *The Economics of Global Turbulence: The Advanced Capitalist Economies from Long Boom to Long Downturn, 1945-2005 (New York: Verso, 2006).*

[23]   See G. Arrighi, N. Aschoff, and B. Scully, "Accumulation by Dispossession and its Limits: The Southern Africa Paradigm Revisited," *Studies in Comparative International Development* 45:4 (2010): 411; David Harvey, *The New Imperialism*, 154-156.

[24]   Bob Jessop, "Liberalism, Neoliberalism, and Urban Governance," *Antipode* 34:3 (2002): 461.

[25]   David Harvey, *The New Imperialism*, 147.

[26]   Peter B. Kenen, *The International Financial Architecture: What's New? What's Missing?* (Washington, D.C: Institute for International Economics, 2001).

in October 1987, to the bursting of the dot.com bubble in 2000-2002 that wiped out trillions of dollars in assets and savings.

These crises indicate that in the transition from the Keynesian era to the neoliberal era state support for capital accumulation has, in many instances, come to take substantially new forms. John Loxley argued that a key strategy for resolving the international debt crisis of the 1980s involved socializing private banking sector debt through official intervention so as to avoid bank collapse.[27] Efforts of this sort were repeated throughout the 1990s in reaction to national and regional financial crises. Peter Gowan argued that the process of neoliberal globalization itself has been driven forward through official intervention following debt and financial crises. He suggested that the entire regime relies on crises as "the IMF covers the risks and ensures that the US banks don't lose" (i.e., countries pay up through structural adjustments).[28] These sentiments were echoed by Wade and Veneroso with regard to the Asian Financial Crisis of 1997-8, when they wrote that "the combination of massive devaluations, IMF-pushed financial liberalization, and IMF-facilitated recovery may even precipitate the biggest peacetime transfer of assets from domestic to foreign owners in the past fifty years anywhere in the world".[29] Despite the fact that financialization clearly benefits capital rather than labour, this process has also paradoxically ensured that the average citizen's material interests are now wrapped up with the health of finance capital given that pension funds, mortgages, and credit card debt are now integrated into global financial markets.[30]

Attempts to support capital accumulation through neoliberal policies come at the expense of concrete legitimation, rendering the contradictions and conflicts of neoliberal era particularly evident and making legitimation largely ideological rather than tangible. Ideological legitimation creates the impression of responding to social conflicts and related problems without actually doing much to resolve them.[31] Yet despite the lack of material benefits offered by neoliberalism (and instead

---

[27]   John Loxley, *Interdependence, Disequilibrium and Growth (London: Macmillan, 1998)*, 29.

[28]   Peter Gowan, *The Global Gamble: Washington's Faustian Bid for World Dominance* (London: Verso, 1999), Chapter 4.

[29]   R. Wade and F. Veneroso, "The Asian Crisis: The High Debt Model versus the Wall Street-Treasury-IMF Complex," *New Left Review* 228 (1998): 3-23.

[30]   Leo Panitch and Sam Gindin, "The Current Crisis: A Socialist Perspective," *The Bullet 142 (2009)*.

[31]   Stephen McBride, *Not Working, 21.*

an actual erosion in the position of the working class) a curious feature of the past thirty years has been that rising protest and dissatisfaction, for example the massive Quebec student protests in 2012, have emerged within a generalized condition of political apathy and cynicism. Apathy is clearly expressed through the persistence of low voter turnout and cynicism is revealed through the low level of trust that exists with formal political democracy. Canada fares poorly on both accounts, and is now ranked 110th out of 152 countries in terms of its registered voter turnout count[32] and has experienced a dramatic decline in trust for the government (for example, in 1965, 58 percent of Canadians reported that they had trust in government, but by 1993 this had dropped to a dismal 33 percent[33]). We call the growing condition of generalized cynicism and apathy leading to democratic decline, along with overall dissatisfaction and lowered expectations of citizens, 'democratic malaise'.[34] Insulation of key decision-making functions from public input and key aspects of the economy from politicians,[35] another hallmark of the neoliberal era, has certainly contributed to this generalized malaise.

The earlier string of crises in the 1980s and 1990s were later followed by even greater and more widespread economic problems beginning in late 2007 with the subprime debt crisis. This triggered banking and financial institution bankruptcies, a lengthy credit crunch, and the onset of a 'Great Recession', the effects of which continue to linger. These events cannot be blamed on financialization and financial market re-regulation alone, rather they are indicative of deep, structural problems within the realm of production (overaccumulation), a lack of effective demand creating an excessive reliance on credit, and other related imbalances (in the international trade regime, for example).

Thus throughout the recent crisis (2007 and beyond) the role of the state in capitalist society has maintained the familiar accumulation and legitimation activities described earlier, but these have recently

---

[32]   Nation   Master   (2010)   www.nationmaster.com/graph/ dem_par_ele_reg_vot_tur-parliamentary-elections-registered-voter-turnout

[33]   Neal J. Roese, "Canadians' Shrinking Trust in Government: Causes and Consequences," in *Value Change and Governance in Canada*, ed. Neil Nevitte (Toronto: University of Toronto Press, 2002), 152.

[34]   See Stephen McBride and Heather Whiteside, *Private Affluence, Public Austerity, Chapter 6*.

[35]   Stephen Gill, "Globalisation, Market Civilisation, and Disciplinary Neoliberalism," *Millennium Journal of International Studies* 24:3 (1995): 412.

taken new forms to match the needs of a system embroiled in crises.[36] This includes unprecedented attempts to rescue leading capitalist sectors like banking and auto (in the form of bailouts, quasi nationalization, and other asset guarantees), and Keynesian-style stimulus packages aimed at promoting job creation and investment. With connections now deeply established between financial markets and the average citizen's savings and debt, and with many jobs threatened by bankruptcy within the North American auto sector, these policies also supported labour despite their obvious benefits for capital.[37] However, it is important to note that stimulus packages have been designed to be temporary and shallow, bailouts have not been tailored to maximize taxpayer investments and instead have served mainly to socialize private debt, and little re-regulation of global financial markets has occurred. In the sphere of global financial governance the policy reaction has been focused on encouraging better surveillance, reporting, and transparency of financial markets, rather than introducing capital controls or the creation of novel regulatory institutions. Furthermore, deep disequilibrium remains between surplus and deficit trading countries, and in the EU in particular this has exacerbated sovereign debt crises.[38] To make matters worse, the lack of real recovery remains a persistent feature of the global economy, labour is in an ever more precarious position, and fiscal austerity is back with a vengeance. We

---

[36] Coercive measures, such as routine back-to-work legislation by the federal government whenever the right to strike is exercised, plus draconian legislation in some provinces, has also been a feature of the recent period, see http://labourrights.ca/restrictive-labour-laws

[37] With roughly 400,000 people in Ontario employed in the auto industry, government action aimed at saving these jobs was arguably in the best interest of all. However, this support was also contingent upon wage and benefit concessions made by labour. In newspaper commentary this came across in a more muted fashion, with Tony Clement, then Minister of Industry, merely stating that the Canadian Auto Workers union "[would] have to be part of the solution to the industry's problems See The Guardian, "GM won't close any more Canadian plants but needs money to survive," *The Guardian, February 20, 2009,* This 'solution', however, later translated into pressure placed on the union to slash labour costs, and ultimately, in April 2009, CAW-Chrysler negotiations produced a $19 per hour reduction in labour costs. See Greg Keenan, Shawn McCarthy, and Karen Howlett, "CAW, Chrysler Ordered to Resume Negotiating," *Globe and Mail, April 21, 2009,* Despite this financial support, however, General Motors announced in 2012 that it would be closing one of its plants in Oshawa, Ontario, which will likely affect at least 2,000 GM workers by 2013.

[38] See Stephen McBride and Heather Whiteside, *Private Affluence, Public Austerity, Conclusion.*

will now turn to a more in-depth examination of the most recent crisis of capitalism, and the role that the state has played in promoting recovery for capital at the expense of labour – an ultimately problematic solution to the crisis.

The most recent crisis

The broad contours of the recent financial and economic crisis are now familiar.[39] Financial deregulation in the neoliberal heartlands led to innovation and intense speculation in toxic financial instruments and, ultimately, a crash of epic proportions. The problems first became apparent with the collapse of a number of US investment banks and mortgage giants Fanny Mae and Freddy Mac. With the major exception of Lehman Brothers, which was allowed to collapse, these were bailed-out out by the US government through massive debt purchasing schemes. The crisis in financial markets soon revealed serious accumulation problems within the so-called 'real economy'. In November 2008 the S&P stock market index was down nearly 45 percent compared to its 2007 high.[40] Major firms like GM and Chrysler became insolvent and were bailed out by US authorities through $17.4 billion in emergency loans in 2009 alone.[41] Because of the highly integrated

---

[39]   For example, see Greg Albo, Sam Gindin, and Leo Panitch, *In and Out of Crisis: The Global Financial Meltdown and Left Alternatives* (Oakland: PM Press, 2010); J. Guard and W. Antony, eds., *Bankruptcies and Bailouts* (Winnipeg & Halifax: Fernwood Publishing, 2009); David McNally, *Global Slump: the Economics and Politics of Crisis and Resistance* (Winnipeg & Halifax: Fernwood Publishing, 2011).

[40]   Roger C. Altman, "The Great Crash, 2008," *Foreign Affairs* (January/February 2009).   http://www.foreignaffairs.com/articles/63714/roger-c-altman/the-great-crash-2008

[41]   Soyoung Kim and David Lawder, "GM Repays US Loan, Government Loss on Bailout Falls," *Reuters* (April 21 2010). http://www.reuters.com/article/idUS-TRE63K56920100421. In fall 2008 Ford, GM, and Chrysler had launched their first request for a bailout from the US government, initially asking for $50 billion in emergency loans. See Chris Isidore, "Big Three Bailout May Be Around Corner," *CNN Money* (September 5 2008). http://money.cnn.com/2008/09/04/news/economy/automakers_Congress/index.htm. However, in 2009 GM and Chrysler ended up receiving a different form of assistance than Ford. Rather than using the $9 billion line of credit that it had requested in December 2008, Ford instead received a $5.9 billion loan from the Energy Department, a $62 million grant through the US stimulus package, and benefited from a $5 billion bailout of the supply network, "Factbox," Reuters, accessed August 5, 2010, http://www.reuters.com/article/2010/08/05/obama-ford-idUSN0517179420100805.   Ford Credit also received support from the US Federal Reserve through its Commercial Paper Program (see http://www.federalreserve.gov/monetarypolicy/cpff.htm).

North American auto industry these bailouts were ultimately cost-shared between the US and Canadian governments.

Within North America, unemployment grew rapidly in the US, but less so in Canada, which escaped the worst effects of the crisis.

Table 1. Unemployment: Canada, US				
	Unemployment Rate 2007	Unemployment Rate 2010	+	Percentage Increase (rounded)
United States	4.6	9.7	5.1	110
Canada	6.0	8.1	2.1	35
OECD average	6.0	8.3	2.3	38

What began as a US banking and financial market crisis quickly spread around the world, particularly to countries with highly internationalized financial sectors, highly leveraged banks, and high levels of exposure to toxic assets associated with the US subprime mortgage market. Thus a US financial crisis turned into a global economic crisis including a global recession. Core neoliberal countries with interest rates at already historical lows (so low that monetary tools were essentially exhausted) resorted to stimulus spending in order to avert complete economic collapse.

Fiscal stimulus may have averted a deeper recession but it did not represent a change of strategy on the part of dominant elites. The Canadian response in particular appears to have taken a 'business as usual' approach to crisis management – denial, minimalism, and bilateralism/policy harmonization with the US.[42] Indeed, in the face of such a traumatic crisis, the development of which was completely at odds with the expectations of the dominant neoliberal approach to policy-making, the continuity of policy once the immediate shock had passed, and the disinclination to re-examine fundamental policy choices that had been made over previous decades, is striking.

---

[42] See Stephen McBride, "The Global Economic Crisis," in *Readings in Canadian Foreign Policy, 2nd ed* , eds. C. Kukucha and D. Bratt (Toronto: University of Oxford Press, 2011).

The 2007 Financial Crisis

By early 2007 the US subprime industry, worth at that time an estimated $1.3 trillion, was poised for collapse. From February, when
Mortgage Lenders Network USA, the country's 15th largest subprime
lender, filed for Chapter 11 bankruptcy protection, a series of other
mortgage lenders declared bankruptcy, or put themselves up for sale.
By August 2007 a worldwide "credit crunch" emerged, as it became
clear that subprime mortgage-backed securities were widely distributed in the portfolios of banks and hedge funds around the world.
A series of coordinated central bank efforts were made to re-inject
liquidity into global capital markets. But in 2008 the subprime disaster
spread to other sectors of the economy. Global stock markets sank in
value – from the highs experienced in early 2007, paper losses on US
stocks totaled $8.4 trillion (USD) by October 11, 2008 – and bankrupt-
cies and collapses of key institutions also began.

Policy Responses

Although the crisis had clearly hit as early as mid- to late-2007, it
was not until a 2008 IMF declaration that the US was in the grips
of "the largest financial crisis... since the Great Depression" that
policy makers began to take decisive, coordinated action.[43] Policy
interventions seriously lagged behind market realities.[44] Even when
the G-7 met in Washington, in October 2008 and agreed to coordination in an attempt to avoid a global depression, no concrete
plan for dealing with the crisis was announced. A month later the
G-20 also met in Washington to discuss policy harmonization.
The proposals centered around strengthening transparency and
accountability, improving regulation, promoting market integrity,
and reinforcing cooperation – all of which were consistent with
earlier technocratic ideas about how to reform the international
financial architecture. Those members of the G-20, notably France

---

[43]   Heather Stewart, "IMF says US crisis is 'largest financial shock since Great
       Depression'," *The Guardian*, April 9, 2008, *http://www.guardian.co.uk/busi-
       ness/2008/apr/09/useconomy.subprimecrisis.*
[44]   Although Dumenil and Levy should be consulted for their description of the
       range of measures taken in the US to support the financial sector from mid-
       2007 to early-2009. See Gerard Dumenil and Dominique Levy, *The Crisis of
       Neoliberalism (Cambridge: Harvard University Press, 2011), 228-243.*

and Germany, which desired more rigorous reform of international institutions, and even the creation of a new international organization capable of managing and/or regulating global financial markets, were unable to prevail.

In responding to the crisis, the preferred policy instrument of the neoliberal era – monetary policy – was unlikely to be effective since interest rates were already at very low levels. Cutting them further would produce little stimulus. Even so, a round of interest rate cuts was implemented by the several central banks in October 2008, with rates lowered to approximately 1.5 per cent by early 2009. This effectively exhausted the ability to achieve further economic stimulus through this means.

Instead, public sector initiatives took the form of bailouts and stimulus packages, the latter comprising a mix of spending increases and tax cuts, and the former remaining consistent with private sector debt socialization as a familiar neoliberal practice. In the neoliberal worldview commitment of public funds must, of course, be repaid through future reductions in public spending.

Table 2. Size of Fiscal Stimulus Packages 2008-2010			
Net effect on fiscal balance [% of GDP]			
	Spending	Tax Revenue	Total
Canada	-1.7	-2.4	-4.1
US	-2.4	-3.2	-5.6
OECD average (unweighted)	-0.7	-1.2	-2.0
Source: OECD 2009: 110			

Canada's Response: Denial, Minimalism, Bilateralism, and Business as Usual

In the face of serious economic and financial turmoil occurring around the world, the initial Canadian policy response was both muted and timid. This has largely been attributed to the country's avoidance of some of the worst effects of the crisis. Long-standing regulatory practices in the financial sector and, arguably, a more conservative managerial culture meant that Canadian banks did not become over-leveraged against their asset base in the way that US and many European banks did. Similarly, sub-prime mortgages had not developed very strongly in Canada.[45] However, it is also likely that a commitment to neoliberal ideals prompted the lack of speed and urgency displayed. This is best exemplified through the government's limited interference in the operation of market forces overall, with an important exception being the commitments made in the 2009 Budget to establish a $200 billion fund, called the Emergency Financing Framework, to support these banks should they need to borrow money. It has been estimated that Canada's banks received $114 billion in cash and loan support between September 2008 and August 2010, though this has not been widely publicized and, as David McDonald argues, secrecy and denial regarding the nature and extent of support offered to Canadian banks can hardly serve as the basis for a healthy and resilient banking sector.[46]

Notwithstanding Canada's *relative* immunity to the effects of the crisis, income per capita did fall, employment dropped and unemployment rose. But aside from the commitments made to capital, the Canadian policy response to the crisis was one which seriously lagged behind market events, failed to display a sense of

---

[45]   The Harper government had begun to introduce forms of deregulation just prior to the onset of the global crisis. In 2007 the federal government began allowing US banking sector competition into Canada, thus prompting rule changes by the Canadian Mortgage and Housing Corporation which contributed to the exposure of Canadian banks and encouraged risk taking behaviours – such as dropping the down payment required on a house purchase to zero and extended amortization periods to 40 years. Bruce Campbell, *The Global Economic Crisis and its Canadian Dimension* (Ottawa: Canadian Centre for Policy Alternatives, 2009, July 1). These measures directly contributed to the need for the federal government to later pump very large sums of money into supporting financial institutions, as Canadian banks have had to write down billions of dollars in bad loans. However, the deregulatory thrust was discontinued. Perhaps as a result, Canada has not had to nationalize banks as has been the case elsewhere. John Loxley, "Financial Dimensions: Origins and State Responses," in *Bankruptcies and Bailouts*, eds. J. Guard and W. Antony (Winnipeg & Halifax: Fernwood Publishing, 2009), 70-71. Even so, complacency is hardly warranted. It does seem that questionable lending and mortgage practices were starting to creep into the Canadian financial system just prior to the onset of the crisis. See Derek Ireland and Kernaghan Webb, "The Canadian Escape from Subprime Crisis? Comparing the US and Canadian Approaches," in *How Ottawa Spends 2010-2011: Recession, Realignment, and the New Deficit Era,* eds., G. Bruce Doern and Christopher Stoney (Montreal: McGill-Queen's University Press, 2010).

[46]   See David McDonald, *The Big Banks' Big Secret* (Ottawa: Canadian Centre for Policy Alternatives, 2012).

urgency as was exhibited elsewhere, and aimed for harmonization with the US at the expense of made-at-home initiatives. We can term these denial, business as usual, and bilateralism.[47] Together, these responses indicate a government that was committed to returning to "normality" as fast as possible, a position which it pressed in international gatherings, as well as on its home base.

The government of Canada's initial response to the crisis was one of official denial during and beyond the election campaign that occurred in October 2008. Indeed, the post-election posture of the minority Conservative government was to emphasize its business-as-usual approach in the face of the economic crisis that was unfolding around the world whilst engaging in a series of policy provocations with the opposition parties which launched the country into a short but bitter constitutional crisis as a coalition of opposition parties representing a majority of seats in the House of Commons unsuccessfully attempting to oust the minority Conservative government.[48]

As global economic conditions continued to deteriorate, the federal government's denial in 2008 turned to a minimalist response in early 2009. The January 27 budget admitted that the crisis had reached Canada and that the economy was in recession. However, stimulus measures in Canada were weighted towards tax cuts rather than spending (see Table 2 above), despite general agreement that spending measures had stronger multipliers and were hence able to stimulate further economic activity more effectively than tax measures. Moreover tax cuts were viewed as permanent features of the fiscal landscape. The Canadian Centre for Policy Alternatives (CCPA) calculated that only 4 percent of the budget tax cuts were directed to low income Canadians, the group most likely to spend any money received, and thus help stimulate the broader economy.[49] As well, the spending component of the stimulus package was explicitly declared to be temporary in order to enable a quick return to balanced budgets.[50] Thus program spending, 13 per cent of GDP in 2007-8, was projected to rise to 14.7 per cent

---

[47]   See McBride, "The Global Economic Crisis," for a fuller account.

[48]   See Peter Russell and Lorne Sossin, eds., *Parliamentary Democracy in Crisis* (Toronto: University of Toronto Press, 2009).

[49]   Centre for Policy Alternatives (CCPA), *Federal Budget 2009: CCPA Analysis* (Ottawa: CCPA, 2009), 3.

[50]   Canada. Department of Finance, *Canada's Economic Action Plan: Budget 2009* (Ottawa: Department of Finance, 2009), 12.

in 2009-10, before falling back to 13.1 per cent in 2013-14.[51] This clearly illustrates that the stimulus package was crafted so as to minimize the amount of government intrusion in the economy in the long run.

Just as Canada's early domestic stance on the crisis could be characterized as 'business as usual' so too was its reaction in international circles. Early manifestations of crisis in 2007 were met with the Bank of Canada's refusal to ease monetary conditions or resort to economic stimulus. At the IMF meeting of finance ministers and central bank governors in October 2007 Canada backed the idea that the private sector was responsible for developing solutions to rectify the credit crisis.[52] By the spring of 2010, Canada would play a more active international role by championing a swift return to neoliberal-style global governance. Prime Minister Harper and Finance Minister Flaherty also used their status as host country representatives at the June 2010 G-20 summit in Toronto to avoid discussing initiatives at the meeting that went beyond neoliberal-style governance, despite the obvious need to address the problems experienced by most other countries through significant institutional reforms. Instead they urged that the G-20 should focus on previously agreed upon commitments to bolster capital requirements, strengthen liquidity, and discourage excessive leveraging.[53] According to John Kirton, Canada was on "the minimalist end of the spectrum and is probably even more minimalist than the United States".[54] At the top of the Canadian agenda was prevention of a bank tax proposed by the IMF and backed by France and Germany. This proposal recommended the creation of two new bank taxes, the first was a Financial Stability Contribution which would be levied at various rates to discourage risky banking practices, and would provide a fund which could be used bailout banks in the event of a future crisis; and a Financial Activities Tax, which would be a tax imposed on bank profits, salaries and bonuses.[55] Finance Minister Flaherty maintained that "Canada will not go down the path of excessive, arbitrary or punitive regulation of its financial

---

51   Ibid., 29.
52   Fletcher Baragar, "Canada and the Crisis," in *Bankruptcies and Bailouts*, eds. Julie Guard and Wayne Antony (Winnipeg: Fernwood Publishing, 2009), 88.
53   Ibid.
54   Paul Viera and Eoin Callan, "Canada set to fight Europe over financial cure," *Financial Post*, November 5, 2008, 1.
55   Bill Curry and Jeremy Torobin, "Canada, EU at loggerheads over bank tax," *The Globe and Mail*, May 5, 2010.

sector".[56] Notwithstanding periodic criticism of the US, a stance made easier by Canada's superiority as far as financial regulation is concerned, Canada had to adapt to US initiatives. One example was signing up for its portion of auto bailout funding, in order to protect its share of North American auto production by the major auto manufacturers.[57] In the auto area in particular Canada was a "policy-taker" in that it was the US which devised the package, leaving Canadians as "ultimately passive observers, who can only cross our fingers and hope that the Obama administration's plans save Canadian autoworkers' jobs".[58] Notwithstanding the rhetoric of the Canadian government about its financially superior situation, the reality was that Canada had little latitude and, where it did have some, often exercised this in the direction of closer bilateral relations with the United States.

This was the response when, for example, Canada was faced with a US stimulus package that contained provisions barring foreign suppliers from participation in funded projects. As most of the money in question was to be spent by state and municipal governments, which are mostly exempt from WTO and NAFTA government procurement provisions, US officials considered the measures compliant with trade agreements. Canadian politicians and officials unsuccessfully pleaded for a Presidential veto of the legislation or for exemptions to be made for Canadian suppliers.[59] Threatening action under trade treaties was an empty gesture since state and municipal procurement was excluded. Canadian governments, backed by business, then pressed for reciprocal procurement liberalization.[60]

In February, 2010 a deal exempting Canadian firms was concluded. This came late in the day as the majority of the US stimulus money had already been allocated.[61] In exchange for limited access

---

56   Heather Scoffield, "Ottawa rejects IMF bank tax recommendations, shows flavour of summit to come," *The Canadian Press,* April 21, 2010.

57   In the event, the Ford Motor Company decided not to access the bailout funds.

58   J. Ibbitson, "When it comes to the Canadian economy, Obama may as well be PM," *The Globe and Mail,* May 20, 2009, A19.

59   Brian Laghi and Kevin Carmichael, "Canada Takes Battle Over 'Buy American' to US Senate," *Globe and Mail,* February 3, 2009, A1.

60   CBC, "Buy American Exemption Deal in the Works," *CBC News,* September 30, 2009, http://www.cbc.ca/canada/story/2009/09/29/buy-american.html.

61   CBC, "'Buy American' deal exempts Canadian firms," *CBC News,* February 5, 2010, http://www.cbc.ca/canada/story/2010/02/05/ott-buy-american-deal.html.

to remaining US contracts, Canadian provincial and municipal governments agreed to sign onto the WTO's government procurement agreement, thereby agreeing to allow US companies to bid on future public works projects at the sub-national level. As usual when Canada is the 'demandeur' in bilateral trade negotiations with the US, it seemed that Canada had made the greater concessions. Moreover, notwithstanding NAFTA rhetoric concerning the "three amigos" of North America, Canada's proposal entirely ignored Mexico.

Other Canadian trade initiatives fall outside the bilateral dimension of Canadian foreign economic policy. For example the negotiations for a comprehensive economic and trade economic agreement (CETA) with the EU are at one level an effort to diversify Canada's trade relations whilst, at an another, intensifying the neo-liberal approach to international trade by opening up new areas, such as government procurement, to foreign suppliers. The EU is said to have insisted that Canadian provinces be represented at the negotiating table because they want access to provincial procurement as part of the chapter on government procurement.

An end to stimulus, a return of austerity, and an uncertain economic recovery

STIMULUS

Despite the widespread use of stimulus packages around the world, within a few short years advocates of government spending began to urge a retreat from stimulus and the implementation of fiscal austerity in order to reduce public sector debt levels. The stimulus measures themselves can be said to have aided both capital and labour, thus contributing both to accumulation and legitimation. Arguably, if they had been better designed, their job creation impact, and hence benefits to labour, would have been enhanced. It is clear, though, that through budgetary austerity measures, labour will pay the price of what stimulus was delivered. There has been some debate in Canada as to the actual impact that the Economic Action Plan had on the economy. How effective was this at creating jobs and promoting economic recovery? Was it too little and too late? Was it needed at all or did the economy improve on its own?

A series of reports released in 2010 suggest different answers to these questions.

In March 2010 the Fraser Institute released a report which claimed that data from Statistics Canada pointed to private consumption and business investment as being the drivers of growth in the second quarter of 2009 and net exports as drivers of growth in the third quarter, not government spending and government investment.[62] The report calls the contribution of these latter two "negligible". The CCPA countered that government support for the construction industry had a positive impact on this hard hit sector and that most new job creation during late 2009/early 2010 was in the public sector, as a result of the stimulus package.[63] Improvements to the package could have been made, however, and Iglika Ivanova argues that making it easier to qualify for employment insurance and welfare would have held greater benefit for household income, and that the Economic Action Plans should have focused less on tax cuts and more on targeted spending such as green infrastructure.[64]

In the fall of 2010 the Auditor General of Canada looked into how the $40 billion Economic Action Plan was being delivered.[65] Here several problems were identified, importantly that the quarterly progress reports released by the federal government contained incomplete information on job creation. The Auditor General called the information provided "anecdotal", and stated that the quarterly reports "did not present a complete picture of all jobs created, nor did it include information on jobs created or maintained for all Economic Action Plan programs".[66] The report also warned of exemptions offered from

---

[62]   Amela Karabegovic, Charles Lammam, and Niels Veldhuis, "Did Government Stimulus Fuel Economic Growth in Canada? An Analysis of Statistics Canada Data," *Canada Fraser Institute* (March 23, 2010).

[63]   Iglika Ivanova, "In defense of the stimulus," *Policy Note* (BC: Canadian Centre for Policy Alternatives, 2010, March 25) http://www.policynote.ca/in-defense-of-the-stimulus/

[64]   Ibid.

[65]   In Budget 2009 the Economic Action Plan had committed $40 billion to stimulating housing construction, building infrastructure, and supporting businesses and communities; the provinces and territories would also fund an additional $12 billion. These amounts were later increased to $47 billion and $14 billion, respectively. Auditor General of Canada, "Chapter 1 – Canada's Economic Action Plan," *Fall Report of the Auditor General of Canada*, http://www.oagbvg.gc.ca/internet/English/parl_oag_201010_01_e_34284.html.

[66]   Auditor General of Canada, "Chapter 1 – Canada's Economic Action Plan."

environmental assessments, and raised concerns about project delays which threatened their ability to receive Infrastructure Stimulus Fund money since this was not supposed to be made available to projects completed after the deadline of March 31, 2011.[67]

However, it is the December 2010 report by the Parliamentary Budget Officer (PBO) that is particularly damning of the way the stimulus program was designed. Based on a survey of municipalities that received Infrastructure Stimulus Fund (ISF) money, the PBO found that 43 per cent of those surveyed felt that the funds had no impact on job creation.[68] At a news conference, the PBO Kevin Page suggested that the impact of the economic stimulus on community welfare had been "moderately positive" but that its effect on the labour market was "more muted, less positive, less glowing".[69] Also, more targeted spending was clearly needed as some projects created more jobs than others (infrastructure projects versus waste management, for example).

Altogether these reports point to a half-hearted Economic Action Plan of relatively poor design. Economic stimulus, especially for hard hit sectors, was certainly needed. However the opportunity to target spending in ways that would have maximized benefits for labour and initiated a new, more sustainable direction for future economic growth was largely squandered. Directing funds towards green infrastructure projects, for example, would have satisfied both. The weak effort on the part of the Harper Conservatives reveals an underlying aversion to go beyond anything but a token effort to fix what ails the neoliberal policy paradigm. Thus Canada's larger crisis reaction of denial and minimalism explained earlier is mirrored in the Economic Action Plan itself. This is also a prime example of ideological legitimation[70] given that public spending to rescue capital and provide for some modicum of legitimacy was quickly used to justify a return to spending retrenchment. This

---

[67]   In December 2010 Prime Minister Harper extended the completion deadline for infrastructure projects that receive stimulus cash, from the end of March 2011 to October 31, 2011.

[68]   David Pinet and Peter Weltman, *Update – Infrastructure Stimulus Fund. Annex A.* (Ottawa: Office of the Parliamentary Budget Officer, 2010, December 1).

[69]   CTV, "Stimulus plan 'not so good' at job creation: watchdog," *CTV News,* December 2, 2010, http://www.cp24.com/servlet/an/local/CTVNews/20101202/ottawa-stimulus-deadline-101202?hub=OttawaHome.

[70]   Promoting the jobs plan did not come cheap, with a cost of over $53 million, see http://www.theglobeandmail.com/news/politics/harper-government-spends-26-million-on-winter-ad-blitz/article1940253.

echoes the familiar pattern of using neoliberal crises to excuse the promotion of additional neoliberal reforms.[71]

A RETURN TO AUSTERITY

No sooner had stimulus spending been approved than it seemed the search for "exit strategies" was under development. For instance, a May 2010 OECD editorial instructed that an "exit from exceptional fiscal support must start now, or by 2011 at the latest",[72] and in its 2010 Economic Outlook the OECD proclaimed that "in those countries that have not yet begun the consolidation process, public finances need to start being brought credibly onto a sound footing by next year at the latest"[73]. In 2009 the TD Bank Financial Group had also counseled that Canada should return to an aggregate budget balance of zero, achieved through fiscal restraint and structural reforms to social programs.[74]

Recent provincial and federal budgets in Canada indicate that austerity will soon be making a comeback. The 2010 federal budget concerned itself with tax cuts for business, spending cuts to federal departments, and further freezes placed on operating budgets.[75] Summarizing recent fiscal policy, the Canadian Labour Congress (CLC) argued, "The Conservatives responded to the recession by raising spending grudgingly and under pressure, both domestically and internationally. Deficit-financed stimulus measures taken in the 2009 Budget which continued into 2010 — especially investment in municipal infrastructure and somewhat enhanced access to Employment Insurance and training — had some positive impact in alleviating the full force of the Great Recession on working people and on hard-hit communities. But these measures have come to an

---

[71] See McBride and Heather Whiteside, *Private Affluence, Public Austerity*, Chapter 5.

[72] OECD, "A Strengthening Recovery, But Also New Risks," *OECD Editorial*, 2010, 6, http://www.oecd.org/dataoecd/4/50/39739655.pdf.

[73] OECD, "General Assessment of the Macroeconomic Situation," *Economic Outlook*, 2010, 9, *http://www.oecd.org/dataoecd/36/57/43117724.pdf.*

[74] TD Bank Financial Group, "The Coming Era of Fiscal Restraint," *Special Report*, October 20, 2009, http://www.td.com/economics/special/db1009_fiscal.pdf.

[75] Canadian Union of Public Employees (CUPE). "Budget 2010: Overview and Summary," March 4, 2010, http://cupe.ca/budget/budget-2010-overview-analysis-summary.

end, and the focus is now on fiscal austerity."[76] Focusing specifically on the 2011 Budget the CLC was of the view that: "The hidden focus of the Budget is upon reducing an already modest deficit. Big spending cuts amounting to $4 billion per year are to take place over the next few years, though no details are provided on where the axe will fall. The Budget hints that these cuts will be used to fund further tax cuts".[77] Thus, government deficits run up by a crisis induced by capital will not be paid through increased corporate tax, but through spending restraint and program cuts. The same pattern continued through the 2012 budget with program spending projected to decline to 12.9 percent of GDP in 2015-16 (compared to 14.1 percent in 2011-12).[78] The same is true at the provincial level. For example, the Ontario government seeks to balance the budget through expenditure restraint, and by imposing a pay freeze on government workers and implementing several tax breaks for business.[79]

RECOVERY

Early on in the recent global financial crisis, Canada held the enviable position of being a relatively safe haven from some of the worst ravages of the economic turbulence and financial volatility experienced at the time. Yet this has only led to a lingering misunderstanding of Canada's position in terms of later recovery from the crisis. This misunderstanding has also been actively promoted by politicians, with

---

[76] Canadian Labour Congress (CLC), "CLC Analysis of the 2011 Federal Budget," March, 22, 2011, http://www.canadianlabour.ca/news-room/publications/clc-analysis-2011-federal-budget.

[77] Originally the March 2011 budget had forecast a return to surplus by 2015-16. Following the May 2011 federal election, the revised 2011 budget (released in June) now indicates a return to surplus one year earlier – by 2014-15. Balancing the budget one year earlier during a particularly gloomy period for the global economy will require expenditure cuts, especially in light of problems in the US and European economies which likely means lower economic growth in Canada than government projections suggest. Treasury Board President Tony Clement is charged with cutting 5 percent from annual program spending, and the review of which programs will be affected is currently underway. See CBC, "Flaherty sticks to deficit pledge, but adds no details." *CBC News,* June 6, 2011, http://www.cbc.ca/news/politics/story/2011/06/06/pol-federal-budget-flaherty.html.

[78] Canadian Labour Congress (CLC), "CLC Analysis of the 2012 Federal Budget".

[79] Daily Commercial News, "Ontario Budget: Austerity for Workers, Tax Cuts for Bay Street," *Daily Commercial News,* March 25, 2010, http://www.daily-commercialnews.com/nw/17681/en.

finance minister Flaherty boasting at the October 2010 G-20 meeting that Canada is "the best place in the G7 to do business" and the typical rhetoric emanating from the finance department in 2009/10 was that Canada would survive the global downturn better than most industrialized countries.[80] However, by early 2011 economist Jim Stanford was warning against such eager proclamations, citing several key indicators which signaled that Canada was being surpassed by other G-7 countries by late 2010.[81] These problems relate to GDP, jobs, Canada's trade balance, and productivity.

For instance, between spring 2010 and January 2011, growth was virtually non-existent; and almost no new net jobs were created between August 2010 and January 2011. The unemployment rate dropped over this period but this was due not to growth but instead to a decline in the labour force participation rate. Examining a less deceptive measure of labour market health – the employment rate – indicates that Canada was fifth in the G7 in the third quarter of 2010. Canada's trade position has also deteriorated, and the country's current account deficit reached an annualized $65 billion in the third quarter of 2010 – an all time high for Canada and the second worst in the G7. Little improvement in production has been made either, and between 2007 and early 2011 cumulative productivity was at zero. In contrast, over that same period, Australia, Norway, Brazil, China, Germany and France suffered less damage to GDP and labour markets due in large part to more pro-active government efforts. Economic woes of this sort must now be resolved in the context of state retrenchment and fiscal austerity, making the federal government's "business as usual" approach to supporting capital accumulation and providing for legitimation an increasingly threadbare exercise.

Conclusion

The intrinsic nature of crises and contradictions in the capitalist mode of production stimulates state engagement with a combination of accumulation, legitimation, and coercion-related roles

---

[80]   For example, see Canada. Department of Finance, "Government Acts to Support Canada's Economic Recovery," December 7, 2010, http://news.gc.ca/web/article-eng.do?nid=578989.

[81]   For more detail, see Jim Stanford, "Halo Came Off Canadian Recovery as 2010 Drew to Close," *The Bullet* 451 (2011).

(the balance between them changing over time). No matter how these roles manifest, crises have proven to be an ongoing feature of the system yet what has become ever more obvious is the particularly persistent nature of economic crises within the neoliberal period (especially, but not exclusively, in contrast to the Keynesian era). This makes the neoliberal policy paradigm problematic on a number of levels, not the least of which includes these important roles played by the state. Long wave and overaccumulation theories discussed here provide salient explanations for why the extra-economic institutions and spatio-temporal fixes of the neoliberal era are unlikely to promote growth and stability in the long run. Further, as both symptom and partial cause of ongoing economic instability, policy efforts to promote accumulation over the past few decades have often been designed in such a way as to substitute material benefits conceded to subordinate classes with ideological and coercive measures. The latter two are now being pursued to an ever-greater extent as the legitimacy of the system wears thin.

Canada's policy response to the most recent economic crisis and associated 'Great Recession' are prime examples of the entrenchment of these trends. Denying that problems existed meant that very few pro-active strategies were implemented. Next, once bilateral and international pressures became too great for the federal government to ignore, taking a minimalist approach to institutional and spending reform was adopted – making stimulus efforts both temporary and uncreative, and also strategic given that token public spending is now being used to justify a return to draconian fiscal austerity.

As time passes, a speedy recovery from the crisis becomes less and less assured. This places a spotlight once more on changing balance of the state's activities vis-à-vis accumulation, legitimation and coercion. While the future is uncertain, what is becoming clear is that not only is neoliberalism a troubled solution to global accumulation problems, but the policy responses to the most significant challenge of neoliberal rule to date have only aggravated these problems. The sum total of state efforts to support accumulation since 2007 thus amount to little more than the rescue of capital at the expense of labour (once more). Not only is this of serious consequence for all citizens, but ultimately it threatens to undermine the legitimacy of the system as well.

FROM THE GREAT RECESSION OF 2008-2009 TO FISCAL AUSTERITY: THE ROLE OF INEQUALITY

Akhter Faroque & Brian K. MacLean

Introduction

The global slump of 2008-2009, often dubbed the Great Recession, saw global output contract for the first time since World War Two.[1] Real GDP in Canada sank by the second quarter of 2009 back to the level of the first quarter of 2006 and the official unemployment rate rose from 5.9 percent in January 2008 to a peak of 8.7 percent in August 2009.[2] As Chart 1 indicates, the decline in Canada's real GDP growth rate ranks with the declines observed in the severe recessions of the early 1980s and early 1990s. It could have been worse. The global slump was most severe in countries that experienced a housing boom-bust cycle combined with a banking crisis, as in the United States, the United Kingdom, Ireland, and Spain, among others. Table 1 shows selected economic indicators for 25 large economies in 2009, the worst year of the slump, and points to the widespread nature of negative economic growth, high

---

[1]   Rogoff argues for the term "Great Contraction" on the grounds that the term "contraction applies not only to output and employment, as in a normal recession, but to debt and credit, and the deleveraging that typically takes many years to complete." This characterization certainly applies to the United States and several European economies but not to most other economies. Kenneth Rogoff, "The Second Great Contraction," *Project Syndicate* (August 2, 2011): pp??, http://www.project-syndicate.org/commentary/rogoff83/English.

[2]   For real GDP (inflation-adjusted output), we have used the Statistics CANSIM series v v1992067 (real GDP in chained 2002 dollars). For the unemployment rate, we have used the Statistics Canada CANSIM series V2062815 (unemployment rate, both sexes, seasonally adjusted).

unemployment, either deflation or very low inflation, and large
government budget deficits.

Chart 1: Real GDP Growth Rate, Canada, 1962-2010

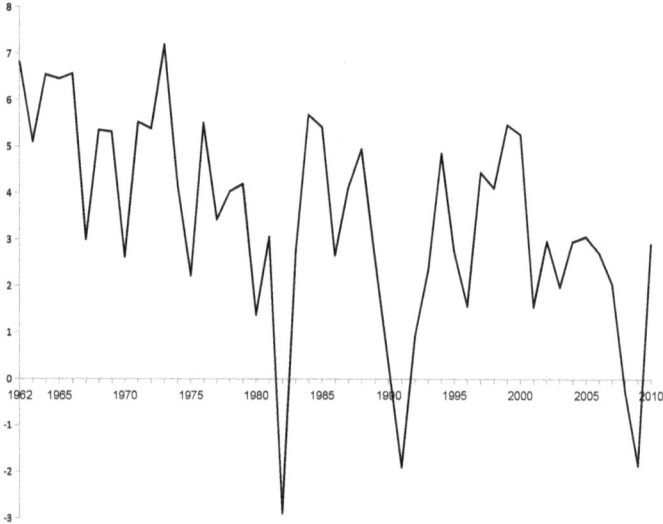

Source: Adapted from Statistics Canada, CANSIM series v41707175.

Even though the impact of the recession on Canadian government finances was relatively mild compared to the impact in
most other high-income countries, political pressures mounted
in favour of government austerity measures similar to those that
have gained ground in the United States and Europe in the wake
of the recession. These measures involve targeted cuts to the wages
and benefits of public sector workers, general cuts to programs that
support the social wages of workers in general, and also rolling
back the collective bargaining rights of public employees.[3]

As the Great Recession of 2008-2009 unfolded, even the editors
of the pro-finance *Economist* newsweekly fretted about the possibility that the "populist argument" that Anglo-Saxon capitalism had

---

[3]   Peters summarizes the situation in the advanced capitalist economies in early
        2011 as governments implemented "exit strategies" from the period of deliber-
        ate fiscal stimulus. John Peters, "Boom, Bust and Crisis: The Challenges of
        Capital and the State for Canadian Workers and Unions in the 21st Century,"
        Laurentian University (2011).

Table 1: Select Economic Indicators, Large Advanced Economies, 2009					
Economy	GDP growth rate (%)	Export volume change	Unemploy-ment rate (%)	Inflation rate (%)	Budget balance to GDP
Australia	1.3	2.8	5.6	1.8	-4.1
Austria	-3.9	-16.1	4.8	0.4	-3.5
Belgium	-2.7	-11.4	8.0	0.0	-6.0
Canada	-2.5	-14.2	8.3	0.3	-5.5
France	-2.5	-12.2	9.5	0.1	-7.6
Germany	-4.7	-14.3	7.5	0.2	-3.0
Greece	-2.0	-20.1	9.4	1.4	-15.4
Ireland	-7.6	- 4.1	11.8	- 1.7	-14.4
Italy	-5.2	-25.6	7.8	0.8	-5.3
Japan	-6.3	-24.1	5.1	- 1.4	-10.3
Netherlands	-3.9	- 9.6	3.4	1.0	- 5.4
Portugal	-2.5	-12.4	9.6	- 0.9	-9.3
South Korea	0.2	- 0.8	3.7	2.8	0.0
Spain	-3.7	-11.6	18.0	- 0.2	-11.1
Sweden	-5.3	-12.5	8.3	2.0	- 0.8
Switzerland	-1.9	- 8.7	3.6	- 0.5	0.8
U.K.	-4.9	-10.1	7.5	2.1	-10.3
U.S.	-2.6	- 9.5	9.3	- 0.3	-12.7
China	9.2	-10.3	4.3	-0.7	- 3.0
Brazil	-0.6	-10.8	8.1	4.9	- 3.0
India	6.7	0.7	—	10.9	- 9.4
Indonesia	4.6	5.3	7.9	4.8	- 1.8
Poland	1.7	-6.8	8.2	3.5	- 7.2
Turkey	-4.7	-8.1	14.0	6.3	-5.6
Russia	-7.8	-8.8	8.4	11.7	-6.3
Source: International Monetary Fund, *World Economic Outlook Database, April 2011*, http://www.imf.org/exter-nal/pubs/ft/weo/2011/01/weodata/index.aspx					

failed could continue to gain ground, and that not only would "politicians from Beijing to Berlin" resist further moves to free trade,
but that arguments for "market solutions in, for instance, health
and education" would be "made with less conviction."[4] Not surprisingly, some progressive economists thought that the crisis would
decisively demonstrate the folly of the free-market fundamentalist
model that had guided economic policy in many countries, and
herald a historic shift in the general direction of economic policy
in a more social democratic direction reminiscent of the so-called
golden age of capitalism from the 1950s to the 1970s. But, instead
of being forced to admit to any failures in the old model, in country
after country the "powers that be" have managed to turn the crisis
into an opportunity to promote policies even more regressive than
previously considered attainable.[5]

The main purpose of this chapter is to provide a Canadian perspective on the causes of the Great Recession of 2008-2009 and on the
question of why the experience of the Great Recession has not resulted
in a shift of economic policy in a more progressive direction. The first
section of the paper explains the Great Recession and its fiscal consequences. While the policy responses we have observed since 2010 in
the high-income capitalist economies – such as income tax cuts combined with government program expenditure cuts – have little basis
in economic logic as means of dealing with a fiscal crisis in economies with lingering high unemployment, they do make sense given
the change in the power structure of society associated with growing
inequality of income over the past few decades.

The second section presents a political economy theory of
income distribution to explain mounting inequality of income in
Canada in recent decades. The central idea is that distributional
outcomes in high-income capitalist democracies are determined
through the interactions of three sets of institutions: markets, government, and labour unions.

---

[4]   See "Capitalism at Bay," *Economist*, October 16, 2008, http://www.economist.
       com/node/12429544.
[5]   Stiglitz, for example, states: "I was among those who hoped that, somehow, the
       financial crisis would teach Americans (and others) a lesson about the need for
       greater equality, stronger regulation, and a better balance between the market
       and government. Alas, that has not been the case." Joseph E. Stigliz, "The
       Ideological Crisis of Western Capitalism," *Project Syndicate* (2011b): http://
       www.projectsyndicate.org/commentary/stiglitz140/English.

The third section describes and explains the sources of rising inequality of income. We provide empirical evidence that after-tax income inequality has been mounting in recent decades in Canada and the United States. Based upon this evidence and our political economy theory of income distribution, we identify the root causes of mounting income inequality in Canada since the early 1980s.

The paper concludes with some important considerations from our research as economists, including our research for this paper, that relate to the achievement of greater economic stability and equality of income in Canada and elsewhere. We touch upon countercyclical macroeconomic policies, the balance of power within countries, re-regulation of finance, and international cooperation.

The Great Recession and its Fiscal Consequences

Economists have proposed many alternative explanations for the Great Recession, but most explanations focus on the role of the U.S. housing bust beginning in 2006 and the subsequent financial panic in the fall of 2008, at least in terms of proximate causes.[6] While there were other economies such as the United Kingdom, Ireland, Spain, and Iceland that also experienced a U.S.-style housing boom-bust cycle combined with a banking crisis, it was the U.S.-centred financial panic in the fall of 2008 that triggered the global recession of 2008-2009. Even economies such as those of Australia, Canada, China, Japan, and many others, lacking any particular internal reason to experience a recession in 2008 or 2009, were dragged into recession by the financial panic emanating from the United States. The financial panic triggered credit crises in many countries, stock market crashes, and then declines in exports and private-sector fixed capital formation.[7]

---

[6]   An entertaining and insightful brief summary of alternative explanations can be found at the beginning of "RSA Animate – Crises of Capitalism," a video version of a talk by David Harvey: http://www.youtube.com/watch?v=qOP2V_np2c0. A good brief guide to books on the origins of the Great Recession is Andrew Jackson, "Best Books on the Crisis," *Relentlessly Progressive Economics* (June 26, 2011), http://www.progressive-economics.ca/2011/06/26/best-books-on-the-economic-crisis/.

[7]   Our view of the Great Recession is based upon too many sources to list here. Among those we would recommend are Dean Baker, *Taking Economics Seriously* (Cambridge, Mass.: MIT Press, 2011), and Joseph Stiglitz, *The Price of Inequality* (New York: W. W. Norton, 2012).

Speculative booms are a normal occurrence in capitalist economies, and do not necessarily require any special explanation, but the
one affecting housing markets in numerous countries during the
2000s, especially in the United States, was particularly extreme.[8] The
rapid increase in house prices in a wide range of countries over several
years leading up to the Great Recession seems partly related to low
interest rates during those years, which in turn were due to a number of
causes, including the "global savings glut" mentioned by U.S. Federal
Reserve Chairman Bernanke.[9] What was special about the U.S. housing boom of 2000-2006, other than the sheer size of the U.S. housing
sector, is that it was associated with a host of "innovations" associated
with housing finance – from *ninja loans* to collateralized debt obligations to credit default swaps – that intensified both the build-up of
the bubble and its subsequent collapse. The extreme leveraging by the
least regulated of U.S. financial institutions provided massive gains to
top management and shareholders during the bubble. Moreover, the
bundling of high-risk mortgages into tranches that were rated as low
risk by the bond rating agencies, and the sale of those tranches across
the globe ensured that when the bubble burst the eventual losses on
bad loans were not limited to U.S. financial institutions but were
shared by financial institutions in many countries.[10] The financial
innovations behind the U.S. housing boom and bust, of course, had
been made possible by financial deregulation, which is why the pro-
finance *Economist* newsweekly feared that there would be a populist
backlash against "Anglo-Saxon capitalism" or what others would call
"neo-liberalism."

By comparison with the United States, house price appreciation
in Canada during the 2000-2006 period was more restrained. (See

---

[8]   See, for example, Robert Shiller, *Irrational Exuberance*, 2nd ed. (Princeton,
      N.J.: Princeton University Press, 2005).
[9]   See Ben Bernanke et al., "International Capital Flows and the Returns to Safe
      Assets in the United States, 2003-2007," *Board of Governors of the Federal
      Reserve System International Finance Discussion Papers*, no. 1014 (February
      2011). http://www.federalreserve.gov/pubs/ifdp/2011/1014/ifdp1014.htm.
[10] After the Japanese housing bubble which developed in the latter half of the
      1980s and burst in the early 1990s, the "bad loans" were concentrated among
      Japanese financial institutions, and the international financial repercussions
      were negligible. The Japanese housing bubble is discussed in Brian MacLean,
      "Avoiding a Great Depression but Getting a Great Recession: The Bank of
      Japan and Monetary Policy, 1991-2004," *International Journal of Political
      Economy* 35, no. 1 (Spring 2006): 84-107.

Chart 2.) The starting point for an explanation would seem to be that in Canada regulatory and especially supervisory standards were tighter over the same period than in the United States.[11] The Canadian housing finance and banking system contains many features and legal provisions that prevented large scale securitization, relaxed lending standards, and a consequent subprime lending debacle.[12]

Chart 2: U.S. and Canadian House Price Indices, February 1999 to February 2011

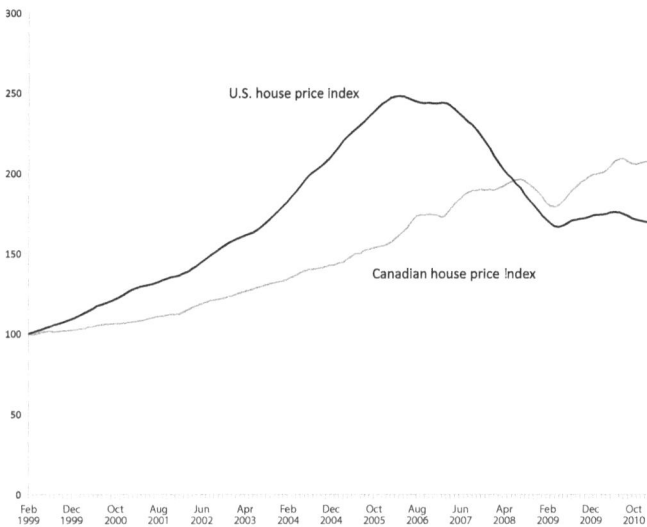

Sources: The Canadian house price index is the Teranet –National Bank House Price Index, Composite 6, from http://www.housepriceindex.ca/; the U.S. house price index is the S & P/Case-Shiller House Price Index, Composite-10, from http://www.standardandpoors.com/indices/economic/en/us/?assetName=Economic&assetID=1221186708649. Both indices have been adjusted to equal 100 in February 1999.

The Great Recession therefore manifested itself in substantially different ways in Canada and the United States. The United States slipped into recession earlier – in December 2007, by the dating of the National Bureau of Economic Research. The first

---

[11]   See Julie Dickson, "Too Focused on the Rules; The Importance of Supervisory Oversight in Financial Regulation?," Remarks by Julie Dickson. Office of the Superintendent of Financial Institutions Canada to the Heyman Centre on Corporate Governance. (New York: March 16, 2010).

[12]   See James MacGee, "Why Didn't Canada's Housing Market Go Bust?," *Economic Commentary* (2009), http://www.clevelandfed.org/Research/commentary/2009/0909.cfm.

component of real quarterly expenditure to make a negative contribution to expenditure growth was residential investment, which exhibited negative growth in the second quarter of 2007, and registered negative growth in each quarter of the following recession. (See Chart 3 for a graphical presentation of the U.S. expenditure data). By the first quarter of 2008, consumption growth also turned negative; by the second quarter of 2008, nonresidential investment growth turned negative; and from the third quarter of 2008 to the second quarter of 2009, residential investment, consumption, and nonresidential investment all continued to shrink. Throughout the recession the only components pulling output in the direction of positive growth were net exports and government purchases.

Chart 3: Contributions to U.S. Expenditure Growth, Third Quarter 2007 to Second Quarter 2009

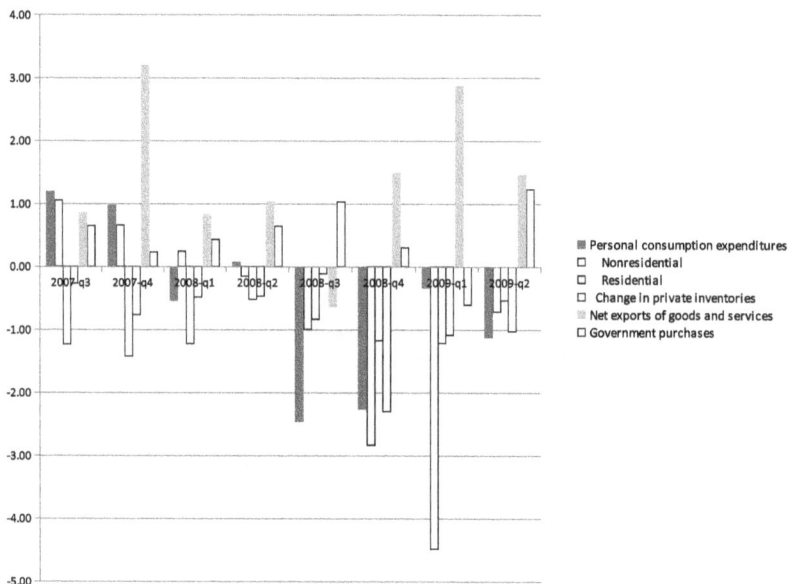

Source: Adapted from U.S. Bureau of Economic Analysis, Table 1.1.2. Contributions to Percent Change in Real Gross Domestic Product, http://www.bea.gov/national/nipaweb/GetCSV.asp?GetWhat=SS_Data/Section1All_xls. xls&Section=2

Chart 4: Exports and Private-Sector Fixed Capital Formation, Canada, 2008-2011, Quarterly Data (in billions of dollars)

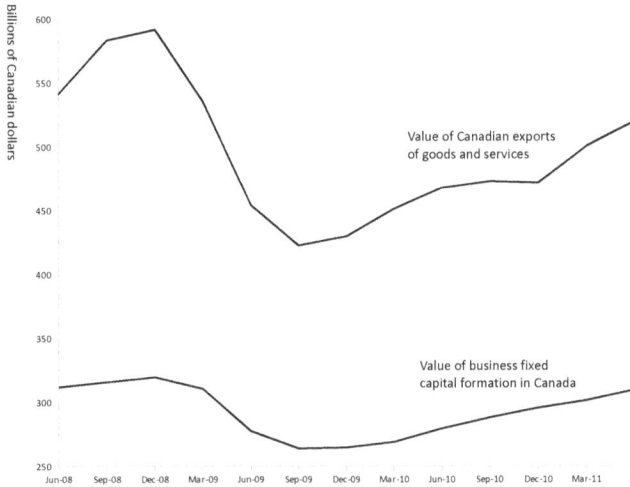

Sources: Statistics Canada CANSIM series v498103 (exports) and v498095 (fixed capital formation).

In Canada, the recession is dated from the third quarter of 2008.[13] The onset of the recession was directly triggered by the loss of export markets and the associated drop in business fixed capital formation. (See Chart 4). As in the United States, government purchases pulled in the direction of positive growth throughout the recession, and rose as a percentage of GDP. (See Chart 5). The peak to trough drop in real (inflation-adjusted) GDP was less in Canada than in the United States – 4 percent as opposed to 5.4 percent.[14] Both countries came out of recession in the third quarter of 2009, making the recession shorter in Canada than in the United States. Also, even by the second quarter of 2011 U.S. real GDP had not returned to the level of the previous peak in the fourth quarter of 2007, but by the third quarter of 2010 Canadian real GDP had surpassed the previous peak of the third quarter of 2008.

---

[13]   See Phillip Cross, "Year-end Review of 2009," *Canadian Economic Observer* (April 2010), http://www.statcan.gc.ca/pub/11-010-x/2010004/part-partie3-eng.htm.

[14]   This paper takes into account the latest revisions to official U.S. and Canadian GDP data as of early August 2011. In late July 2001 the official U.S. GDP data for the 2007-2011 were revised downwards.

Chart 5: Government Purchases as a Share of GDP, Canada, 2007-2011, Quarterly Data

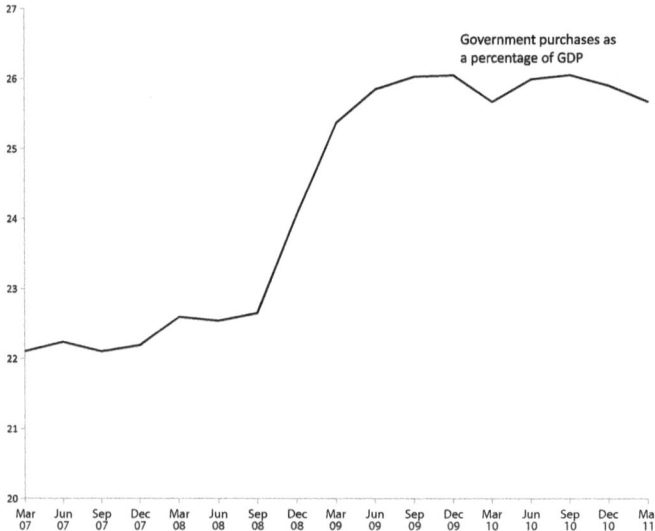

Sources: The numerator is the sum of Statistics Canada CANSIM series v498092 (government current expenditure), v498093 (government gross fixed capital formation), and v498094 (government investment in inventories); the denominator is CANSIM series v498086 (GDP at market prices).

The Great Recession manifested itself differently in Canada and the United States not just with respect to GDP but also with respect to the labour market. For example, employment in Canada peaked in October 2008, fell by 2.5 percent to reach bottom in July 2009, returned to the pre-recession peak by January 2011, and continued to grow. By contrast, employment in the United States fell 6 percent from December 2007 to December 2009, and had only recovered by mid-2011 to a level previously reached in mid-2004. (See Chart 6 on Canadian and U.S. employment levels.) The Canadian unemployment rate rose from 6.1 percent in October 2008 to a peak of 8.7 percent in August 2009, and by June 2011 had fallen steadily to 7.4 percent, which was 1.2 percentage points above the level observed near the beginning of the recession. The U.S. unemployment rate rose from 5.0 percent in December 2007 to a peak of 10.1 percent in October 2009, and was at 9.2 percent in June 2011, a full 4.2 percentage points above the level observed near the beginning of the recession.

Chart 6: Trends in Employment Levels, Canada and the United States, 2005-mid-2011

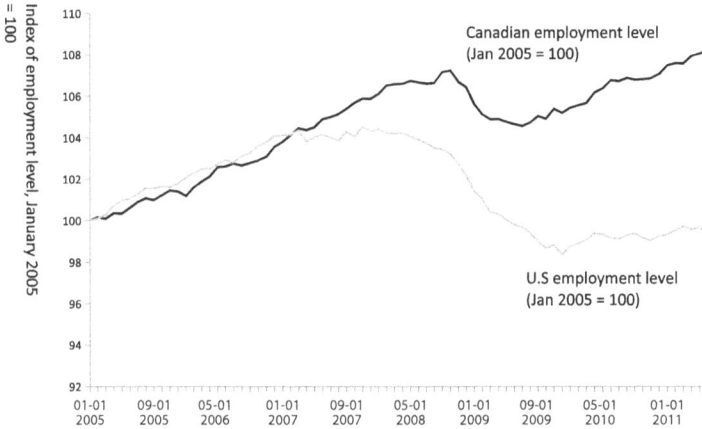

Sources: Adapted from Statistics Canada, CANSIM series v2057603, for Canadian employment, and U.S. Bureau of Labor Statistics, series ID CE160V, retrieved from http://research.stlouisfed.org/fred2/categories/12, for U.S. employment. Employment levels for both countries are converted to indexes with January 2005 as the common base period with employment set equal to 100.

The greater severity of the U.S. recession largely reflects the dramatic housing boom and bust that Canada has so far managed to avoid, and the U.S. financial sector collapse that stemmed from the U.S. housing bust.[15] The greater severity of the recession in the United States was not the result of less aggressive macroeconomic policy response in the United States than in Canada. In both countries fear of a repeat of the Great Depression stirred policymakers to action. The Federal Reserve and the Bank of Canada each aggressively lowered their key policy interest rate close to the zero (see Chart 7), but the Federal Reserve also undertook several unconventional monetary policy measures that included participation in the Wall Street bailout, emergency lending, toxic asset purchases, and quantitative easing. Both countries also initiated fiscal stimulus packages (in the first quarter of 2009). But the U.S. stimulus relative to GDP was larger: Caldentey and Vernengo (2010: p. 25), for example, claim that the accumulated fiscal deficit over the 2008-2010 period resulting from discretionary fiscal measures

---

[15]   Another factor supporting recovery in Canada has been rising demand, particularly from the so-called emerging market economies, for Canadian natural resource exports.

amounted to 5.6 percent of GDP for the United States versus 4.1 percent of GDP for Canada.

Chart 7: The Bank of Canada's Overnight Rate Target and Fed's Federal Funds Rate, 2005-2011

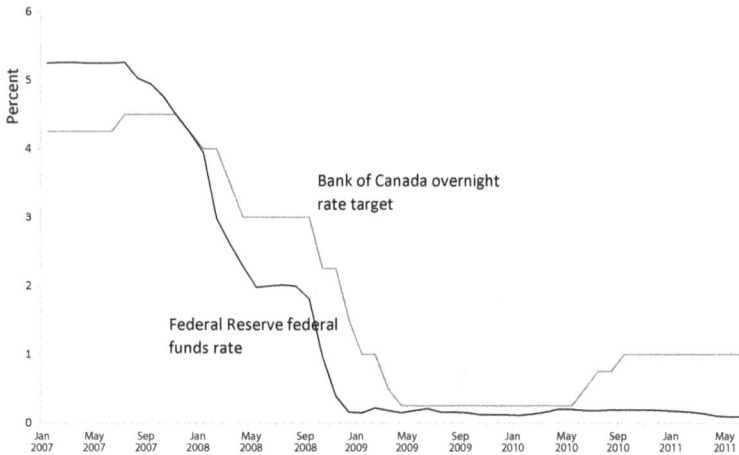

Source: Adapted from the Statistics Canada series v122530 (bank rate) according to the formula overnight rate target = bank rate − 0.25, and the U.S. federal funds effective rate, H15/H15/RIFSPFF_N.M

Given the origins of the Great Recession, there was much talk in the early months of the recession about the need to strengthen financial market regulation in various high-income countries and at the international level. But reflecting the continued power of the financial oligarchies of various countries, financial market re-regulation has not gone far.[16] Indeed, as the fears of another Great Depression subsided, the policy debate in high-income countries soon turned to the alleged ills of government budget deficits and dangers of monetary expansion. One side in this debate called for immediate reductions in government budget deficits despite still-weak recoveries in many high-income countries, warning that the deficits would drive up long-term interest rates and crowd out private-sector investment. The same side argued for higher policy interest rates from central banks, claiming that all the

---

[16]   Macklem provides an official Canadian perspective on current international initiatives regarding financial regulation. Tiff Macklem, "Global Financial Reform: Maintaining the Momentum," Bank of Canada, 2011, http://www.bankofcanada.ca/wp-content/uploads/2011/07/remarks_070711.pdf.

money created by the central banks through quantitative easing and similar policies was on the verge of creating an era of high inflation. The other side (progressives) argued that so long as the economy remained depressed with high unemployment and low aggregate demand at near-zero interest rates, there was no fear of high inflation igniting or of higher interest rates crowding out private-sector investment. Indeed, as predicted by the progressives, to this day, almost three years since the start of the global recession, there is little sign of runaway inflation or of rising interest rates either in the United States or Canada.

The push for monetary and fiscal austerity in Canada, the United States, and other high-income countries has been aided by two facts. One is that the U.S. fiscal stimulus, while large relative to the fiscal stimulus of many other countries, was small relative to the loss of aggregate demand associated with the collapse of the housing bubble.[17] Consequently, although the stimulus worked to prevent a repeat of the Great Depression, it did not produce a robust recovery. Moreover, the stimulus spending together with the operation of automatic stabilizers left the United States with large fiscal deficits. Because the fiscal stimulus was marketed by the Obama administration with forecasts assuming that it would be adequate to produce robust recovery, and this has not happened, advocates of fiscal austerity have been able to use the mistaken administration forecasts to claim that the fiscal stimulus has done nothing other than to expand the government deficit and consequently add to the U.S. government debt.[18]

The other fact is that as the recession unfolded some Eurozone countries, beginning with Greece, began to experience problems with government borrowing. The problems with government borrowing were manifested in a rising gap between the market interest rates that the economically weaker Eurozone countries had to pay for borrowing

---

[17] Calculation of the magnitude of fiscal stimulus in the United States is complicated by the fact that state governments generally have balanced budget laws, and their efforts to balance budgets during a downturn offset to some degree stimulus measures enacted at the federal level.

[18] The U.S. debt ceiling negotiations in the summer of 2011 and the Standard & Poor's downgrading of the U.S. government bonds in August 2011 may also have contributed to public perceptions of runaway U.S. government debt and the need for fiscal austerity measures. Canada underwent a similar downgrading in 1994 that was most helpful for proponents of government spending cuts.

compared with what Germany had to pay. The higher interest rates paid by Greece, Ireland, and Portugal, and then even Spain and Italy, reflected not only their high government deficit to GDP and government debt to GDP ratios, but also the severe constraint that membership in the Eurozone posed on their policy options for economic recovery. Lacking their own national currencies and hence the option for sharp currency depreciation as a means of stimulating economic recovery, they were left with the grim option of restoring competitiveness in international markets through wage and price reductions. Rather than recognizing this inherent limitation of the euro project, proponents of fiscal austerity were able to portray it as further evidence of the folly of counter-cyclical fiscal policy. In fact, some authors view the euro project as being inherently biased towards the wealthy within the core countries.[19] In one country after another, the public was informed that any delays in implementing fiscal austerity measures would result in that country going the way of Greece – that is being forced to pay ever higher and higher interest rates on government borrowing, and eventually having to go cap in hand to the International Monetary Fund and elsewhere to beg for loans.

In spite of all of the evidence against them, the advocates of fiscal austerity and the inflation hawks won a political victory at the level of policy. Politicians in the United States and Europe, where the recession has been deeper than in Canada, have been able to sell fiscal austerity, deep cuts in social programs, and, in some cases, rollback of the power of unions.[20] In Canada, similar moves for fiscal austerity have been made by the government, in spite of the milder Canadian recession, and the exceptionally low Canadian government debt-to-GDP ratio.[21]

---

[19] See Mark Weisbrot, "Why the Euro is Not Worth Saving," *The Guardian* (July 11, 2011), http://www.guardian.co.uk/commentisfree/2011/jul/11/eurozone-crisis-euro-monetary-union.

[20] The most publicized case in the United States is probably in the state of Wisconsin (on which, see, e.g.,.Paul Krugman, "Wisconsin Power Play," *The Conscience of a Liberal* (February 21, 2011b), http://krugman.blogs.nytimes.com/.) In Canada signs of a similar trend include the federal government's intervention on behalf of management in the Air Canada and Canada Post negotiations in 2011.

[21] Jackson summarizes key statistics placing Canadian fiscal austerity measures in a comparative international context. Andrew Jackson, "Public Sector Austerity: Why is Canada Leading the Way?," *Relentlessly Progressive Economics* (August 3, 2011b), http://www.progressive-economics.ca/2011/08/03/public-sector-austerity-why-is-canada-leading-the-way/.

From a technocratic economic point of view, widespread moves towards contractionary fiscal policy in the midst of weak economic recovery seem inexplicable. Writing in March 2011, the liberal U.S. economist Brad DeLong surveyed the situation in the high-income countries and lamented that: "Right now, the global economy is suffering a grand mal seizure of slack demand and high unemployment. We know the cures. Yet we seem determined to inflict further suffering on the patient."[22]

But the advocates of fiscal austerity are not simply misguided. If the true concern were with reducing government deficits and bringing government debt-to-GDP ratios down, then fiscal austerity measures would not be characterized as they are by a one-sided emphasis on government spending cuts. They would be heavily weighted towards tax increases, even tax increases combined with government spending increases in line with the balanced-budget multiplier theorem of macroeconomics.

The form that the fiscal austerity takes reflects the power of the wealthy, especially wealthy business owners and managers. They have a great deal of influence on what governments do.[23] They prefer government spending cuts, particularly social program spending cuts, to tax increases. They benefit from slack labour markets in the high-wage economies. A period of slow growth in the high-income countries is compatible with high rates of after-tax profit. From the standpoint of the advocates of fiscal austerity, this is the key indicator of its success.[24]

The only danger for the wealthy is that if fiscal austerity goes too far the result will not be mere slow growth of GDP, but a so-called double-dip recession. Indeed, in the midst of the stock market declines that followed the Standard and Poor's downgrade of U.S. government debt in early August of 2011 many economic forecasters recognized this possibility.[25]

---

[22]   J. Bradford DeLong, "Pain without Purpose," *Economists' Voice* 8, no. 1 (2011): 2 article 4, http://www.bepress.com/ev/vol8/iss1/art4.

[23]   See, e.g., the work by the U.S. political scientist Jacob Hacker, including Jacob S. Hacker and Paul Pierson, *Winner-Take-All-Politics: How Washington Made the Rich Richer—and Turned Its Back on the Middle Class* (New York: Simon and Schuster, 2010).The Laurentian University political scientist John Peters has been extending the analysis of Hacker and colleagues to Canada. Peters, "Boom, Bust and Crisis."

[24]   Our critique of DeLong is similar to that of Barbara Bergmann, "Comment on Delong," Economists' Voice, vol. 8, issue 1, www.bepress.com/ev/vol8/iss1/art6/.

[25]   For a strong prediction of recession from the economist known as "Dr. Doom," see Nouriel Roubini, "Mission Impossible: Stop Another Recession," *Financial Times* (August 7, 2011), http://www.ft.com/intl/cms/s/0/f443f640-c115-11e0-b8c2-00144feabdc0.html#axzz1UZCRuC11.

Why would fiscal austerity in high-income countries be taken so far as to raise concerns that it would trigger a double-dip recession? In short, it is a reflection of the growth of inequality of income (and of power) in these countries over the past few decades, as we analyze in the following sections.

A Political Economy Theory of Income Distribution

There are many extremely detailed, lengthy, and useful accounts of the various root causes for the mounting income inequality in Canada, the United States, and numerous other high-income countries during the past three decades, some of which relate these root causes to the 2008-2009 global recession.[26] Such nuanced accounts are necessary for understanding the intricate twists and turns of the relevant politics in many countries. Our aim is less ambitious. This section presents a simple and general framework for a political economy theory of income distribution focused on Canada and the United States that only seeks to explain the key stylized facts of mounting income inequality. The framework we propose argues that distributional outcomes in high-income market democracies are determined primarily through the interactions among three institutions: the power elite (the corporate elite and other wealthy power holders), labour unions, and markets.[27] The framework is informed by four major hypotheses.

---

[26]   See, e.g., David Harvey, *The Enigma of Capital* (New York: Oxford University Press, 2010); Thomas Palley, *From Financial Crisis to Stagnation: The Destruction of Shared Prosperity and the Role of Economics* (Cambridge, Mass.: Cambridge University Press, 2012); and Joseph E. Stiglitz, *The Price of Inequality: How Today's Divided Society Endangers Our Future* (New York: W. W. Norton & Company, 2012).

[27]   Our focus is on the high-income countries in part because Canada is one. Also, the high-income countries have been more seriously impacted by the Global Recession than middle-income and low-income countries, and in the past decade or so globalization has had a different impact on income distribution and politics in most high-income countries compared to many middle-income countries, notably the Latin American countries that have been part of the so-called Pink Tide (see, e.g.,) beginning in the late 1990s. Christopher Chase-Dunn *et al.*, "Neoliberalism, Populist Movements and the Pink Tide in Latin America," *Institute for Research on World-Systems Working Paper*, no. 58 (2010), http://irows.ucr.edu/papers/irows58/irows58.htm.

The first hypothesis is that through the operation of market forces capitalist economies tend to produce growing inequality of income and wealth. Under capitalism of the past few decades perhaps the most pervasive of the inexorable market forces that increase inequality over time are rent-seeking activities by monopolistic corporations, the forces of globalization, and skills-biased technical change.

Most real-world markets are not competitive, but instead are dominated by large corporations that garner monopolistic profits. The giant corporations rely, for example, upon state power to protect their intellectual property rights and the monopolistic profits they confer, which contribute to rising inequality. A major feature of numerous trade agreements since the 1990s has been the inclusion of provisions dealing with intellectual property rights.

Globalization of production and trade also contribute to growing wage and income inequality in high-income developed countries such as Canada and the United States. For example, increased globalization increases the threat of offshoring of production, which keeps wages down in Canada. Furthermore, increased trade pushes Canada to specialize in the production of goods that require more of its abundant factor (natural resources), and import more manufactured goods instead of producing them domestically. So globalization tends to bid up the incomes of shareholders benefiting directly and indirectly from natural resource exports while, at the same time, bidding down the wages of the blue-collar workers in the manufacturing sector.

Skilled-biased technological change has an effect on inequality similar to that of globalization. The new communications and information technologies have contributed to income and wage inequality because they increase the demand for workers with college and higher degrees and decrease the demand for workers with high schools diplomas or less. The result is to increase the wages of highly-educated workers and to decrease the wages of workers with average levels of education.

Our second hypothesis runs counter to what might be called the liberal umpire view of the state, that the government in a capitalist democracy is an overarching institution with the means and the responsibility to reverse the effects of anti-egalitarian market forces. In the liberal umpire view, the responsibility of the government does not end with the implementation of aggregate stabilization (monetary, fiscal and exchange rate) policies; it has the additional responsibility to ensure that the benefits from economic growth are enjoyed by all groups in society. The government can achieve the latter objective through progressive income taxation, policies on health care and education, and by establishing a strong social safety net.

But, in practice, many government policies actually serve to redistribute income upwards. An important reason for the non-egalitarian policies of the government is that capitalist democracies typically permit a grossly disproportionate influence of the corporate elite and their allies in policy-making relative to other groups in society.[28] When the rich and powerful are able to interact with the political system to influence regulations and otherwise generate conditions favourable to business such as tax cuts and fiscal austerity, government policies, instead of reducing inequalities among citizens, tend to amplify them.[29]

The third hypothesis is that labour movement can function as an important countervailing power to the power elite, both in workplaces and in the broader political sphere. In our political economy theory of income distribution, unions and labour movements provide a counterweight to the anti-egalitarian market forces and also to the non-egalitarian government policies described above. Unions also help institutionalize norms of equity, thereby reducing the dispersion of overall wages in highly unionized regions and industries.[30] Even among economists who might not have appreciated the role of unions a couple of decades ago, there are those who today see the countervailing power role of unions, as when Krugman (2011a) writes about the United States that:

> On paper, we're a one-person-one-vote nation; in reality, we're more than a bit of an oligarchy, in which a handful of wealthy people dominate. Given this reality, it's important to have institutions that can act as counterweights to the power of big money. ... You don't have to love unions ... to recognize that they're among the few influential players in

---

[28]   See, e.g., Linda McQuaig and Neil Brooks, *The Trouble with Billionaires* (Toronto: Penguin Books, 2010).

[29]   See, e.g., Daron Acemoglu, "Thoughts on Inequality and Financial Crisis," Slides. (Denver: MIT, January 7, 2011).

[30]   See Bruce Western and Jake Rosenfeld, "Unions, Norms, and the Rise in American Earnings Inequality," *American Sociological Review*, (Forthcoming 2011).

our political system representing the interests of middle-and working-class Americans, as opposed to the wealthy.

But, of course, the strength of the union counterweight may vary within countries over time and also across countries. During the past three decades the power of the labour movement has declined dramatically within the United States and somewhat in Canada compared to the previous three decades.

The fourth hypothesis is that power elites and the labour movement struggle not just over the direct fiscal matters such as the forms of taxation and social programs, but also over more structural features of the economy that determine the scope and nature of markets, such as over which sectors of the economy are most exposed to international competition, over protection of intellectual property rights, over corporate governance, and so on.[31]

Depending on the nature and the relative strength of the power elite and the labour movement, and the scope and nature of markets, the net outcome may be a society that is relatively egalitarian by today's standards, as was true of the 1950s to 1970s in Canada and the United States, or it may be a society in which economic and social inequality amplify over time, as has been the case during the past three decades in these same countries. The processes and the nature of the influence that each of these institutions exert on income distribution are described below.

Evidence and Explanation for Mounting Inequality in Canada and the United States: 1980 - 2007

THE EVIDENCE ON MOUNTING INEQUALITY

This section assembles empirical evidence of mounting after-tax income inequality within Canada and the United States over the past three decades and also attempts to identify the causes for the rising inequality based on the political economy theory of income distribution outlined above.

---

[31]   Our views on this hypothesis have been especially influenced by the work of the U.S. economist Dean Baker, especially Dean Baker, *The Conservative Nanny State: How the Wealthy Use the Government to Stay Rich and Get Richer* (Lulu Press, 2006).

Table 2 presents several alternative measures of after-tax income inequality within Canada and the United States over the period 1979-2007. The first is the Gini coefficient - a common measure of income inequality (dispersion) used in the social sciences. The higher the value of the Gini coefficient, the greater is income inequality.[32] It is clear from Table 2 that after-tax income inequality has trended upward in both countries over the period 1979-2008 and comparatively, the rise in inequality has been starker within the United States (where the Gini coefficient has increased from 30 to 37) than within Canada (where the Gini coefficient has increased from 28.3 to 31.5).

Table 2: Rise in Inequality in Canada and the U.S., 1979-2008		
	Canada	United States
Year	1979 2008	1979 2008
Gini (1)	28.3 31.5	30.0 37.0
Total Income Shares (2)	6.2 6.1	
Lowest Quintile	55.6 50.5	4.1 3.4
Middle 60 Percent	38.2 43.4	51.7 46.6
Highest Quintile		44.2 50.0
Year	1977 2007	1978 2007
Richest 1 Percent (3)	7.7 13.8	7.0 23.5
Earnings-Productivity Gap (4)	1980-2007	1980-2007
Labour productivity	1.27	1.73
Median real hourly wage	0.01	0.33
Total Gap	1.26	1.40

Sources: (1) Statistics Canada, *Survey of Consumer Finances*, and Luxembourg Income Study (Picot and Myles, 2005); (2) .CANSIM Table 202-0405 (total income includes income from all sources including government transfers before deductions of federal and provincial income taxes); U.S. Census Bureau, *Current Population Survey*, Annual Social and Economic Supplements; (3) Yalnizyan (2010); (4) CSLS Research Note 2009-2.

The increase in the Gini coefficient, however, cannot tell us exactly where in the distribution inequality has increased: whether the rich have become richer, or the poor have become poorer or

---

[32]   For a concise explanation of the Gini coefficient, see Robert Frank et al., *Principles of Microeconomics*, 3rd Canadian ed. (Toronto: McGraw Hill Ryerson, 2012b), 364-366. The Gini coefficient can be constructed so that it can take on values between 0 and 100, as reported above, or between 0 and 1, which is also frequently employed.

inequality has risen in the middle of the distribution. We therefore in Table 2 supplement the Gini measure with the income shares of the lowest quintile (poorest 20 percent), the middle 60 percent, and of the highest quintile (richest 20 percent) of the population. This shows that, both in Canada and the United States, inequality has increased largely because of a 'hollowing out' of the middle income groups (middle 60 percent of the earners): both the middle-income and the poor have lost ground to the richest 20 percent (top quintile), but this upward redistribution has occurred mainly from the middle 60 percent of earners to the top 20 percent of the earners.

To see the degree of income polarization, we also report the income share of the richest 1 percent of the population over the period 1977-2007 for both countries. The income share of the richest 1 percent of Canadians grew substantially from 7.7 percent in 1977 to 13.8 percent in 2007. But the degree of income polarization was even greater in the United States where the share of the richest 1 percent has grown from 7.0 percent to 23.5 percent over the same period.

Some economists have argued that since higher productivity and growth are the only sustainable way to support gains in the real wages of workers, public policy should be concerned only with the promotion of productivity and growth, without regard to income distribution.[33] But many Canadian and U.S. studies have found that, during the past decades, real wages of workers have lagged behind economic growth and workers' productivity growth. The final rows of Table 2 show how dramatically wages have lagged behind productivity growth in both Canada and the United States over the 1980-2007 period.

Factors Contributing to the Rise in Inequality: 1980-2007

Economic historians have referred to the decades of the 1950s, 1960s and the 1970s as the "golden age" for income and wealth inequality in the United States and Canada. It has been argued that this

---

[33]   Even within orthodox economics, opposing views have been expressed. Berg and Ostry have argued that income inequality can, in fact, be destructive to growth. They find that the countries that have a more equal distribution of income also enjoy growth spells of longer duration. Andrew G. Berg and Jonathan D. Ostry, "Inequality and Unsustainable Growth: Two Sides of the Same Coin," Research Department, International Monetary Fund (April 8, 2011).

is largely because the regulatory standards, progressive taxation and labour laws that were put in place after the Great Depression led to broad-based economic growth, high rates of unionization, rising wages, and declining inequality in the United States and Canada during this period.[34] We argue below that the U-turn that has occurred in the trend towards greater equality since the early 1980s is the result of dramatic reversals of these equalizing forces.

In addition to the market forces described in section III, two other specific types of structural changes in the economy have contributed significantly to rising inequality in Canada and the United States in recent decades. These are de-unionization and a shift in the balance of power to employers, and financialization of the economy and rise of financial power within the power elite. These two factors have contributed to a political environment in which the power elite has been able to bring about change not just in the pattern of government taxation and expenditure for upward redistribution but also in the structure of the economy.

1. DE-UNIONIZATION AND SHIFT IN THE BALANCE OF POWER

The level of unionization of the workforce and a political system that institutionalizes and represents the interests of the workers together can provide a powerful counterweight to the non-egalitarian market forces and also anti-egalitarian government policies within a country. Historically, Canada has enjoyed both a higher level of unionization than has the United States, and also has had an influential social democratic party (the New Democratic Party of Canada, NDP) that has held power in various provinces from time to time.[35]

The Organization for Economic Cooperation and Development (OECD) has recently released updated time series for the percentage of employees in a country that belong to a union over the period 1960-2008. We compare this series for Canada to that of the United

---

[34]   See, e.g., Kari P. Levitt, "The Great Financialization" (John Kenneth Galbraith Prize Lecture, June 8, 2008), http://karipolanyilevitt.com/documents/The-Great-Financialization.pdf.

[35]   Some writers have characterized these differences between Canada and the United States as the result of cultural differences. See, for example, M. Seymour Lipset, "Trade Union Exceptionalism: The United States and Canada," *Annals of the American Academy of Political and Social Science* 538, no. 1 (March 1995): 114-130.

States in Chart 8. Notwithstanding possible measurement differences between the countries, Chart 8 clearly shows that the level of unionization has been significantly higher in Canada than in the United States throughout most of the period 1960-2008. This is consistent with the evidence of a more egalitarian income distribution in Canada than in the United States noted previously.

Chart 8 also shows that the process of de-unionization in Canada began in 1982 when union density peaked at 36.8 percent and, with a short break in the downward slide over the period 1987-1990, it continued throughout the rest of the period, ending at 27.1 percent in 2008. By contrast, this process of decline in the unionization rate has persisted in the United States throughout the entire period, starting at 30.9 percent in 1960 and ending at 11.9 percent in 2008.

Chart 8: Canadian and U.S. Union Density, 1960-2008

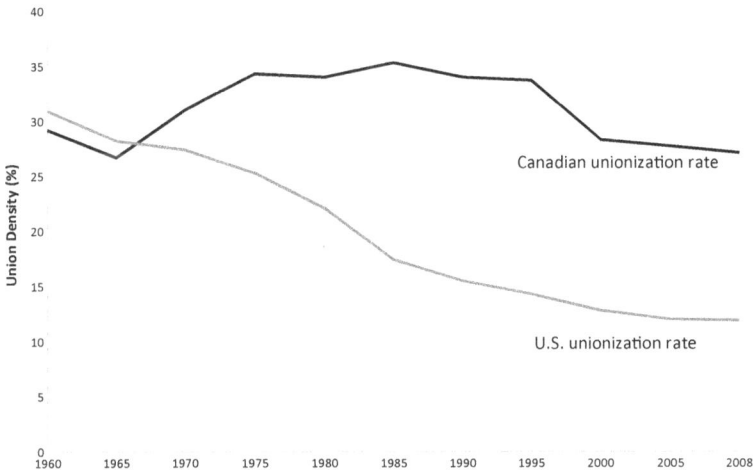

Source: OECD estimates: http://www.oecd.org/dataoecd/37/2/35695665.pdf

2. FINANCIALIZATION AND THE RISE OF FINANCIAL POWER

Stagnant wage growth and decline of unions have coincided with explosive growth of financial markets and financial power during the past three decades. The term "financialization" is related to this shift in the balance of power. Financialization involves such economic developments as a larger relative share of financial activities (Finance,

Insurance, and Real Estate, often abbreviated as FIRE) in total output
and a corresponding decline in the share of real activities (goods and
services). Financialization has also meant a political process whereby
financial markets, financial institutions and financial elites gain
greater influence over economic policy and economic outcomes.

Chart 9 plots one measure of financialization: the share of
output of the FIRE sector in GDP for Canada and the United States
over the period 1981-2009. This clearly shows that the level of financialization (as measured by the FIRE to GDP ratio) has increased
in both countries over this period. Perhaps contrary to common
perceptions, the level has risen by slightly more in Canada (output
share of FIRE has risen from 16 percent to 21.4 percent of GDP)
than in the United States (output share of FIRE has risen from 17
percent to 20.0 percent of GDP).

Chart 9: Finance, Insurance, and Real Estate Sector to GDP Ratios for Canada and the United States, 1981-2009

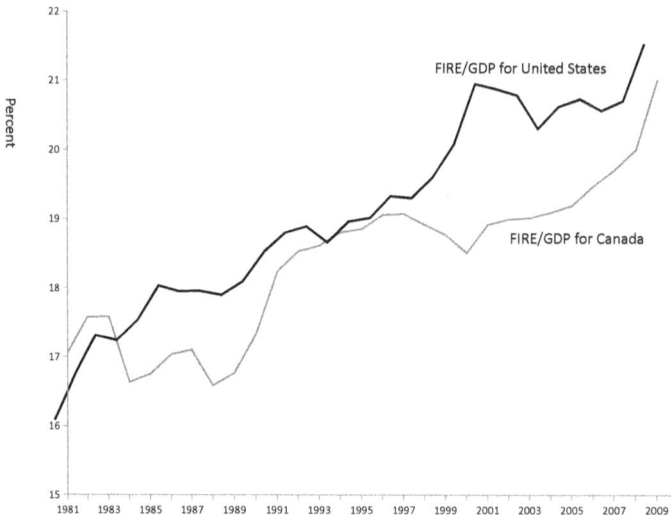

Sources: For the Canadian shares, adapted from CANSIM series v41881724 for FIRE output and v41881478 for output
of all industries, both in 2002 constant prices. The U.S. shares are adapted from U.S. Bureau of Economic Analysis
data series.

Another financialization metric is a Financial Index (FI) developed by the International Monetary Fund (IMF 2006) to capture the
degree to which the financial system of a country is bank-based or

market-based. The index value ranges between 0 and 1, with lower values indicating greater dependence on bank-based financial intermediation. The index values for Canada are 0.44 in 1995 and 0.53 in 2004 and for the United States they are 0.64 in 1995 and 0.74 in 2004. They point to increased financialization in both countries but also show that the U.S. financial system is significantly more market-based (largely due to the presence of a significant shadow banking system) than the Canadian financial system. This evidence is consistent with the greater instability of the U.S. financial system.

Both theory and evidence suggest that excessive financialization contributes to mounting income inequality through various channels. [36] A key channel is that as financial markets play a bigger role in the economy financial forces exert greater influence over the management of corporations in the non-financial sector of the economy and create greater pressure to boost profits at the expense of wages. Another channel is that financialization creates greater opportunities for massive gains to the financial elite from various forms of financial fraud or near fraud including excessive risk-taking by too-big-to-fail financial institutions undertaken with the understanding that the state will be forced to fund bailouts in the worse case scenarios. [37] Yet another channel is that with increased financialization the economy takes on a more of a "casino" character with households bearing greater risks and with earnings less related to effort due to the increased importance of financial gains and losses associated with random events ("luck"). This is especially so to the extent that the financial oligarchy is able to influence public policy to promote or maintain practices that benefit financiers at the expense of work-

---

[36] On the cross-country evidence, see, e.g., A. David Zalewski and Charles J. Whalen, "Financialization and Income Inequality: A Post Keynesian Institutionalist Analysis," *Journal of Economic Issues* XLIV, no. 3 (2010): 757-777. On theory, see, e.g., Thomas Palley, "Financialization: What it is and Why it Matters" (Paper presented at a Conference on "Finance-led-Capitalism? Macroeconomic Effects of Changes in the Financial Sector," Berlin, Germany, October 26-27, 2007).

[37] On normal fraud by hedge funds, see Dean P. Foster and H. Peyton Young, "Hedge Fund Wizards," *Economists' Voice* 5, no. 2 (2008) Article 1, http://www.bepress.com/ev/vol5/iss2/art1. The widespread fraud associated with the U.S. housing boom is mentioned in all of the books reviewed in Andrew Jackson, "Best Books on the Crisis," *Relentlessly Progressive Economics* (June 26, 2011), http://www.progressive-economics.ca/2011/06/26/best-books-on-the-economic-crisis/.

ers – practices such as defined contribution plans versus defined benefit, private pensions as opposed to social security, educational loans as opposed to subsidized education, private health care rather than public health care, and so on.[38]

3. STRUCTURAL CHANGES PROMOTED BY THE POWER ELITE

It is widely recognized and well-documented in sources such as McQuaig and Brooks (2010) how the power elite have over the past few decades successfully pushed for changes in government taxation and expenditure that have promoted upward redistribution of income and wealth. Less widely recognized are several other mechanisms – analyzed by Baker (2006), Baker (2010), and Stiglitz (2011), among others – through which the rich and powerful have used their control of governments to structure markets in ways that have also furthered upward redistribution. Many of these mechanisms would appear to be operational not just in the United States but also in the Canadian economy.

For example, monetary policy has contributed to an upward redistribution of income. During the past three decades – the period of the so-called Great Moderation – monetary policy in Canada has been more focused on controlling inflation than preventing recession. Much of the input into the formulation of the government's inflation control policy has come from the financial markets and the financial elite and very little from other social groups.[39] When the Bank of Canada raises interest rates and engineers a recession in order to control inflation, the people who get laid off first are factory workers and store workers, not corporate executives nor even doctors and lawyers. Indeed, any hint that wage growth is approaching or exceeding productivity growth is taken by the central bank to mean that monetary policy must be tightened in order to bring about a moderation of wage growth.[40]

In addition, government trade policies pursued during the past three decades, most notably the North American Free Trade

---

[38]   See, e.g., Jacob S. Hacker and Paul Pierson, *Winner-Take-All-Politics: How Washington Made the Rich Richer—and Turned Its Back on the Middle Class* (New York: Simon and Schuster, 2010).

[39]   See Linda McQuaig, "StatsCan Reports rising inequality," (2008), http://www.lindamcquaig.com/Columns/ViewColumns.cfm?REF=71.

[40]   For more on this issue, see Brian K. MacLean and Lars Osberg, eds., *The Unemployment Crisis* (Montreal: McGill-Queen's University Press, 1996).

Agreement (NAFTA), have put blue-collar workers into more direct competition with low-paid foreign workers, and have contributed to income inequality in Canada, and also the United States.[41]

Another example is that the benefits from government allocation of patents and copyright monopolies flow overwhelmingly to people at the very top of the income distribution. Seen in this perspective, the legal changes by various governments that have extended the number of years covered by patent protection –in Canada from 17 to 20 years – constitute an anti-egalitarian policy. This emphasis on the protection of intellectual property rights has also found support from developments in international trade legislation.

A final example is that both the Canadian and the U.S. governments write rules for corporate governance and have allowed new compensation mechanisms for corporate executives that have been implemented in recent decades.[42] These rules have permitted enormous growth of the salaries of top executives while the incomes of most workers have stagnated, thereby contributing to rising inequality.

The Way Forward

Canada experienced a severe recession in 2008-2009, but not as severe as in the United States and some other countries that experienced the bursting of a housing bubble and severe problems with their financial sectors prior to and during the recession. We have argued that income distribution is important for understanding the unfolding of the Great Recession.

We have shown that a rough guide to developments in the income distribution can be provided by a framework in which

---

[41]   Immigration policies can have similar consequences for domestic wages as trade policies do. See, for example, Stanford on Canada's Temporary Foreign Worker program that accounted for "almost 30% of all net new paid jobs created in Canada between 2007 and 2011." Jim Stanford, "Temporary Foreign Workers and the Labour Market," (May 7, 2012), http://www.progressive-economics.ca/2012/05/07/temporary-foreign-workers-and-the-labour-market/. See also Dominique Gross and Nicolas Schmitt, "Temporary Foreign Workers and Regional Labour Market Disparities in Canada," *Canadian Public Policy* 38, no. 2 (June 2012): 233-263.

[42]   An insightful source on executive compensation is Lucian Bebchuk and Jesse Fried, *Pay without Performance: The Unfulfilled Promise of Executive Compensation* (Cambridge, Mass.: Harvard University Press, 2006).

income distribution is seen as being determined by the interactions of market forces, government, the power elites, and labour unions. In our framework, unions have provided a positive counterweight to the anti-egalitarian market forces and government policies in Canada and the United States. But union density and power have declined significantly in both countries during the past three decades, less so in Canada than in the United States. There has been a corresponding rise in the power of financial markets and the financial elite, which have contributed significantly both to the mounting inequality in Canada and the United States and also to the current economic crisis. The greater inequality in the United States, and the greater power of financial capital there, largely accounts for the more severe recession that country has experienced.

During the Great Recession, fiscal policy in Canada, as in many other high-income countries, was initially employed together with monetary policy to prevent a repeat of the Great Depression. Also, as in many other high-income countries, the direction of Canadian fiscal policy has shifted since 2009 in the direction of a fiscal austerity characterized by social program spending cuts and no increase in taxes for the wealthy. It has also been accompanied by government measures against unions.

This sharp shift in fiscal policy in Canada and other high-income countries is incomprehensible on technical economic grounds, but it can be understood as a logical development in a world of sharp income inequality. In this world, fiscal and other public policies are crafted to serve the interests of the rich and powerful with little need for modification to meet the interests of the rest of society. Indeed, the push to fiscal austerity has been sufficiently pronounced in such a range of high-income countries that it runs the risk of going too far even for the interests of the rich and powerful and triggering a so-called double-dip recession across the high-income countries.

How can Canadians avoid a U.S.-scale recession in the years ahead and enjoy a future characterized by greater stability and equality of income? We are not especially qualified to develop a detailed policy package and accompanying political strategy to answer this question. And policy packages and strategies with many attractive and sensible elements have already been developed with input from a wide range of experts by organizations such as the Canadian Centre for Policy Alternatives and by its counterparts in other countries, such as the

Economic Policy Institute in the United States.[43] We would, however, like to close by pointing to a few important considerations from our research as economists, including our research for this paper, that relate to the achievement of greater economic stability and equality of income.[44]

First, counter-cyclical monetary and fiscal policy – in the current context, especially fiscal policy – are potentially very important for economic stability and lowering high unemployment rates. Keynesian economists are generally reliable in their analysis of monetary and fiscal policies, and their analyses can be extremely helpful for seeing through overblown claims about government debt, the possibility of hyperinflation, and so on, and for formulating a coherent macroeconomic policy response to the current situation.[45] Particularly insightful are Keynesian economists who recognize the central role that the formation and bursting of asset price bubbles has played in the economic instability of high-income countries in recent decades.

Second, policies that will alter the balance of power in society are critical. The power of workers needs to be strengthened relative to the power of employers in society at large. A key finding of the new economic research in the wake of the crisis is that restoring the bargaining power of ordinary households can be very effective in reducing inequality and also lowering the risk

---

[43]   See, e.g., Canadian Centre for Policy Alternatives. *Alternative Federal Budget 2011* (Ottawa: Canadian Centre for Policy Alternatives, March 15, 2011). See also Jim Stanford, *Economics for Everyone* (Halifax and Ottawa: Fernwood Publishing and Canadian Centre for Policy Alternatives, 2008), especially Chapter 26. On the thinking behind the alternative budget approach followed by the Canadian Centre for Policy Alternatives, see John Loxley, *Alternative Budgets: Budgeting as If People Mattered* (Halifax: Fernwood Publishing, 2003).

[44]   Since writing these considerations in an earlier draft, we have read a newly-published book by Palley that provides similar reasoning as ours but in much greater detail (and from a U.S. perspective). Thomas Palley, *From Financial Crisis to Stagnation: The Destruction of Shared Prosperity and the Role of Economics* (Cambridge, Mass.: Cambridge University Press, 2012).

[45]   This point may sound obvious but it is useful to recall that in the federal election campaign of October 2008 all of the federal political parties, including the New Democratic Party, loudly proclaimed that they would never run government deficits if elected. For a brief critique, see Mike McCracken, "No Party Will Admit to Running a Deficit During a Recession," *Toronto Star*, October 4, 2008.

of future crises.[46] In this same vein, Krugman (2011) writes: "So if we want a society of broadly spread prosperity, education is not the answer – we'll have to go about building that society directly. We need to restore the bargaining power that labour has lost over the last 30 years, so that ordinary workers as well as superstars have the power to bargain for good wages." This goal can be aided through higher rates of taxation on high-income households and on corporations.

Third, in terms of reducing the power of employers, it seems particularly important to reduce the power of the financial sector and its potential for negative impact on the rest of the economy. In the wake of the current crisis, many remedies for reducing the risks posed by the financial system to the economy have been proposed, ranging from raising capital requirements on banks to taxation of speculative financial transactions. Understandably, because of the great interconnectedness of financial markets across national boundaries, these remedies are generally discussed at international forums, although some countries have adopted additional country-specific measures. From the perspective of the Canadian economy, perhaps the most important of these remedies has come in the form of Basel III agreement which requires higher capital standards on banks and which the government of Canada has accepted. It should be noted, however, that while most countries have lauded Basel III as 'giant leap' for regulators, many prominent economists have noted that while Basel III is a step in the right direction, it is not sufficient to prevent another financial crisis.[47] Many economists and political leaders in Canada, the United States and Europe have also endorsed the idea of a financial transactions tax (also known as a Tobin Tax) to be imposed on short-term financial transactions that contribute to economic instability without adding to long-term productivity. Even a very small amount of such tax can raise a

---

[46]   See, e.g., Michael Kumhof and Romain Ranciere, "Inequality, Leverage and Crises," (International Monetary Fund Working Paper. WP/10/268., 2010) and A. B. Atkinson and S. Morelli, "Inequality and Banking Crises: A First Look" (Paper prepared for the Global Labour Forum in Turin organized by the International Labour Organization ILO, 2010).

[47]   See, e.g., Mervyn King, "Banking: From Bagehot to Basel, and Back Again" (Speech by the Governor of the Bank of England, Buttonwood Gathering, New York City, NY, October 25, 2010), http://www.bankofengland.co.uk/publications/speeches/2010/speech455.pdf.

large amount of government revenue that can finance new egalitarian initiatives.[48]

Finally, that unions and left-of-centre political parties need to cooperate at the international level to resist the corporate-led form that globalization has been taking; that is, to fight for the establishment of rules and regulations to support greater economic stability and a more equal distribution of income.[49] This would mean, among other things, new rules for trade, new standards for labour markets, and genuine efforts to suppress tax havens.[50]

---

[48] This idea has been rejected by the Conservative government of Canada with claims that to be effective such a tax must be implemented internationally and that Canada's financial system has performed much better than those in the United States and Europe in the recent crisis.

[49] The issue of cooperation to deal with international capital flows and financial stability was raised by many after the Asian financial crisis. See, e.g., Brian K. MacLean, "The Transformation of International Economic Policy Debate, 1997-1998," in *Out of Control: Canada in an Unstable Financial World*, ed. Brian K. MacLean (Toronto: James Lorimer & Company Ltd., 1997), 67-94.

[50] Several such proposals are discussed in Chapter 10 of Thomas Palley, *From Financial Crisis to Stagnation: The Destruction of Shared Prosperity and the Role of Economics* (Cambridge, Mass.: Cambridge University Press, 2012).

NEOLIBERALISM, CAPITALIST CRISIS, AND CONTINUING AUSTERITY IN THE ONTARIO STATE

Tim Fowler[1]

Introduction

This chapter looks at the particular response of the Ontario government to the Great Recession, examining how the government used the crisis of capitalism to attack organized labour within the province. It does so primarily by focussing on the 2010 provincial budget, which included a government mandated wage freeze for two years for all public sector workers. In a very real sense the Ontario government was planning on compelling public sectors to help solve a crisis these workers had no hand in causing. The chapter then shifts to the response of many of the unions in Ontario to this budget. The Ontario government could not unilaterally introduce a wage freeze on unionized public servants, as this would violate the union's charter rights to collectively bargain, so the government set up a series of 'consultations' in an attempt to get unions in Ontario to agree to the wage freeze.

Many of the unions in Ontario which were facing a wage freeze chose to participate in the consultation process - some to attempt to convince the government there were other ways to solve Ontario's fiscal mess besides freezing wages (advocating a raise in the corporate tax rate was a common suggestion) while other unions seemed willing to negotiate with the government. A small contingent of the Ontario labour movement refused to participate in the consultation process

---

[1] I would like to thank George Rigakos at Red Quill, as well as the two anonymous reviewers, for their comments on this chapter.

at all, claiming participating would give the process legitimacy. The chapter argues that the unions which participated in the process *did* give the Ontario government a degree of legitimacy to impose wage freezes, and were slipping towards the reactionary positions of business unionism.

In the past fifteen years, all three major political parties in Ontario have formed government at least once. One may expect the changes in government to bring about divergent public policies, and this may be true in some specific policy areas, however much neoliberalism has restricted policy options. With labour and union rights, however, the policies of the Rae, Harris/Eves and McGuinty regimes have been remarkably similar. All three governments have introduced legislation to restrict union freedoms. The Rae government is perhaps best remembered for its *Social Contract Act* and the Harris and Eves years were marked by labour unrest in the public sector. When campaigning in 2003, McGuinty promised to restore fairness and balance to labour relations in Ontario, counteracting the turbulence under NDP and Progressive Conservative governments.

McGuinty has been successful in creating and maintaining some level of labour peace in the province during his tenure as premier, however this peace has almost exclusively been in the education sector. While there have been sporadic strikes in the public sector during his time in office, there has been nothing like the province wide waves of unrest under the previous two administrations. The labour peace has been marked, in part, by McGuinty's desire to be seen as the 'education premier,' and thus wanting relatively easy labour relations in the education sector. Further, McGuinty has enjoyed the support of certain sections of the labour movement during his election campaigns - the Canadian Autoworkers (CAW), the province's teachers' unions, and many of the building trades have come together under the umbrella organization 'Working Families Coalition' at election time to support the McGuinty Liberals.

The peace in education aside, in many ways, the McGuinty government has simply been an extension of the 'Common Sense Revolution,' the hard right, neoliberal agenda of the Progressive Conservatives under leadership of Harris and Eves, and has continued to take an aggressive neoliberal approach to labour relations in the province. McGuinty has readily relied on the coercive power of the Ontario state to restrict trade union freedoms: for example, back-to-work legislation has been used to end legal strikes, the government has acted as an intervener in court cases to prevent agricultural workers in the province from gaining union protection, and part-time workers at Ontario colleges have been subjected to numerous restrictions on their right to organize - stemming from a loophole in Ontario labour legislation which McGuinty promised to close, but did not. While in many ways this has not been different from the Common Sense Revolution, the rhetoric surrounding these assaults on trade union freedoms has been. When intervening in labour disputes, McGuinty has masked his coercion as part of a consensual process, claiming he is intervening not to take sides, but to defend the interests of all Ontarians.

The provincial budget of 2010 set off a major wave of labour discontent in Ontario. The budget sought to legislate a wage freeze on all public sector workers in an attempt to help Ontario recover from the effects of the Great Recession. The implementation of austerity measures through legislation is not a new phenomena; it has been an ongoing feature of neoliberalism. Neoliberalism has involved an assault on trade union freedoms, as neoliberal theory sees trade unions as a roadblock to high levels of capitalist accumulation. To neoliberals, trade unions act as an impediment in the free market, and thus their power must be curbed, or altogether erased, in order to facilitate high levels of profit. The 2010 Ontario budget was lockstep neoliberal in this regard, as the goal of the budget was to prop up the ailing Ontario economy, and the policy devices introduced came directly from neoliberal orthodoxy.

This paper is divided into four main parts. The first provides an overview of the challenges neoliberalism presents to trade unions. The second looks at the way McGuinty has masked coercion as consent, using the two examples of the strike by the ATU against the Toronto Transit Commission (TTC) and of part-time academic workers organized in CUPE against York University. The third section, the main case study, examines the provincial budget of 2010, the subsequent call for public sector wage freezes, and trade union response to the consultation process in Ontario. The final section concludes.

The Neoliberal Challenge to Trade Unionism

Neoliberalism is an ideology, and a set of policies and practises, which emerged out of the crisis of the Keynesian national welfare state and the Fordist mode of production. Fundamentally, neoliberalism seeks to restore power to the capitalist class - power which was diminished during the so-called 'post war compromise' underpinning Keynesianism and Fordism. Neoliberalism has dramatically increased the profitability of national and multinational capital, in both realms of finance and production. One of the major successes of neoliberalism has been to redistribute wealth *upwards*, transferring wealth from the working classes to capital. As unions are seen as a barrier to profitable capitalist accumulation part of the neoliberal program has been to attack and severely limit the freedoms of trade unions.

The rise of neoliberalism is often contextualized by the governments of Margaret Thatcher in the United Kingdom and Ronald Regan in the United States; specifically, the opening salvos of the neoliberal onslaught are often identified as Thatcher attacking trade union power and Reagan's firing of striking air traffic controllers.[2] The governments' of Thatcher and Reagan went to war with unions in order to 'open up' the markets of their respective countries. Of all the various policies and practises of neoliberalism this one, the opening up of markets, is paramount to neoliberal ideology and practise. Perhaps the most important and ongoing restructuring of labour markets under neoliberalism has been a move towards 'labour market flexibility.'

At its simplest 'flexible labour' appears to mean, to capital, low-cost labour. Capital sees low cost labour as casual and disposable.[3] Casual and disposable labour allow for greater levels of capitalist accumulation, as capital is not tied to providing for a fixed labour force. Labour can be discarded to increase profits, and capital can outsource labour to low-cost jurisdictions as another way to increase profits. Rather than the high wage jobs for life (for men)

---

[2]   David Harvey, *A Brief History of Neoliberalism* (Oxford: Oxford University Press, 2005), 22 - 25.

[3]   Dave Broad, Jane Cruikshank, and James P. Mulvale, "Where's the Work? Labour Market Trends in the New Economy," in *Capitalism Rebooted? Work, Welfare and the New Economy,* eds. Dave Broad and Wayne Anthony (Halifax: Fernwood Publishing, 2006), 60.

that were typical under Keynesianism, neoliberal norms are low wage, temporary jobs. This, of course, runs contrary to unionism: unions, through collective bargaining, seek high wages and job security. Unions seek to regulate work and expand full-time employment from part-time employment, to raise the average wage of their members - and many trade unions actively campaign for a higher minimum wage to ensure well-paying jobs for all workers, not just union members. The ideological shift to self-employment under neoliberalism also undermines union power, as self-employed workers, by definition, cannot organize.[4]

Neoliberal orthodoxy holds that 'unions operate to distort the natural price flexibility of the marketplace, resulting in higher levels of unemployment and wage-based inflationary pressures. Consequently, government policy should be directed towards eliminating these sources of inflexibility.'[5] Hence, neoliberal governments have introduced wide ranging policies to restrict trade union rights and freedoms, and to narrow the scope of the activities of unions. Restrictions on union organizing and union security arrangements are a cornerstone of neoliberal trade union legislation.[6]

Neoliberal policies have made it much harder for workers to join trade unions. This serves the neoliberal agenda twofold. On the one hand, fewer unionized workers means a more 'flexible' and lower-waged workforce, which means greater capitalist accumulation. On the other hand, unions' declining membership mean less economic resources for unions. This has broad implications for trade unions. Fewer economic resources often mean that unions have less political clout, and are restricted in their ability to advance an agenda.

---

[4]   Of course, these 'self employed' workers are often simply just workers who are 'self employed' doing work on a contract-by-contract basis that used to be done by a full-time, unionized worker. In this capacity, many 'self-employed' workers have sought collective bargaining rights as the actual reality of the situation is that they are employees or dependent contractors. See Cynthia J. Cranford, Judy Fudge, Eric Tucker, and Leah F. Vosko, *Self-Employed Workers Organize* (Montreal and Kingston: McGill Queen's University Press, 2005).

[5]   Stephen McBride and John Shields, *Dismantling a Nation: The Transition to Corporate Rule in Canada*, 2nd ed. (Halifax: Fernwood Publishing, 1997), 26.

[6]   Jim Stanford and Leah F. Vosko, "Challenging the Market: The Struggle to Regulate Work and Income," in *Challenging the Market: The Struggle to Regulate Work and Income*, eds. Jim Stanford and Leah F. Vosko (Montreal and Kingston: McGill-Queen's University Press, 2004), 13; Gary Teeple, *Globalization and the Decline of Social Reform: Into the Twenty-First Century* (Aurora: Garamond Press, 2000), 118.

Further, it means that less money can be directed towards broad organizing campaigns to bring new workers into the union. Hence, a vicious circle is born: lower union density decreases the money unions have, which means unions can dedicate less money to organizing efforts, which means fewer workers in unions.

Restrictions on the right-to-strike are also very prevalent under neoliberalism. Neoliberal governments have introduced growing legal restrictions on where and when union members can picket and have drastically increased restrictions on secondary picketing.[7] To these restrictions can be added legislation which outright bans strikes in certain sectors by expanding the definition of 'essential' workers.[8] Essential workers cannot, by definition, engage in strike action. There has also been a dramatic increase in the use of back-to-work legislation to bring a legislated end to legal strikes. Neoliberal trade union legislation has made it much harder to strike, has restricted what activities are allowed during strikes, and have often introduced back-to-work legislation to end strikes. Further, there are growing legal penalties for unions which engage in 'illegal' strikes, which refuse back-to-work order, engage in secondary picketing or other activities proscribed by neoliberal policies.

Labour market restructuring and the assault on trade union freedom has come in two successive waves. Peck and Tickell note that the early stages of neoliberalism could be characterized as "roll-back" neoliberalism: 'blaming the economic crisis of the 1970s on Keynesian financial regulation, unions, corporatist planning, state ownership and "overregulated" labour markets.'[9] Thus, the neoliberal roll-back of the late 1970s involved 'freeing up markets, restoring the right to manage, and asserting individualizing opportunity rights.'[10] One of the major sets of early neoliberal rollbacks were restrictions on union organizing, strikes, and rollbacks of collective bargaining rights. Roll-back neoliberalism stripped away the protective coverings established under Keynesianism, many of which had been established by trade unions. Trade union powers were curbed and dismantled and, subsequently, 'flexible' labour markets were established.

---

[7]   Stanford and Vosko, "Challenging The Market," 13.

[8]   Teeple, *Globalization and the Decline of Social Reform*, 118.

[9]   Jamie Peck and Adam Tickell, "Neoliberalizing Space," *Antipode* 34, no. 3 (July 2002): 388.

[10]   Ibid.

The second wave of neoliberalization, in the 1990s, was characterized as 'roll-out' neoliberalism. Roll-out neoliberalism involved 'new forms of institution-building and government intervention which have been licensed within the neoliberal project.'[11] Roll-out neoliberalism involved the active neoliberal state restructuring and remaking institutions to better facilitate capitalist accumulation. Of particular importance to roll-out neoliberalism was the creation of a more flexible labour market. In the mid 1990s, the OECD *Jobs Study* was released, which called for an increase to labour market flexibility.[12] This study provided the impetus the capitalist class needed to restructure labour markets. It was roll-out neoliberalism which saw the normalization of part-time, low wage contingent work, the rise of self employment, and the switch from welfare to workfare, amongst many other labour market changes. These rolled out policies also involved a major challenge to trade unions. The expansion of management rights saw collective agreements, many of which had been in place for decades, come under attack as management demanded more and more concessions in the name of 'the right to manage.' The reorientation of negotiations of wage and working conditions to the individual level, rather than the workplace, saw the *raison d'étre* of collective bargaining challenged. While roll-back neoliberalism assaulted the gains that organized labour had made during the Keynesian compromise, roll-out neoliberalism challenged the very nature of trade unionism, and posed challenges that the union movement had never faced before.

Roll out neoliberalism also involved a renewed ideological attack on trade unions. While trade unionism has certainly been challenged and attacked by neoliberal policies at all stages of neoliberalism, the ideological undermining of trade unions was intensified in the 1990s. Stephen Gill argues that neoliberalism 'tends to generate a perspective on the world that is ahistorical, economistic, materialistic, 'me-oriented', shortermist and ecologically myopic.'[13] Perhaps most important to the analysis of neoliberalism and trade unions are the 'me-oriented' and shortermist nature of

---

[11]   Ibid., 389.
[12]   Stanford and Vosko, "Challenging the Market," 11.
[13]   Stephen Gill, "Globalisation, Market Civilisation, and Disciplinary Neoliberalism," *Millennium - Journal of International Studies* 24, no. 3 (1995): 399.

the neoliberal project. Both of these fundamentally challenge trade unionism's perspective on collective economic action and long term workplace planning through collective agreements. Neoliberalism is exceptionally hostile to collective activity, especially economic or social collective activity, and attacks collective action at its core.

The next section of this chapter looks at the McGuinty Government's approach to labour relations. McGuinty has often intervened in labour disputes in the province in the name of acting for 'all Ontarians.' These interventions further the advancement of neoliberalism in Ontario. McGuinty's approach of treating coercive measures as consensual can be understood in the language of 'roll-out' and 'roll-back' neoliberalism. As the Ontario government has rolled back trade union rights, it has concurrently rolled out a new 'common sense,' in the Gramscian sense, surrounding organized labour.[14]

Masking Coercion as Consent

While McGuinty originally campaigned in 2003 on restoring balance to labour relations in Ontario, the McGuinty Government's approach to labour relations has been anything but balanced. The McGuinty government has restricted trade union freedoms and has been as coercive towards unions as the previous Progressive Conservative and NDP governments were. McGuinty has, however, masked his coercion as consent. He has often argued that the coercive policies he has introduced are for the best interests of Ontario or Ontarians, suggesting that he is not anti-union *per se*, just that the unions have 'gone too far' or that a labour dispute has lasted too long and the Ontario government needs to step in. Consider, for example, the strike between CUPE 3903 and York University: the McGuinty government legislated an end to this strike; the premier argued that he was doing this for the best interests of the students at York - because the two sides had reached an impasse, back-to-work legislation was supposedly necessary. McGuinty's labour policies, while being masked as consensual, were just as coercive as the policies of Rae or Harris. McGuinty has introduced back-to-work

---

[14]   Gramsci argued that 'common sense' differs from 'good sense' in that 'common sense' is 'sense that is held in common.' Thus, for Gramsci, common sense are ideas and thoughts that supported the dominant ideology, and went unquestioned.

legislation ending legal strike and restricting the right to strike, he has enacted legislation restricting the rights of workers to organize into unions, and has also brought about numerous other policies and laws which restrict trade union activity.

The McGuinty government's approach to labour relations is decidedly neoliberal in character. McGuinty has further entrenched neoliberalism in Ontario, especially when dealing with labour rights. The Liberal regime has acted to restrict and circumscribe union freedoms, and highlighted the supremacy of the consumer (often masked as an 'average Ontarian') in its rhetoric. The government has championed the interests of capital when dealing with labour relations, this is quite apparent, for example, in the quest of agricultural workers to gain unionization rights where the Ontario government has intervened on behalf of the Ontario Agriculture Association to prevent these workers from unionizing.

There are multiple examples of the McGuinty government masking coercive actions towards trade unions as consent. Generally, the government will initially refuse to get involved with labour disruptions, claiming they believe in collective bargaining. At some point, though, the government is willing to intervene, claiming they are standing up for all Ontarians - making it clear that they are not 'taking sides,' that their action is to simply benefit all of Ontario. Of course, these interventions are all implicitly on the side of capital, meaning that by acting for 'all Ontarians' the government is acting against organized labour. Further, by allowing strikes to continue for a short period of time, or initially suggesting that the government has no interest in intervening, coercive actions are masked further masked as consensual by framing the government as an impartial mediator between two sides that cannot agree. In April of 2008 the McGuinty government passed back to work legislation, ordering striking ATU workers at the Toronto Transit Commission (TTC) back to work. The strike was rather short-lived: the ATU workers went on strike on 26 April 2008, and were ordered back on the 27th. While the time it took for the Ontario government to intervene in a legal strike was quite short, what was interesting were promises by the McGuinty government to declare the TTC an essential service, thus baring future strikes.

On 18 April 2008, during bargaining and before the ATU workers had walked off the job, McGuinty offered to declare the TTC an essential service, thus barring them from striking, if the City of Toronto approached the provincial government and asked him to do so.[15] McGuinty was more than willing to intervene in free collective bargaining to ban workers from striking *before* the negotiations had even reached an impasse. This marks an impressive display of coercion by the province and the premier: the willingness to intervene, as a third party which has no direct stakes in the negotiations at hand, to restrict the right to strike. That said, McGuinty was only willing to step in and declare the TTC an essential service if the City of Toronto asked the Ontario government to do so.[16] This suggests that McGuinty was attempting to shield himself from appearing to be anti-labour. By declaring the TTC an essential service, at the request of the City of Toronto, McGuinty could claim he was simply carrying out the will of Torontonians, and it should be the City of Toronto, not the government of Ontario, who is responsible for the essential service declaration. Indeed, this is exactly what happened: on 30 March 2011 the Ontario Government declared the TTC an essential service, at the request of conservative Toronto mayor Rob Ford.[17]

In 2009, the Ontario government intervened to end a strike between CUPE 3903, representing part time academic staff at York University, and the University itself. The strike, which started in November 2008, was brought to a legislated end at the end of January 2009. In intervening, McGuinty claimed that the sides were at a deadlock, and for the good of the students at the university, the Ontario government would intervene to pass back-to-work legislation.[18] Here, again, McGuinty claimed that governmental involvement in the collective bargaining process was *not* about picking sides between capital and labour, but was about acting for the best interests of the citizens of the province.

These two examples are indicative of the direction that McGuinty takes with labour relations. The Ontario government is more than willing to intervene in free collective bargaining to end legal strikes by

15   Keith Leslie, "McGuinty Says Province Would Consider Declaring Toronto Transit Essential Service," *The Canadian Press*, Toronto, April 18, 2008.

16   Ibid.

17   Rob Ferguson and Tess Kalinowski, "Ontario Bans Strikes by the TTC," *The Toronto Star*, March 30, 2011.

18   Mark McAllister, "NDP Blocks McGuinty Plan to End York Strike; Back-to-Work Legislation Likely to Take Several Days Without All-Party Support," *The Ottawa Citizen*, January 25, 2009.

workers. In doing so, the government constructs the intervention not as a coercive act by the Ontario state, but simply that the government is intervening to do what is best for the province as a whole. This masking coercion as consent became the main theme for the attacks on the Ontario working class coming out of the 2010 provincial budget. In this budget, discussed below, the Ontario government proposed to freeze the wages of all public sector workers for two years. The language the government used was not of coercion, but suggesting that Ontario workers all needed to 'chip in' to help solve the economic crisis caused by the Great Recession - a sort of 'we're all in this together' rhetoric. Further, the Ontario government 'invited' unions to 'consult' on a proposed wage freeze, again framing a coercive act as something which could be reached by consensus.

The 2010 Budget

On 25 March 2010 the McGuinty government tabled a budget designed to cut Ontario's growing deficit. The budget was an example of typical neoliberal fiscal and monetary doctrine: while facing a budgetary deficit, the province would not consider raising taxes - indeed, there was a commitment to lower the overall corporate tax rate. Along with lowering taxes, the budget documents contained a promise to freeze the wages of the entire public sector in the province.

The budget advanced what Gindin and Hurley have dubbed a 'wage freeze environment.'[19] Gindin and Hurley describe a two pronged attack on public sector workers in Ontario. First, the Ontario government sets itself up as a defender of public services, blaming rising compensation costs for a decline in services. At the same time, workers and unions are oriented to believe that wage and benefit gains are impossible. Both modes of attack were present in the budget document. The Ontario government *did* promise more spending in certain areas of the public sector: $310 million for new spaces in universities in the province and $63.5 million for public day care spaces, for example.[20] At the same time the province was

---

[19] Sam Gindin and Michael Hurley, "The Public Sector: Searching for a Focus," in *The Bullet* 354, May 15, 2010. <http://www.socialistproject.ca/bullet/354.php>.

[20] Robert Benzie, "Ontario Vows Freeze on Public-Sector Wages," *Toronto Star*, March 25, 2010.

promising more spending for public services, the budget document also contained a promise of a two-year wage freeze for over 1.06 million workers in the broader public sector.[21] This seemingly contradictory position - promising support for the public service on the one hand, while on the other attacking those workers who deliver public services - has been in lock-step with the past practises of the McGuinty government. Elected, in part, with the support of the provincial labour movement and a promise to return 'balance' to labour relations in the province,[22] the McGuinty regime has overturned some of the most extreme elements of the previous Progressive Conservative government's anti-union legislation, but has generally continued on a path very similar to the Harris and Eves 'Common Sense Revolution': lowering corporate taxes, restricting union rights, and cutting social spending in order to balance the budget.

Dwight Duncan, the minister of finance, and McGuinty used the budget as an opportunity to make political hay by attacking the opposition parties at Queen's Park. First, the government attacked the Progressive Conservatives, noting that the Liberal government was adding money to the public service, and that their record of labour relations was much better than the previous PC's. In their attack on the NDP, McGuinty and Duncan promised that the wage freeze for *unionized* workers would be negotiated, not legislated (non unionized workers and managers in the public sector had their wages frozen through legislation). Recalling the spectre of the Bob Rae NDP government and the incredibly unpopular *Social Contract Act* and the 'Rae Days' that stemmed from the *Act* - unpaid days of work used to control a ballooning deficit - the Liberals promised that the wage freeze would be negotiated, not legislated.[23] On the wage freeze, Duncan promised that the government 'will not propose mandatory days off ... we will honour existing collective agreements.'[24]

While Duncan was seemingly promising a more consensual approach to labour relations in the public sector than either the

---

[21]   Ibid.

[22]   Bradley Walchuk, "Changing Union-Party Relations in Canada: The Rise of the Working Families Coalition," *Labor Studies Journal* 35, no. 1 (2010).

[23]   For a complete discussion of the *Social Contract Act* and the Rae Days, see Leo Panitch and Donald Swartz, *From Consent to Coercion: The Assault on Trade Union Freedoms,* 3rd ed. (Aurora: Garamond Press, 2003), chapter 8.

[24]   Quoted in Benzie, "Ontario Vows Freeze on Public-Sector Wages," 2010.

Progressive Conservatives or New Democrats had delivered in their tenure in office, this was simply because the coercive route could not be undertaken. Canadian judicial precedent has long been that section 2(d) of the *Canadian Charter of Rights and Freedoms* protects the freedom to associate, but does *not* protect the right to strike nor the right to bargain. In June 2007, however, the Supreme Court of Canada seemingly undid twenty years of judicial president and ruled, in *Health Services and Support - Facilities Subsector Bargaining Association v. British Columbia* that section 2(d) did, in fact, protect the procedural right to bargain. Essentially, the legal framework as of the 2010 Ontario budget prevented the Ontario government from unilaterally legislating a wage freeze without 'consulting' the unions involved.

The response from organized labour to the proposed wage freeze was fast and, not surprisingly, hostile. Sid Ryan, president of the Ontario Federation of Labour (OFL) condemned the wage freeze, as did Fred Hahn, president of the Canadian Union of Public Employee's Ontario Division (CUPE-O), and the Ontario Nurses Association (ONA).[25] For his part, Warren (Smokey) Thomas, president of the Ontario Public Service Employee's Union (OPSEU), noted the class character of the wage freeze: 'It's difficult for workers to swallow some of this stuff when you see bankers and investment houses ... going back to multi-million bonuses after just being bailed out.'[26] After this initial salvo by prominent public sector union leaders, and a promise of a negotiated wage freeze by the province, the issue seemingly went silent until July 2010, when the province announced it was ready to begin a 'consultation' with unions in order to begin working towards the promised wage freeze.

The Consultation Process

On 20 July 2010, Dwight Duncan made a speech in Toronto to assembled business and union leaders where he claimed that he would meet with unions in the next months to tackle the 'single biggest line in our budget - public-sector compensation.'[27] The

25   Karen Howlett, "Ontario's Deep Freeze," *The Globe and Mail*, March 26, 2010.
26   Robert Benzie, "The Big Freeze: Duncan Points to Deficit as He Ends Pay Raises for About 1 Million Public Sector Employees," *The Toronto Star*, March 26, 2010.
27   Quoted in Linda Nguyen, "Duncan's Freeze Pitch Finds Silence; Labour May Go to Court Over Wages," *National Post*, July 21, 2010.

'consultation process,' as Duncan labelled it, apparently began on 20 July 2010, with Duncan claiming that the speech he gave was the first step in the consultation process. Union leaders had a varied response to Duncan's announcement - Sid Ryan, of the OFL, said the unions would attend the consultations with 'an open mind' but would go to the courts if the province brought about an 'unwanted' wage freeze.[28] This is somewhat indicative of the direction that the Ontario labour movement has been taking for the past decade - increasingly relying on institutional measures, such as court action and short term alliances with political parties, to advance labour's agenda. Conversely, some unions, like OPSEU and the Canadian Autoworkers (CAW), lashed out against the consultations, claiming that they would not grant wage concessions through bargaining.[29] Ken Lewenza, president of the CAW, not only spoke out against the wage freeze, but questioned the economic merit of restricting the purchasing power of the working class: 'To suggest that the provincial deficit should be borne by public sector workers is tremendously short-sighted and unfair. Ontario can only get out of a deficit position by growing the economy, not by making it even more precarious. This will in no way protect services as the province is claiming.'[30] Many unions, such as CUPE-O, found themselves in the middle - speaking out against the wage freeze, but not outright refusing to participate in the consultations, and offering up no alternatives to a wage freeze.[31]

Shortly after the announcement that there would be a consultation process to bring about a wage freeze, and the union outcry to these developments, the Ontario government fired back. The McGuinty government took this time to position themselves as a defender of public services, who were taking necessary but difficult steps to both balance the budget in Ontario and also keep providing high levels of public services. The assistant deputy minister of labour relations, Tim Hadwen, defended the consultations thusly: 'The purpose of the consultations is to provide opportunities for

[28]   Quoted in Ibid.
[29]   Robert Benzie, "Wage-Freeze Plan Rebuffed: Finance Minister's Proposal for Two-Year Freeze of Public-Sector Wages 'Horrible Idea,' Says OFL," *Toronto Star*, July 21, 2010.
[30]   Sonja Puzic, "Union Calls Wage Freeze 'Unfair Attack'; Duncan's Two-Year Plan has Critics Warning of Strikes," *The Windsor Star*, July 21, 2010.
[31]   Nguyen, "Duncan's Freeze Pitch Finds Silence."

broader public sector bargaining agents, employers and the government to engage in a dialogue about how we can work together to manage compensation expense in a fair manner that protects key public services.'[32] This statement reveals the ideological position of the McGuinty government with regard to the budgetary deficit. First, the government had positioned itself as the sole defender of public services: the government wished to provide a full and robust welfare state to all Ontarians, but could not because of the deficit. The money, the government argued, to protect public services had to come from somewhere, and it was the unions and their high levels of compensation that were eating up all the budget for the public service. Hence, according to these logics, it is not the McGuinty government's refusal to even consider raising the corporate tax rate, nor their cutting of service budgets that is the problem: it is solely the unions, and their overcompensated members, that must be dealt with. According to this script it is the unions and their workers - those who actually deliver public services on a day-to-day basis, that are the problem, and the government would stand up to them in order to ensure the continual delivery of public services.

The first round of consultations, held in August 2010, met with fierce resistance from the unions involved, and did not produce the results the government was looking for. OPSEU walked away from the table, not one full day into the consultation process, with their president claiming the consultation process was 'a half-baked plan that has disaster written all over it.'[33] OPSEU took the position that the wage freeze was unnecessary, and that the union would deal with the freeze at the bargaining table, not during the consultation process. OCUFA, the Ontario Confederation of University Faculty Associations, similarly walked away from the consultation table, albeit after sitting with the government for one week. The union publically rejected the idea that wage freezes were the only way to deal with the budgetary deficit and, similarly to OPSEU, said that the thirty-three faculty associations the confederation represented would deal with the wage

---

[32]   Quoted in Elizabeth Church and Karen Howlett, "Ontario to Propose Wage Freeze for Public Sector," *The Globe and Mail*, July 23, 2010.

[33]   Elizabeth Church, "First Round of 'Wage Freeze' Talks Strike Out with Professors, OPSEU," *The Globe and Mail*, August 26, 2010.

freezes individually, at the bargaining table.[34] The CAW, which was at the table representing workers in nursing, long term care, and the university sector, also walked away from the consultation process, decrying them as a sham. Lewenza, president of the CAW, took things a step further and threatened job action if the government went ahead with the proposed wage freeze.[35]

The second phase of negotiations involved CUPE, the Ontario Nurses Association (ONA), and the Steelworkers (USW). These unions seemed more willing to participate in the consultations. For their part, the ONA sat at the table with the government, but refused to talk about a wage freeze. Instead, the union argued that the only way out of the budgetary deficit would be for the government to raise the corporate tax rate.[36] This was, to say the least, a non-starter with the Ontario government, and talks subsequently reached an impasse. The Steelworkers followed suit, meeting with the government at the table, but rejecting a wage freeze and calling on McGuinty to raise the corporate tax rate.[37] For its part, CUPE-O took the most tame and passive approach to the consultation process of all the unions asked to sit at the table. While CUPE-O did condemn the wage freeze, Fred Hahn, the president of the Ontario Division, claimed "We're interested in engaging the government in a real discussion. ... We're not interested in walking away."[38]

While a third phase of consultations was planned, the wheels came off the proverbial cart in late September and early October as provincial arbitrators began handing out compensation increases when negotiations were referred to binding arbitration. In late September, Norm Jesin, ruling on outstanding issues in private, for-profit long term care facilities, granted members of SEIU a 2% wage increase. In his ruling, Jesin argued "I cannot accept that compensation should be frozen because of the (provincial) budget, particularly as there

34   Ibid.
35   Rob Ferguson, "Trouble Ahead, Union Warns: Years of Peace in Public Sector Could End if Premier Keeps Wage-Freeze Plan, CAW Says," *Toronto Star*, August 31, 2010.
36   Ontario Nurses Association, *Front Lines: The Members' Publication of the Ontario Nurses' Association* 10, no. 5 (October 2010): 1.
37   United Steelworkers, "Steelworkers Reject Assaults on Working Families' Incomes"   <http://www.usw.ca/workplace/campaigns/campaigns/freeze?id=0004>
38   Ferguson, "Trouble Ahead, Union Warns."

has been no legislation by the government requiring such a freeze."[39] This was followed in early October by a ruling much celebrated by the Ontario labour movement, arbitrator Martin Teplitsky awarded 2.5% to professors at University of Toronto, arguing that the increase mirrored the average increase of 2.3% in private sector compensation that year. While the increase itself encouraged the labour movement, it was Teplitsky's claim that he awarded the increase because he would not 'compromise his independence' and did not want to 'appear [to be] a minion of government.'[40] In early November arbitrator Kevin Burkett granted 16 000 hospital workers a 2% wage increase, arguing he would not freeze compensation unless there was a legislated directive to that effect.[41] At this point, most unions seemed content to press for wage increases at the bargaining table, relying on the precedent set by the provincial arbitrators. If wage increases could not be negotiated using this precedent, most unions were confident in their ability to receive wage increases from arbitrators.

While the consultation process has come and gone, and many unions were able to negotiate or win a wage freeze, there has been some limited long term campaigns against austerity measures in Ontario. The USW ran a campaign which extended into late 2010, educating locals and members on the wage freeze, and urging those locals in bargaining not to accept a wage freeze at the table. The most overarching and lengthy campaign was from OPSEU, which ran a campaign from November 2010 to January 2011. OPSEU mobilizers made presentations to most of the locals in the union, and the union held over forty demonstrations province wide. The campaign culminated in the tongue-in-cheek 'People for Corporate Tax Cuts,' a campaign which highlighted how the corporate tax cuts were paid for by cutting public services around Ontario. The campaign, which involved advertising across the province and a website (http://www.peopleforcorporatetaxcuts.ca/), "encouraged" every Ontarian to raise $500 to help pay for McGuinty's corporate tax cuts. The obvious goal of the campaign was to juxtapose the

---

[39] Robert Benzie and Rob Ferguson, "Labour Ruling Chills Liberals: Arbitrator Rejects Bid by Nursing Homes to Freeze Wages of 17,000 Workers," *Toronto Star*, September 17, 2010.

[40] Louise Brown, "Ruling Gives U of T Profs 4.5 Per Cent Over Two Years," *Toronto Star*, October 12, 2010.

[41] Robert Benzie, "Raises Ordered for 16,000 Health-Care Workers Despite Pay Freeze," *Toronto Star*, November 9, 2010.

cuts being made to the public service at the same time that the province was cutting the corporate tax rate. It is interesting to note, however, that OPSEU ran the campaign by itself after extensive consultations with eight other unions in the province had failed to arrive at an agreement on a cross union fight-back campaign.[42]

Analysis and Conclusions

The first, and perhaps most obvious, conclusion that can be drawn from the Ontario labour movement's response to the wage freeze consultations is that the Ontario labour movement remains exceptionally fragmented. There was no clear response from labour to the consultations - some unions walked away from the bargaining table, other remained at the table, and others still used the consultations as a chance to eschew a wage freeze and to propose other options to the government's deficit. The fractured nature is perhaps best highlighted by OPSEU's inability to coordinate a cross union fight-back campaign to the wage freeze, simply because the major public sector unions in Ontario could not reach a consensus on what the fight-back campaign might look like. If, as some have suggested, we are currently experiencing an era of 'permanent austerity' where governments will increasingly look to the public sector as a space to cut budgets, the labour movement needs to seriously begin working towards common goals on common campaigns.

This, of course, is much easier said than done. The Ontario labour movement, much like the greater Canadian labour movement, remains fractured along ideological lines, there still exists a gulf between the private sector and public sector unions, and many unions still have a business unionism (or sometimes a business unionism plus the NDP) orientation. In Ontario, the ideological divide between the unions in the province is quite pronounced - some unions work within the Working Families Coalition to promote strategic voting against the Progressive Conservatives, which realistically means providing financial support to and encouraging members to vote for the Liberal Party of Ontario. Other unions in Ontario maintain a close relationship with the Ontario

---

42   Bryan Evans, "The Politics of Public Sector Wages: Ontario's Social Dialogue for Austerity," Paper presented at *The Annual Meeting of the Canadian Political Science Association*, Wilfred Laurier University, Waterloo, Ontario, May 16-18, 2011: 3.

NDP. Both of these party affiliations must be questioned. The Liberals, with the 2010 budget, have shown (again) that they are no friend to the labour movement, and have no problem extracting concessions from the working class in times of financial crisis. For its part, the Ontario NDP remained muted on the issue of consultations, with party leader Andrea Horwath refusing to publically condemn the mandated wage freeze. Indeed, after avoiding the issue of the wage freeze at a press conference shortly after the 2010 budget speech, when asked point-blank if Horwath supported the wage freeze, the leader responded 'workers will understand that they have to do their part as well.'[43]

Perhaps the larger issue that unions in Ontario need to grapple with is the continual movement towards bureaucratic and legalistic responses to challenges facing labour. The initial response by many unions in Ontario, including the OFL, was to threaten to take legal action to uphold the right to bargain. This was, of course, in the wake of the HEU decision that seemingly protected the right to bargain. There are two major flaws with turning to the legalistic route. First, the Canadian courts are notoriously fickle, and can and will turn on labour unexpectedly. While the HEU decision was celebrated by the labour movement, it was mostly undone by the Fraser decision of April 2011, which ruled, in regards to agricultural workers in Ontario, that the Charter of Rights and Freedoms does not provide a constitutional right to bargain.[44] Working within the legal system opens the labour movement up to unexpected decisions that may have the effect of rolling back union rights. Further, relying on the legal system serves to shift power away from the rank-and-file union members and to the union's legal team. This has the effect of dulling class consciousness within the labour movement.

The consultation process itself reveals the problems with relying on institutional solutions to challenges. LeGay and Cummings argue that the consultations were a legal trap: the Supreme Court decision in *HEU* used the phrase 'meaningful consultation' in multiple places. The ruling has implied that governments may constitutionally justify restricting bargaining rights to implement wage

---

[43]   Quoted in Adam Radwanski, "Opposition Flubs Attack on McGuinty Budget," *The Globe and Mail*, March 30, 2010.

[44]   With *Fraser* the constitutional status of the right to bargain is murky, at best. It is unclear if *HEU* still stands with regard to public sector unions and *Fraser* for private sector ones.

restraints *if* the government in question undertakes 'meaningful consultation' with the unions in question.[45] Thus the trap: if the unions refuse to engage in consultations, they are not bargaining, so governments may act unilaterally and introduce wage freezes. If, conversely, the unions *do* participate in the consultation process, they have fulfilled the 'meaningful consultation' requirement, and governments may act unilaterally to introduce wage freezes.

By participating in the consultation process some of the unions in Ontario, particularly OPSEU and the CAW, used the opportunity to show that there were opportunities available beyond freezing public sector wages to curb the deficit in Ontario. That said, no union, save OPSEU, used the attack on the labour movement as an opportunity to organize a meaningful political campaign to fight back. Much of the current literature on union renewal suggests that there are two major orientations a union can take: business unionism or social movement unionism. Many of the unions that engaged in the consultation process behaved like business unions: participating in agreements with their employers (in this case, the Ontario state) in order to allow their employers to remain 'competitive.' While a shift towards adopting many of the principles of social movement unionism (organizing both the unorganized and organized, creating more and better activists, taking equity seriously, etc) is the first step to union renewal, it is a necessary step - not a sufficient step towards a new unionism.

A new unionism must have a class basis to it. Rather than relying on legalistic and institutional methods to face challenges, unions must work towards taking issues to the bargaining table and picket line - and show a willingness to engage in strike activity regardless of the legality of said activity. Short term institutional solutions may help the labour movement, but these solutions must be augmented by building a working class unionism. Agreeing to participate in state-sponsored 'consultations' in order to ensure the profitability of the capitalist system is short-sighted, and only serves to undermine the long term interests of the working class in Ontario.

---

[45]   Jordy Cummings and Patrick D. LeGay, "Public Sector Unions and the Consultations for Austerity," in *The Bullet* 446, December 27, 2010. <http://www.socialistproject.ca/bullet/446.php>.

COLLECTIVE BARGAINING IN A TIME OF AUSTERITY: PUBLIC SECTOR UNIONS AND THE UNIVERSITY SECTOR IN ONTARIO

Mathew Nelson and James Meades

Introduction

The recessionary squeeze on governments in the name of austerity is impacting unions and public sector workers worldwide. Across Europe, workers and students have joined together in mass protest against government strategies of raising tuition fees, cutting public services, laying off public sector workers, and accumulating massive debt to bail out financial and corporate interests. In states across the US, newly elected Republican officials and right-wing pundits have called for cuts to wages and benefits, slashed support to state colleges and universities, and pushed new legislation to limit the power of public sector labour unions in collective bargaining and politics. Likewise, federal and provincial governments in Canada have responded to the global economic crisis by turning to a program of "permanent austerity" in targeting public services and public sector workers.[1] In Ontario, the Liberal government of Dalton McGuinty legislated a two-year wage freeze for all non-unionized public sector workers, and through a series of measures such as dubious public consultations

---

[1]   Bryan Evans and Greg Albo, "Permanent Austerity: The Politics of the Canadian Exit Strategy from Fiscal Stimulus," in *Saving Global Capitalism: Interrogating Austerity and Working Class Responses to Crises*, eds. Carlo Fanelli et al. (Ottawa, ON: Red Quill Books, 2010).

put pressure on public sector unions to follow suit.[2] Such austerity measures have effectively sought to undermine the power of unions to protect and sustain a decent standard of living for their members through collective bargaining. This has been particularly apparent in the universities, where a large number of students already burdened with student loans are facing increasing tuition fees and downward pressure on their wages. To date, however, mass opposition remains largely non-existent and, with the exception of students in Quebec, the student movement in Canada has yet to ally itself with workers' organizations in any significant way.

This chapter seeks to explore the impacts of recent austerity measures on public sector unions in Ontario's university sector. The major goal of our analysis is to situate the restructuring of universities in Canada and Ontario within the broader political and economic context of neoliberalism, a process which seeks to subject every aspect of university life to market logics of corporatization and privatization.[3] The first section examines the impacts of the neoliberalization of the university in Canada and across the world, arguing that in this context, academics and other university workers are increasingly denied the ability to meet students' educational needs and to pursue knowledge for its own sake. The second part provides an overview of the global economic crisis of 2007–08, and suggests that the crisis has intensified the chronic underfunding facing post-secondary education in Canada and the province of Ontario. The third section looks specifically at austerity measures and post-secondary education in Ontario, with a focus on the effects of austerity on the university sector and how both inflationary and tuition increases are increasing the debt and threatening the take-home pay of university employees. Drawing on a particular case study, the fourth section examines the 2010 set of negotiations between the Canadian Union of Public Employees Local (CUPE) 4600 and Carleton University in Ottawa, Ontario. With an emphasis on future steps forward, we conclude with some of the challenges and victories for university sector

---

[2]   Jordy Cummings and Patrick D. LeGay, "Public Sector Unions and the Consultations for Austerity," *Socialist Project: The Bullet* 446 (December 27, 2010), accessed May 24, 2010, http://www.socialistproject.ca/bullet/446.php.

[3]   See Alex Callinicos, *Universities in a Neoliberal World* (London: Bookmarks, 2006); Charles R. Menzies, "Reflections on Work and Activism in the 'University of Excellence,'" *New Proposals: Journal of Marxism and Interdisciplinary Inquiry* 3, no. 2 (February 2010): 40–55.

unions, and suggest that there is no alternative but broad-based student, community, and worker resistance to reduced public funding for post-secondary institutions and the ongoing privatization of universities.

Privatization and the Neoliberal University

The attempt to restructure universities in Canada and across the world in the name of austerity is part of the global political-economic process known as neoliberalism. From a Marxist perspective, David Harvey argues, "Neoliberalism is in the first instance a theory of political economic practices that proposes that human well-being can best be advanced by liberating individual entrepreneurial freedoms and skills within an institutional framework characterized by strong private property rights, free markets and free trade."[4] In response to the inability of the Keynesian welfare state to sustain capital accumulation in the post-war period, the discourses and practices of neoliberalism seek "to deepen and intensify internal competition among competing business interests, thereby pitting workers and workplaces in competition with one another through ever-increasing market compulsions." This can include "efforts to contract-out and privatize provincial and municipal services, extract concessions from its unionized and non-unionized workforce, in addition to an increased reliance on public-private partnerships (P3's)."[5] In the university sector, this means that academics and other university staff are increasingly denied the capacity to pursue knowledge for its own sake and to meet students' educational needs.

One of the main ideas behind the rise of neoliberal ideas is the concept of the "knowledge economy" or "knowledge capitalism." According to Alex Callinicos, proponents of a new knowledge economy make three primary claims:

- A shift is taking place from the production of physical goods to that of immaterial services;

---

4   David Harvey, *A Brief History of Neoliberalism* (Oxford: Oxford University Press, 2005), 2.

5   Carlo Fanelli and Chris Hurl, "Janus-Faced Austerity: Strengthening the 'Competitive' Canadian State," in *Saving Global Capitalism: Interrogating Austerity and Working Class Responses to Crises*, eds. Carlo Fanelli et al. (Ottawa, ON: Red Quill Books, 2010), 33.

- Partly in consequence, production is becoming more "knowledge-intensive"—in other words, products are likely to sell thanks to both the increasingly sophisticated techniques used to make them and the ideas that they represent and that are used to market them, all of which relies on research by highly qualified workers.
- The success of companies and national economies alike is therefore increasingly dependent, not on the physical plant and equipment that they have built up over years, decades, or even longer, but on their "human capital" —that is, on the skills, knowledge and imagination of their workforces. It is through successfully using these skills to supply what the world market wants that individuals, firms and whole countries can prosper.[6]

However, theories of the knowledge economy tend to ignore the centrality of competition to neoliberal capitalism. Competition involves winner and losers, but not every post-secondary institution can proclaim itself to be a "university of excellence." Because "neoliberalism in higher education means that this logic of competition is internalised deep into how universities work,"[7] those universities that appear to 'excel' are increasingly privatized, run like businesses, or pushed to work more closely with them through "partnerships." First, university administrators increasingly draw on business jargon, employing terms such as "quality," "innovation," and "excellence," where institutional effectiveness is monitored through performance indicators and managerial strategies that aim to discipline students and academics by assessing their behavioural conformity in relation to the broader interests of capital. From this perspective, higher education is often seen as a form of job training, where critical thinking is made subservient to skill set assessments. As a result, "the right to an education [...] is replaced by a set of measures that fall under the belief that the imitation of business methods will produce the best results for the university."[8]

---

[6]   Callinicos, *Universities*, 8–9.
[7]   Callinicos, *Universities*, 11.
[8]   Edurne Bagué, Nuria Comerma, and Ignasi Terradas, "An Analytical Proposal for Understanding the 'Higher Education European Space': A View from the University of Barcelona," *New Proposals: Journal of Marxism and Interdisciplinary Inquiry* 3, no. 2 (February 2010): 9–19.

Second, the discourse of business partnerships emphasizes "knowledge transfer," the idea that universities conduct research that immediately benefits private enterprise and businesses. Public-private partnerships between universities and business can take many forms. They can include universities receiving research contracts from private firms, as well as the formation of collaborative projects that involve the exploitation of research developed in the university by private companies. But much like the idea of partnerships, Menzies argues that the discourse of post-secondary "excellence" must also be situated in relation to neoliberal capitalism. The "new corporate university of excellence" entails new forms of privatization, as well as the notion that education as a right is being challenged by a concept of education as a commodity to purchase. The paradigm of excellence as an organizing principle drives academic "output" rather than "content," especially with respect to the quality of publications. Some researchers get lost in the competitive rush to publish, by prioritizing "their own advancement over the people about who they write."[9] As a result, the paradigm of excellence undermines collaboration and cooperation in the workplace. Like the promotion of business partnerships and the concept of the knowledge economy, the discourse of excellence contributes to the subordination of post-secondary education to neoliberal logics of privatization and corporatization.[10]

New forms of privatization and corporatization are connected to reduced public funding for post-secondary institutions, which are being restructured to provide domestic and Canadian corporations with the academic research and the skilled workers they need to stay profitable.[11] Therefore, "the neoliberal university is affected by privatization and underfunding in the same way that all public services are." In particular, "government underfunding reinforces the drive for cost savings, and it also guides university administrators toward forms of privatization—all of which are further encouraged by governments." Different forms of privatization

---

9   Menzies, "The 'University of Excellence,'" 53.

10   Neil Tudiver defines "the corporate university," like the neoliberal university, as a structure that "replaces the traditional learning centre concept of providing services with a profit centre model of selling commodities." See Neil Tudiver, *Universities for Sale: Resisting Corporate Control over Canadian High Education* (Toronto, ON: James Lorimer & Company, 1999), 155.

11   See for instance, Linda McQuaig, "Universities' Corporate Temptation," *The Toronto Star,* February 22, 2011, A19.

can include securing private financing of research, increasing the number of corporations on campuses, and increasing user fees in the form of higher tuition.[12] In this climate, resources per student are reduced, and academics and departments are increasingly forced to compete with each other for funds. Rising tuition fees are forcing many students to work long hours to support themselves and preventing students with working-class backgrounds from attending university. This in turn generates growing pressure on university students to take on unprecedented amounts of student loan debt.[13] For student-workers such as teaching assistants (TAs), contract instructors, and other flexible "contingent faculty,"[14] who often find themselves in precarious working conditions, this neo-liberal assault creates the insecurity of "being permanently on the edge of unemployment, having to make do with casual, temporary, perhaps part-time work, or combining several jobs."[15]

As demonstrated in the following sections, the global economic crisis has intensified the funding crisis facing post-secondary education in Canada and the province of Ontario. In the Canadian context, Fanelli and Hurl draw attention to what they call "capital-preserving federalism," a strategy that imposes constraints and fixes the parameters of political and economic reform to meet the needs of capital accumulation at the expense of public services, social programs, and labour and environmental protections.[16] But while Canada's federal and provincial governments have responded to the crisis by signaling a turn to permanent austerity in targeting public sector workers, this does not necessarily mark the beginning of a new era. Rather, the adoption of austerity measures in response to the global economic crisis should be viewed as an escalation of neoliberal projects that first emerged in the mid-1970s.

---

12   Dan Crow, "Precarious Employment and the Struggle for Good Jobs in the University Sector," *Socialist Project: The Bullet* 160 (November 30, 2008), accessed May 24, 2010, http://www.socialistproject.ca/bullet/bullet160.html.

13   Alan Nasser and Kelly Norman, "The Student Loan Debt Bubble," *Counterpunch* (January 11, 2011), accessed May 24, 2011, http://www.counter-punch.org/nasser01112011.html.

14   See James L. Turk, "Restructuring Academic Work," in *Universities at Risk: How Politics, Special Interests and Corporatization Threaten Academic Integrity,* ed. James L. Turk (Toronto, ON: James Lorimer & Company, 2008), 292–303.

15   Callinicos, *Universities,* 24.

16   Fanelli and Hurl, "Janus-Faced Austerity," 30.

The Global Economic Crisis and Capital-Preserving Federalism

The global economic crisis that originated in the US in 2008 saw billions of public dollars pumped into private American banks and corporations that were deemed "too big to fail." The crisis and the ensuing recession must be understood in terms of the excessive power of finance capital, or what has been referred to as "the financialization of the capital accumulation process," where real capital formation in the realm of goods and services becomes increasingly dominated by speculative finance.[17] This is not to suggest that the crisis can be viewed entirely in financial terms, or that a strict opposition exists between a predatory financial sector and the sphere of the productive economy. Rather, processes of financialization involving credit, speculative capital, and the creation of debt through loans as a means of generating profit are all necessary for the daily workings of the capitalist system. In the neoliberal era, however, the financial sector has greatly expanded and assumed a heightened significance. After a lengthy period of wage repression in the 1970s and 1980s, capital was able to solve the subsequent drop in effective demand in the 1990s by pumping up the credit economy, resulting in the vast amounts of debt in housing markets and elsewhere.

The current crisis originated in the financial sector, where a vast array of complex financial instruments such as mortgage-backed securities, collateralized debt obligations, and credit default swaps were tied to tens of millions of US mortgages worth billions of dollars short of what was initially paid for them. When the financial bubble eventually burst, mortgage owners began defaulting when the houses they had taken mortgages on began to fall in value. In the US, the federal government responded to the economic crisis with the largest financial bailout in world history. While the bailout was ultimately successful in averting a wholesale collapse of the global economy, the public sector austerity measures that followed have meant that workers' conditions continue to steadily deteriorate as income and wealth is redistributed from poor and working people to the rich. According to David McNally, "the bad bank that

---

17   John Bellamy Foster, "The Financialization of Accumulation," *Monthly Review* 62, no. 5 (October 2010): 1.

triggered the crisis in 2008 never went away—it was simply shifted on to governments. Private debt became public debt." With this shift, "the focus of ruling classes shifted toward a war against public services. Concerned to rein in government debts, they announced an age of austerity—of huge cuts to pensions, education budgets, social welfare programs, public sector wages, and jobs. In so doing, they effectively declared that working class people and the poor will pay the cost of the global bank bailout."[18]

The credit crisis in Canadian financial markets first exploded in mid-August 2007, after a relatively sustained period of economic growth from 2003 to 2006. The healthy economic conditions for capital that preceded the 2007 crisis were the result of an expansion of credit, which more than doubled between 1996 and 2006, and exceeded the $1-billion mark for the first time in 2006.[19] Despite widespread claims that there was no bank bailout in Canada, da Silva points out that, apart from guaranteeing hundreds of billions of dollars to pay back new loans made to Canadian financial institutions, the federal government's Insured Mortgage Purchase Program and the Extraordinary Financing Framework are effectively handouts to the big Canadian banks, which were given the option of auctioning their risky mortgage packages to the Canadian Mortgage and Housing Corporation in exchange for public money. Rather than allocating the bailout money towards stimulus spending and the creation of new jobs for unemployed workers, it has been used to restore the balance sheets of the financial sector and fund the future expansion of Canadian finance capital.[20]

The deficit precipitated by the crisis and bailouts of the financial sector has been used to further intensify neoliberal restructuring and austerity measures in Canada.[21] Despite neoliberal arguments in favour of shrinking the state through minimal government intervention in the economy, the crisis appears to have triggered

---

[18]   David McNally, *Global Slump: The Economic and Politics of Crisis and Resistance* (Oakland, CA: PM Press, 2011), 4.

[19]   Fletcher Barager, "The Credit Crisis in Canada: The First Six Months," *Financial Meltdown: Canada, the Economic Crisis and Political Struggle* (Socialist Interventions Pamphlet Series, 2009): 20.

[20]   Steve da Silva, "Bank Bailouts and the 2009 Federal Budget," *Financial Meltdown: Canada, the Economic Crisis and Political Struggle* (Socialist Interventions Pamphlet Series, 2009): 30–36.

[21]   Evans and Albo, "Permanent Austerity," 21.

a consensus among many mainstream economists that forms of intervention are increasingly necessary in order to stabilize the economic system. In this context, "the austerity agenda isn't about big versus small government: it is about increasing the repressive and punitive aspects of governments and shrinking redistributive programmes and democratic gains."[22] In successive federal budgets, for example, the Conservative government has prioritized corporate tax cuts and policy fields such as national defence, state security and surveillance, policing, and prison expansion over areas such as post-secondary education. In a climate of bank bailouts, corporate tax reductions, and cuts to social spending, we have witnessed a shift in the focal point of the crisis from financial institutions to state finance, and finally, onto the public in the form of a long squeeze on federal and provincial spending.

In the area of post-secondary education, the 2010 federal budget did little to address the long-term funding crisis facing universities in Canada, instead prioritizing the commercialization of research, academic–business partnerships, and corporate research funding, with little regard for rising costs of living, increasing enrolment, and aging infrastructure on Canadian campuses. In its response to the budget, the CUPE argued:

> Underfunding has ensured tuition fees and student debt, corporate sponsored and directed research, increased contracting out of services and jobs, and a reliance on underpaid, contract workers. The consequences of underfunding are completely at odds with a public education system based on the principles of accessibility, affordability and equality. [...] Those hardest hit by these trends are women, immigrants, workers/students of color and workers/students with disabilities. The emphasis on science and technology, commercialization of research in this budget, and aspirations to corporatize our campuses through increasing numbers of academic/business partnerships, corporate research funding, patents and intellectual property rights revenue is a threatening trend that is compromising the quality of our public education

---

[22]   Cummings and LeGay, "Public Sector Unions."

system. Without proper public funding this trend will increase, as will an overreliance on tuition fees as a source of private funding.[23]

This strategy of capital-preserving federalism, involving the federal government's chronic underfunding of the current system of general cash transfers to the provinces, has multi-scalar and multi-spatial effects[24] on provincial governments, which are themselves increasingly cutting spending on funds previously designated for post-secondary education. At the same time, public sector employees at universities are being targeted in attempts to legislate away collective bargaining rights and force workers to accept wage cuts and inferior working conditions.

Neoliberal Austerity and Post-Secondary Education in Ontario

While the strategy of capital-preserving federalism is advanced at the federal level, it is reflected in the uneven budgetary and fiscal policies of the Canadian provinces. In Ontario, the Liberal government of Premier Dalton McGuinty was elected in 2003 in part because it claimed it would be less hostile to workers than the previous right-wing government of Mike Harris and its so-called Common Sense Revolution.[25] Despite their rhetoric, however, the Liberals left in place a number of major tenets of the Common Sense Revolution, including reduced welfare benefits and anti-union

---

23 Canadian Union of Public Employees, "Fact Sheet: Post-Secondary Education," (April 14, 2011), accessed May 25, 2011, http://cupe.ca/s4d920c565467d/ sheet-post-secondary-education.
24 Fanelli and Hurl, "Janus-Faced Austerity," 30.
25 Although many unions have a longstanding policy of backing the social-democratic New Democratic Party (NDP), a variety of craft unions and teachers' unions have long supported the federal and provincial Liberal Party. As Walchuk points out, in the lead-up to the 2003 provincial election in Ontario, a number of trade unions and labour councils formed an umbrella group known as the Working Families Coalition (WFC) in an effort to stop the Conservatives from being elected to a third term in office. Rather than campaigning for the NDP, "the WFC's strategy was to actively campaign *against* the governing Tories, and, in the process, implicitly encourage support for the Liberal Party." See Bradley Walchuk, "Changing Union-Party Relations in Canada: The Rise of the Working Families Coalition," *Labor Studies Journal* 35, no. 1 (March 2010): 37.

legislation. Despite modest counter-measures, including heightened post-secondary funding, the provincial government has "re-branded" and "re-packaged" neoliberal policies in a less overt form, through measures such as corporate tax cuts, wage repression, and the streamlining of public sector services.[26] After the Ontario government projected a record deficit of $21.3 billion in March 2010,[27] Premier McGuinty and Finance Minister Dwight Duncan decided to balance the budget on the backs of working-class and poor people and public-sector employees. At the same time it was providing nearly $4.6 billion over two years in tax cuts to corporations, the provincial government froze the salaries of Members of Provincial Parliament and 350,000 other non-unionized public sector workers for two years through the Public Sector Compensation Restraint to Protect Public Services Act. The proposed wage freeze, in effect, served "to conceal a massive transfer of wealth from the pockets of working people to the bonuses of CEOs."[28] In addition, the 2010 Ontario budget included a proposal to cut $200 million from the Special Diet Allowance, which allowed 124,000 people on social assistance to buy food necessary to deal with specific medical conditions. In effect, the government's austerity agenda involved cutting welfare spending to the poor, slashing certain government programs, easing the tax burden on profitable corporations and Ontario's wealthiest sectors, and implementing wage restraint measures for public sector workers.[29]

In an attempt to pit workers against each other, the provincial government initiated a process that would facilitate significant inequity between union and non-unionized workers doing similar work. While McGuinty and Duncan stopped short of imposing a wage freeze on the 750,000 public sector unionized

---

[26] Carlo Fanelli and Mark P. Thomas, "Austerity, Competitiveness and Neoliberalism Redux: Ontario Responds to the Great Recession," *Socialist Studies* 7, no. 1/2 (Spring/Fall 2011): 141–170.

[27] Karen Howlett and James Bradshaw, "The Ontario Public-Sector Wage Freeze that Wasn't," *Globe and Mail*, February 4, 2011, accessed May 25, 2011, http://www.theglobeandmail.com/news/national/ontario/the-ontario-public-sector-wage-freeze-that-wasnt/article1892496/.

[28] Warren (Smokey) Thomas, "Workers Bear Burden of Provincial 'Restraint,'" *Toronto Star*, November 19, 2010, accessed May 23, 2011, http://www.thestar.com/opinion/editorialopinion/article/893386—workers-bear-burden-of-provincial-restraint.

[29] Evans and Albo, "Permanent Austerity."

employees in the province, they called for a voluntary two-year
wage freeze, arguing that there would be no new money from
the province to cover wage increases for new collective agreements. The overwhelming legal position was that the government
could not simply impose a wage freeze on unionized employees.
According to precedent set by the Supreme Court of Canada in
2007, for governments to be able to intervene in the collective bargaining process, they must consult with affected unions and offer
an appropriate rationale before they can table legislation that may
violate an entrenched right under the Canadian Charter of Rights
and Freedoms.

While collective bargaining rights continue to be protected
by the Charter and the Ontario Labour Relations Act, Cummings and LeGay argue that wage restraint consultations were
in essence an attempt by the province to set a trap for organized
labour and to "engage in more repressive restraint measures
because, paradoxically, labour rights are now constitutionally
enshrined via the Charter ruling." While the Supreme Court
recognized labour's right to engage in collective bargaining with
employers, it failed to address the very substance of bargaining,
arguing that "it is the collective bargaining process that is constitutionally protected, not the content of the actual provisions of
the collective agreements."[30] In particular, the Supreme Court's
use of the phrase "meaningful consultation" can be seen as a legal
trap because "it allows the government to justify whatever sort
of wage restraint measures they want as being consistent with
labour rights because the measures come from a process that
putatively respects consultation; and therefore the measures are
'reasonable.'"[31]

In an apparent attempt to circumvent the collective bargaining
process, however, the Liberal government held a number of preliminary talks on restraint with a number of public sector unions.
While a majority of unions walked away from the talks in opposition, including the Canadian Automobile Workers, the Canadian
Association of University Teachers, and the Service Employees

---

[30]   Supreme Court of Canada cited in Sam Gindin and Michael Hurley, "The
       Public Sector: Searching for a Focus," *Socialist Project: The Bullet* 354 (May 15,
       2010), accessed May 25, 2011, http://www.socialistproject.ca/bullet/354.php.
[31]   Cummings and LeGay, "Public Sector Unions."

International Union, others, including the Ontario division of CUPE, decided to engage in a series of "consultation sessions" with the government beginning in August 2010, in an attempt to "act as responsible participants in a pluralistic public sphere, as 'stakeholders' responsibly negotiating with employers over wages and service provisions."[32] In this context, CUPE Ontario, under the leadership of Fred Hahn, largely avoided any widespread defence of free collective bargaining in the province, and did not attempt to put forth "a coherent and militant position shared across the public sector."[33] Rather than engaging with the broader question of class resistance and struggle against neoliberal capitalism, Hahn in particular utilized a reformist discourse centred on economic growth, engaging the government in discussion, and the negative effects of freezing workers' wages, especially in terms of slowing down recovery by inhibiting "consumer spending."[34]

The Ontario University Workers Coordinating Committee (OUWCC), a voluntary association consisting of CUPE locals in the university sector, followed a similar path by drafting an alternative plan for post-secondary education to present to the government ahead of the proposed consultations. The OUWCC had, at the time, collective agreements that were open on 14 of 17 universities, and 28 university locals were at the bargaining table. Member locals were attempting to coordinate their bargaining in pursuit of decent wages and benefits, pensions for precarious workers, and better working conditions. The intended aim of an emergency meeting on August 4, 2010, was for members to decide whether they would give the OUWCC the mandate to engage in consultations with the government and to decide what would be discussed. Representatives decided to give CUPE Ontario the mandate to continue pushing for inclusion in the Provincial Discussion Table that began on August 9, but they agreed to CUPE's business-as-usual approach, which meant the union would not agree to any employer requests to pause or suspend the bargaining process through cancelled dates. A number

---

32   Ibid.
33   Julian Holland, "Ontario University Workers Face Tough Bargaining Challenges," *People's Voice*, September 1–15, 2010, 5.
34   Canadian Union of Public Employees Ontario, "Statement by CUPE Ontario, July 21, 2010 re: Wage Freeze," (July 21, 2010), accessed May 24, 2011, http://www.cupe.on.ca/doc.php?document_id=1199&lang=en.

of representatives did express concern that participation in the government sessions would legitimize a consultation process that they deemed to be illegitimate, but in the end the OUWCC was shut out of the discussions.

Despite the lack of a coherent public sector fight back, the McGuinty government ultimately failed to impose a culture of restraint throughout the public sector, with labour arbitrators awarding employees of universities, hospitals, long-term home care, and police services annual wage increases ranging from 1.5% to 2.75%.[35] In a review of 23 labour agreements, the *Globe and Mail* found that in numerous cases, negotiators decided not to implement a wage freeze, resulting in tens of thousands of workers winning pay increases totalling close to $126.4 million over two years.[36] The same is true in the university sector, where the *Globe and Mail* examined seven of ten university contracts that included wage increases in the first two years. In this sector, arbitrators have avoided, in the words of arbitrator Martin Teplitsky, appearing to be "minions of government."[37] Arbitrator William Kaplan, for example, granted professors and librarians at the University of Toronto a 4.5% raise over two years, and awarded members of the Carleton University Academic Staff Association (CUASA), a union representing faculty, professional librarians, and some lecturers, 1.5% increases in each of the first two years of the agreement. Duncan Watt, Carleton's vice-president of finance and administration, justified the agreement by arguing that

---

35   Karen Howlett and James Bradshaw, "Labour Chaos in Ontario Predicted," *The Globe and Mail*, May 6, 2011, A8.

36   Howlett and Bradshaw, "The Ontario Public-Sector Wage Freeze." *The Globe and Mail* also reported that the Ontario government secretly awarded 38,000 employees of the province's largest public sector union, the Ontario Public Service Employees Union, an additional increase of 1% for 2012. Overall, the secret deal amounts to an increase of 3% for that year, effectively guaranteeing labour peace until after the provincial election of October 2011. The secret deal was made in December 2008, 15 months before the announcement of the province-wide wage freeze. See Karen Howlett, "Employers up in Arms over Ontario's 'Secret' Wage Deal," *The Globe and Mail*, May 5, 2011, accessed May 23, 2011, http://www.theglobeandmail.com/news/politics/employers-up-in-arms-over-ontarios-secret-wage-deal/article2009740/. See also Karen Howlett and James Bradshaw, "Labour Chaos in Ontario Predicted," *The Globe and Mail*, May 6, 2011, A8.

37   William Kaplan cited in Louise Brown, "Ruling Gives U of T Profs 4.5 per cent over Two Years," *The Toronto Star*, October 12, 2010, accessed May 23, 2011, http://www.thestar.com/news/canada/article/874373—ruling-gives-u-of-t-profs-4-5-per-cent-over-two-years.

"a labour dispute would have been far more costly."[38] In 2010, meanwhile, the average wage increase over three years for CUPE locals in the OUWCC was 1.5% for 2010, 1.4% for 2011, and 2.1% for 2012. In particular, CUPE 4600, the union representing TAs and contract instructors at Carleton, secured a modest wage increase without the use of an arbitrator. In the following section, we have elected to concentrate on the most recent rounds of collective bargaining between CUPE 4600 (Unit 1 representing approximately 1,500 TAs and Unit 2 representing approximately 500 contract instructors) and Carleton University as an empirical case study.

Bargaining Against Austerity: CUPE 4600 and Carleton University

For students employed in the university sector in Ontario, including many TAs and contract instructors, the provincial government's plans to implement a "zero-zero" two-year public sector wage freeze effectively amounted to a cut in real wages. Across Ontario, tuition fees are going up while class sizes are growing, programs are being cut, and aging infrastructure is being neglected. Meanwhile, the provincial government is pursuing an aggressive strategy of university expansion involving many universities receiving economic stimulus money for new capital projects. Universities in Ontario already have the highest tuition fees on average in Canada. For example, Statistics Canada reported that in September 2010, graduate fees increased by 10%, and undergraduate fees rose by 5.4%.[39] In addition, the cost of living for workers and students in Ontario is on the rise because of higher rates of inflation, national consumer price index increases, and the recent introduction of the Harmonized Sales Tax by the

---

[38]   Duncan Watt cited in Howlett and Bradshaw, "The Ontario Public-Sector Wage Freeze."

[39]   "Ontario's Record in High Tuition Fees is a National Embarrassment," Canadian Federation of Students (CFS), September 16, 2010, accessed May 25, 2011, http://www.newswire.ca/en/releases/archive/September2010/16/c2418. html. Since 1994, full-time undergraduate tuition rates have more than tripled in Ontario since 1994. See also Armine Yalnizyan, "Austerity Canadian-Style, Now in Britain? Pity," *The Globe and Mail,* November 12, 2010, accessed May 24, 2011, http://www.theglobeandmail.com/report-on-business/economy/ economy-lab/the-economists/austerity-canadian-style-now-in-britain-pity/ article1796379/.

Ontario government in July 2010.[40] With recent budgets calling for increasing enrolment in Ontario colleges and universities, it follows that university sector workers would be compensated less in terms of actual take-home pay, while doing more work. All of these factors have a profound effect on the quality of education in the province.

The recent rounds of bargaining at Carleton University that spanned from June to November 2010 not only offer an avenue to examine how neoliberal austerity measures impact unions in the university sector, but more importantly, present a context for exploring the structural and relational problems that activists face in the broader post-secondary education sector". Securing a modest wage increase was undoubtedly important for the standard of living for the members of CUPE 4600, and it did provide a reference point for unions at other universities in their negotiations. At the same time, however, we would like to underline some of the ways in which membership mobilization, clear communications, and strong collaboration with other allied groups and organizations during any round of contract discussions must be directed towards agitating against the structural problems inherent to the neoliberal university of excellence.

In what follows, we have divided the bargaining process into three overlapping time frames: (1) the initial developmental period from June to mid-September, (2) the bargaining period from early September to late November, and (3) the critical period from mid-October to late November. Given that the bargaining process between Carleton and CUPE 4600 was not the only collective action happening at Carleton during this time, these temporal abstractions should guide the reader in traversing a hectic series of events, processes, and activities. While there are inevitably issues and processes that span the entire frame of our analysis, creating distinct points of reference will allow us to demonstrate how mobilization and communication strategies change throughout the duration of negotiations in response to new developments or concerns. However, before exploring the

---

[40]   At 13%, the Harmonized Sales Tax rate is set at a combination of the Goods and Services Tax (GST) and the Provincial Sales Tax (PST), meaning that the tax rate has not increased, but because it follows the application of the GST, and the GST applies more broadly than the PST, workers and students are currently paying higher taxes on a broad range of goods and services.

2010 round of collective bargaining, there are two contextual matters that must be addressed.

First, during the 2008–09 round of collective bargaining, Unit 1 (the TAs) had failed to achieve a strong mandate, with a strike vote resulting in 51% of the membership opposing the possibility of job action if the bargaining process failed. Not only did this development remove one of the most important tactics available to the union—the strike—it also signalled to the employer that concessions could be tabled and won. The vote, which occurred during a public transit strike in Ottawa and the aftermath of a recently concluded strike of TAs at York University in Toronto, Ontario, created a climate that was less than ideal for the union. The 2008–09 round of bargaining resulted in the loss of fixed tuition indexation, wherein the tuition rate for TAs was fixed to either 2000 or 2005 levels depending on the commencement of a student's program of study. Fixed indexation was instead replaced with a rolling index, which stabilizes tuition rates to the year that a student begins their program. As a result, a student who began their program in the 2010–11 academic year pays approximately 4.5% more than a student who began in the 2009–10 academic year, while a student who begins their studies in 2011–12 will pay approximately 6% more in tuition fees than those students who began in 2010–11. The ineffective strike vote placed downwards pressure on the wages of TA at the same time they are paying more for tuition.

Second, apart from CUPE 4600, several CUPE locals at Carleton had collective agreements that expired in 2010, including CUPE 2424, representing close to 750 clerical, library, administrative and technical staff, and CUPE 910, with close to 80 operational and maintenance staff workers. In addition, the contract for Carleton's faculty association, CUASA, expired on April 30, 2010. As we demonstrate below, the presence of four major unions on campus negotiating new collective agreements at similar times presented several opportunities for strategic and tactical collaboration. There were some issues and limitations as to how far such union solidarity could have been taken, but having allies in a similar situation proved to be an effective tool in achieving a fair settlement. While there is a large difference between having the unions negotiate their contracts at the same time and having the unions negotiate together, this distinction is beyond the scope of this chapter and would require future analysis and elaboration.

The Developmental Period

In the initial developmental period of bargaining, there were four major tasks that faced the CUPE 4600 Executive Council. Having filed our notice to bargain in early June 2010, the most important task involved preparing our bargaining proposals to present to the employer. At this time, the CUPE 4600 general membership had already committed to endorsing the OUWCC's call for no concessions and a key set of coordinated bargaining proposals. The seven core bargaining proposals involved maintaining and strengthening pension and benefit plans, improving job security and job equity, achieving appropriate wage increases, and improving workplace health and safety. Of the seven proposals, two stand out as tactically and strategically important. First, the OUWCC resolutions called for a commitment to resist the pressure from the provincial government to freeze wages for two years. As evidenced in our previous discussions, the motivation behind this resolution was ensuring that public sector workers were not forced to pay for the costs of an economic crisis that was caused by governments and the financial industry. Second, the resolutions pushed for coordinated bargaining settlements, which called on union locals to sign three-year agreements in order to exert further pressure across the province during subsequent negotiations. The central idea here was that the OUWCC could develop collective bargaining strategies to enhance and support locals in the university sector as a whole.

Moving forward from the OUWCC's proposals, the second major task for CUPE 4600 was formulating the initial proposal to present to the employer, Carleton University. The bargaining teams for both the TA and contract instructor units employed a "think big" philosophy to examine the existing collective agreement for areas or clauses that could be inserted or improved. By examining previous collective agreements between the local and Carleton, as well as collective agreements from other union locals in similar conditions of employment, the Unit 1 bargaining committee found possible changes or additions to 17 articles encompassing approximately 40 sub-clauses and three letters of understanding. These changes and additions included such areas as wages, maternity leave benefits, class size limits, fee waivers for the athletics facilities and the public transit pass, payments for deferred duties, union representation on the Board of Governors and University Senate, as well as professional development funding for academic materials, conferences, and other related duties. Rather than take a "demand the impossible" strategy, however, the proposal was presented to the CUPE 4600 general membership in such a manner that while maintaining a core set of priorities, all the proposals would be introduced to the employer in order to see what might be gained overall.

The Executive Council consequently isolated several core issues to move forward with during the bargaining process. This process, in turn, necessitated a third major task for the CUPE 4600 executive involving two central components: communication and mobilization. Both Unit 1 and Unit 2 identified three or four key issues that would be the centre of the communications strategy. For the TAs in Unit 1, the four issues were the proposed wage freeze coupled with an approximate 4.5% tuition increase, class sizes for tutorials and labs, funding for professional development, and control over job duties. For the contract instructors in Unit 2, the three main issues were wages,[41] incumbency and seniority rights for reappointment, and job security protections. Despite numerous other articles in the initial bargaining proposals, the executive agreed that these specific issues presented the best option for appealing for support to the general membership, the wider university community, and the general public if strike action was deemed necessary.

The third central component for the local in the lead-up to bargaining was ensuring strong member mobilization. With the help of a contract worker charged specifically with this task, the major aim was to ensure that members were informed in clear terms about key issues. They were also encouraged to volunteer for the union, resulting in a core contingent of members who were passionate enough to risk individual setbacks for the collective good. Making use of TA orientation sessions, both at a faculty as well as a departmental level, members of the CUPE 4600 Executive Council visited each academic department to explain the role and position of the union and the benefits of union membership, as well as to recruit and encourage new members to become involved. The goal

---

[41]   For instance, at that time contract instructors in the same city at the University of Ottawa were compensated approximately 14% more per course.

was to ensure that every department had a steward to act as a representative at the executive level and to see if others would take part in any number of ongoing campaigns endorsed by the union. Because the bargaining units of any union are only as strong as the strength of the membership behind them, devising strategies to engage a membership constitutes an essential task for any union during the bargaining process.

The fourth major task was to coordinate and organize with the other key stakeholders on the Carleton campus. This meant ensuring that representatives of the faculty (CUASA), the administrative and support staff (CUPE 2424), the physical plants (CUPE 910), the Carleton University Students' Association, and the Carleton Graduate Students' Association had an open forum to discuss their own bargaining developments, campaigns, and strategies. Through a semi-informal organization called Campus United, these representatives met at several points over the summer months to explore avenues for joint action and collective pressure. Through a "strength in numbers" approach that viewed coordination and solidarity as essential, Campus United provided an invaluable resource, and in certain ways became more important as the bargaining process wore on. As we will see, however, in other respects, solidarity between unions is often easier to establish in principle than in practice.

The Bargaining Period

The second period, beginning in early September and continuing to late November, can roughly be represented as the actual bargaining process. With a bargaining proposal ready to be submitted to the Carleton University bargaining committee, and with a membership outreach and communication strategy in place, the next major goal of the union was getting to the bargaining table. As is the case at many universities, the employer's committee attempted to stall the bargaining process in the summer by largely ignoring the union until the start of the fall semester. This is part of a broader strategy aimed at isolating the union from the broader student population, a large proportion of which would be disadvantaged in the event of a work stoppage later in the school year. Despite requesting meeting dates throughout the latter part of August, it was not until September 8, 2010, that Unit 1 was able to exchange proposals with the employer. With three hours scheduled, the university's committee adjourned the meeting after only an hour, citing the large proposal from the union as something they were not yet prepared to address. The lack of serious negotiations resulted in a request from CUPE 4600 for the use of a conciliator from the Ontario Ministry of Labour to attain further dates for Unit 1 and an initial meeting for Unit 2.[42] While the request for conciliation is common during public sector bargaining, especially since it is legally necessary before strike action can occur, it is uncommon that a union should have to request conciliation to simply exchange bargaining proposals.[43]

Following the initial struggle to begin bargaining, it soon became clear that all four bargaining units at Carleton shared a similar sense of frustration at the process. This frustration led to strike votes by each union that proved effective at gauging how members would support strike action if necessary. On September 27, 2010, CUPE 2424 held its strike vote, with 83% of members voting in favour of strike action; CUASA held its strike vote on October 4 and 5, receiving 88.5% in favour; and CUPE 4600 held its strike vote from October 25 to 28, which resulted in a 74% mandate for Unit 1 and an 89% mandate for Unit 2.[44] In comparison to the 51% of CUPE 4600 members who voted in favour of possible strike action during the 2008–09 round of collective bargaining, these results point to the success the local had in communicating with their membership, and sent a strong message to the bargaining committee that they had substantial membership support to pursue an improved collective agreement. Following the success of the strike vote, and during the actual bargaining process itself, executive members and volunteers further developed a mobilization and communications strategy

---

[42] These meetings occurred on September 23, 2010, for Unit 2 and September 24, 2010, for Unit 1.

[43] In addition, following recommendations from the Ontario government for employers to pause or delay bargaining in order to further pursue consultations with public sector unions, Carleton's bargaining committee did ask to delay the bargaining process on August 11, 2010, but CUPE 4600 rejected the request.

[44] Samantha Ponting, "Will Strike if Provoked," *The Leveller* 3, no. 2 (November 2010), accessed on May 24, 2011, http://leveller.ca/wp-content/uploads/2010/11/lvllr_vol3_2.pdf. See also Matthew Pearson, "Carleton University Faculty Gives Union Negotiators Strike Mandate," *The Ottawa Citizen*, October 6, 2010, available at: http://qufa.wordpress.com/2010/10/06/carleton-university-faculty-gives-union-negotiators-strike-mandate/.

through Campus United and the use of information tables, numerous media interviews, and various social events.

In particular, Campus United proved itself to be a valuable resource for CUPE 4600, but often in contradictory ways. In one sense, it offered representatives of the local an avenue to explore the various tensions and limitations of solidarity actions with workers employed in different institutional positions. First, it soon became evident that a distinction could be made between the permanently employed academic and administrative workers of CUASA and CUPE 2424, and the precariously employed academic workers of CUPE 4600.[45] Second, despite many valuable allies within CUASA, it became clear that a certain faction viewed the role of their association in terms of organizational self-preservation rather than as a social and political force. Some members argued that, as a professional association, CUASA should concentrate on "bread and butter" issues rather than union principles of solidarity. In many respects, this faction acted largely in accordance with traditional craft union principles, whereby, to the exclusion of other workers, members of a particular craft are organized together with the aim of preserving their respectability as skilled professionals.[46]

Despite possessing different institutional interests, the solidarity and collaboration between CUPE 2424 and CUPE 4600 involved cost sharing and joint community and membership outreach events.[47] Most importantly, Campus United attempted to engage

---

[45]   In terms of job security, at Carleton TAs are employed for anything from a semester to four years, while contract instructors are generally hired on four month contracts.

[46]   David Camfield, *Canadian Labour in Crisis: Reinventing the Workers' Movement* (Halifax and Winnipeg: Fernwood Publishing, 2011), 106. For more on craft unionism in the late 1800s see Craig Heron, *The Canadian Labour Movement: A Short History*, 2nd ed. (Toronto, ON: Lorimer, 1996), 6.

[47]   These events included a "picketpalooza" (designed for participants to make picket signs for an information picket and possibly a strike line picket) on November 10, an information picket on November 15, and an event entitled "Recipe for Fair Bargaining Give-Away." With respect to the latter, Campus United representatives, at the direction of CUPE 2424, developed a recipe card for fair bargaining. The recipe cards highlighted the necessity of respect and good faith during the bargaining process and were designed to have union members as well as other staff and students sign them so that they could be sent to the Carleton University Board of Governors. Each person that signed a recipe card was offered a free cookie, made all the more significant by the fact the Carleton University President, Dr. Roseann Runte, had previously handed out cookies to undergraduate students to appear more approachable.

the Ottawa community by publishing a full-page advertisement in local print media on November 10. Formatted as an open letter to the Ontario Minister of Training, Colleges and Universities, John Milloy, the letter called attention to how Carleton University was employing a "scorched earth" policy for dealing with its key stakeholders. It highlighted how labour negotiations had been "acrimonious" and how such conduct by the university was not only threatening the reputation of the school but would jeopardize Carleton's potential of achieving the prestigious "research intensive" designation. In its closing statements, the open letter requested a meeting with Minister Milloy to discuss creative ways to stabilize and improve relations between the university administrations, its workers, and students.[48] While it certainly caught the attention of the Carleton administration, Ministry Milloy failed to reply.

The need for membership mobilization to prepare for a possible strike was made all the important during the bargaining process itself, because CUPE 4600 faced serious difficulties in having the central concerns of the members taken seriously. On repeated occasions during bargaining, not only did the employer justify its demand for a zero percent wage increase by insisting the university did not have the available funds, on repeated occasions members of its bargaining team claimed that their hands were tied by a provincial government that was pressing employers to provide no net increases in compensation for public sector workers for two years. In addition, arguments that pointed to questionable expenditures by Carleton's administration, as well as increasing class sizes, costs of living, tuition, and workloads were frequently ignored under the pretence that the university lacked money due to pension insolvency problems, even though TAs and contract instructors at Carleton do not belong to any pension plan. As a result, it soon

---

[48]   See "Carleton's 'Scorched Earth' Approach to Stakeholder Relations is Jeopardizing Bid for Research Designation," accessed May 24, 2011, http:// www.marketwire.com/press-release/carletons-scorched-earth-approach-stakeholder-relations-is-jeopardizing-bid-research-1350542.htm.   At   the time of the publication of the open letter, the Carleton University Students' Association and the Graduate Students' Association were immersed in a dispute with Carleton over the University's refusal to forward to them the student association fees collected on their behalf. See Nick Falvo, "Student Union Busting – Carleton Style," *Rabble.ca*, November 23, 2010, accessed May   24,   2011,   http://rabble.ca/blogs/bloggers/campus-notes/2010/11/ student-union-busting-carleton-style.

became evident that both units would need to increase pressure in order to achieve a fair settlement. Because CUASA and CUPE 2424 were facing similar difficulties, through Campus United the four bargaining units prepared to set coordinated strike deadlines in relation to successive requests for no-board reports.[49] In coordination, CUASA set a legal strike deadline for November 15, CUPE 2424 set a strike deadline for November 17, and CUPE 4600 set a strike deadline for November 22.

The Critical Period

The third period of the bargaining process constituted the critical phase for CUPE 4600. This phase was the most stressful, yet the most exciting period of the entire process. With the no-board report requested and strike deadlines set by each bargaining unit, membership communication and mobilization were intensified, and the logistics of strike preparation were initiated. In the lead-up to potential job action, members were largely concerned about lost wages, picket line crossing, the time required to perform picket duties, and the possibility that a strike would impact external sources of funding such as the Ontario Graduate Scholarship and funding from the Social Sciences and Humanities Research Council. Despite widespread misinformation, the union executive, volunteers, and departmental stewards worked to calm the fears of members and assure them that TAs who withdrew their labour would not be impacted in their role as university students. Since TAs occupy a hybrid position as student-workers, it was critical to dispel myths concerning this dual role in the context of possible strike action.

The University, in particular, attempted to deploy a number of potentially divisive strategies during the final period of the bargaining process. First, Carleton's administration largely ignored

---

49   A "no-board report" can be requested by either side in the negotiation at any point after the first meeting with a conciliator, which states that conciliation has not produced an agreement. Once the no-board report is received, the parties have 14 days before there is a legal strike or lockout position available to the union or to the employer. The request is frequently used by unions to pressure the employer to negotiate with a greater sense of urgency and to better respect the union's bargaining proposals.

repeated requests for meetings to establish an academic amnesty policy for students in the event of a strike. Such a policy would have included provisions to ensure students were able to avoid losing their semester and tuition fees, and were able to complete their course requirements in some form. Rather, President Runte responded by stating that a motion on amnesty should be rejected by the University Senate, and instead suggested that the Emergency Academic Response Committee would proceed in an ad hoc manner. Second, four days prior to the strike deadline, the University released a Contingency Plan for addressing any possible labour stoppages. This document, sent to all deans, associate deans, and departmental chairs and directors, specified that Carleton would attempt to continue offering courses without the use of TAs or contract instructors. In particular, the plan stated that "all documents, files, computer records, e-mails and voicemail that are part of the university's work must be accessible by appropriate supervisors and managers" and that "it will be necessary to recover [...] (1) all ungraded work (2) all graded but unreturned work and (3) all interim term grades." Despite the University's attempt to potentially employ scab labour in the event of a strike, the plan met strong resistance from several departments and many students, faculty members, and instructors.

Despite these tactics, the aggressive communications counter-strategy used by CUPE 4600 proved largely effective. Several general membership meetings were attended by over 100 individuals, a massive feat for a TA and contract instructor union local, and members expressed their commitment to maintaining 24-hour picket lines in order to interrupt mail delivery and garbage collection. In addition, volunteers and members staffed information and strike tables, handed out flyers and leaflets, volunteered for picket captain training (an essential activity for ensuring member safety and effectiveness on picket lines), and began signing up for four-hour segments of picket duty in order to guarantee lines would be staffed at all times. With many logical issues taken care of, including arrangements for an off-campus office and strike trailer near the picket line, both CUASA and CUPE 2424 received new agreements in the week prior to CUPE 4600's November 22 strike deadline. Although a campus-wide strike would have made a strong impact on negotiations, both bargaining teams eventually reached new collective agreements 36 hours before the deadline. The deal resulted in modest wage increases for both units, improved professional and employee assistance plans, and the creation of a health plan for the contract instructors.

Conclusion

Following an overview of the negative effects of the neoliberal processes on universities in Canada, this chapter has argued that the recent economic crisis has intensified neoliberal austerity measures, specifically the chronic underfunding facing post-secondary education in Canada and the province of Ontario. In particular, decades of underfunding for education at the provincial level have resulted in a dramatic increase in privatization and public–private partnerships; budgetary cuts to specific university departments; reliance on part-time, temporary, and precariously employed contract instructors; tuition fees; overall enrolment and class sizes. The neoliberal restructuring of post-secondary education not only forces universities to operate in a more business-friendly manner, with more companies utilizing publicly funded universities for private research and development, it has also increased direct corporate influence on university operations and the production of knowledge.

Nonetheless, the ongoing commercialization of knowledge and increasing corporatization of the university goes beyond the mere sponsoring of research grants. For example, in Carleton University's drive to become a university of excellence, the university's administration has recently initiated a series of preliminary talks with a corporation called Navitas, a for-profit "educational provider." Through its business model, Navitas seeks to enter into agreements with individual universities in order to open "pathway institutes" that are designed to stream undergraduate students who may not qualify for accredited degree programs. In effect, the corporation uses the host university's logo, its reputation, and its campus resources to recruit and teach primarily international students,[50]

---

[50] See for instance Matthew Pearson, "Foreign-Student Plan Stirs Carleton Debate," *The Ottawa Citizen*, October 7, 2010, accessed May 24, 2011, http://www2.canada.com/ottawacitizen/news/city/story. html?id=9c38cc3b-117a-4735-8e8d-b859c73b2d81&p=2.

while charging whatever fees they may wish. Such agreements signal not only the creeping privatization of the post-secondary education, but also the further financial exploitation of international students and continued attempts to undermine the strength of unionized academic faculty, TAs, and contract instructors.

As we have seen, federal and provincial governments have turned towards making public sector workers pay for the costs of a meltdown that originated in the financial sector. In this sense, the nature of the economic crisis has shifted the site of class struggle more towards public sector unions. For Harvey, "right now, to the degree that the struggle is likely to be between public sector workers and the state apparatus, this is a very specific form of struggle, which is not based in factories. It's going to be the teachers' unions and these [types of] groups that are likely to be pushed into a more vanguard role."[51] Accordingly, public sector unions must lead the fight to preserve social services by building alliances and community support, developing creative workplace strategies, and finding a basis for potential unity with groups (e.g., students) outside of the official labour movement.

While the response to the Ontario government's proposed wage freeze by CUPE Ontario and sectoral union groups such as the OUWCC proved somewhat limited in this regard, at the local level, collective bargaining can often become the first line of defence in the fight to protect workers' rights and public services. In the case of CUPE 4600's 2010 round of bargaining, the Carleton administration's wholesale attack on labour and student unions opened up a space for broad-based student and worker resistance to the neoliberal agenda on campus. In this sense, the Carleton example can be situated within the context of recent debates concerning union renewal, which have examined "how to reverse the decline of union strength and influence, reinvigorate membership participation and democratic decision-making, increase union visibility in communities, and expand unionization rates through increased organizing and closer links with social movement groups."[52] In particular, CUPE 4600's engagement with the Carleton community

---

[51] David Harvey, "Explaining the Crisis: An Interview with David Harvey," *International Socialist Review* 73 (September-October 2010): 53.

[52] See Pradeep Kumar and Christopher Schenk, eds., *Paths to Union Renewal: Canadian Experiences* (Peterborough, ON: Broadview Press, 2006).

can be seen as a conscious attempt at "social movement unionism," which engages in broad class and social struggles, adopts a "militant stance towards employers," and "commits unions to working against neoliberalism for social change."[53]

Given the litany of challenges facing post-secondary education, we would like to conclude with a number of possible avenues for building powerful alliances between students, community activists, and union members. First, a concerted effort must be made to challenge and reformulate the ways in which post-secondary education is often viewed. This challenge must reiterate that education is a public good that benefits all of society, and is not simply an individual privilege or commodity to be purchased. Second, students and workers across university campuses must recapture and revitalize a militant commitment to class-based and other forms of struggle. This means exploring how direct action tactics, such as occupations and public demonstrations, can pressure administrative and governing bodies to begin to take student and worker demands more seriously. Finally, students, workers, and community members must foster stronger working relationships in confronting federal and provincial governments. In the context of a recent resurgence of right-wing, neoliberal governments, these challenges will continue to mount unless a more proactive and aggressive strategy is developed to place union and progressive issues on the agenda. Ultimately, such a strategy must involve recognizing that, in the words of Callinicos, "preserving and developing what is valuable in existing universities can't be separated from the broader struggle against capitalism itself."[54]

---

[53]   Camfield, *Canadian Labour*, 145.
[54]   Callinicos, *Universities*, 39.

"WE WILL FIGHT THIS CRISIS": AUTO WORKERS RESIST AN INDUSTRIAL MELTDOWN

Bill Murnighan and Jim Stanford

Introduction

This chapter provides a case study in union response to the unprecedented industrial turmoil that accompanied the global financial crisis and resulting recession. The Canadian Auto Workers Union represented about 60,000 auto workers at the time the crisis hit: two-thirds of all workers employed in auto assembly in Canada, and something under half of workers in the auto parts sector. The auto industry is Canada's most important manufacturing industry, and a key source of exports. It was one of the first industries in the "real" economy to suffer the fall-out from the global crisis that ripped through financial markets in 2008. North American auto sales were already weakening as a result of falling consumer confidence, surging imports, and very high gasoline prices in 2007 and 2008. Then, with the collapse of Lehman Brothers and subsequent financial chaos, continental auto sales plunged dramatically. Consumer sales were undermined by tighter credit conditions, which also hampered access of automotive manufacturers (in both vehicle assembly and parts production) to normal working credit. North American auto sales as 2008 drew to a close reached their lowest levels in decades, and the industry's entire production chain experienced a violent shock.

While Canada's financial system was not affected as dramatically by the global financial crisis (due to our large, concentrated banks, tighter banking regulations, and huge government financial support provided to banks during the crisis), the impacts of the financial crisis and resulting recession in the U.S. economy (which is the final market for about 85% of Canadian final auto output) were quickly felt by the auto industry in this country. Indeed, several important vehicle and powertrain manufacturing facilities were shut in 2008 and 2009, as producers adjusted to the sharp downturn in demand and acute financial conditions by reducing capacity. General Motors permanently closed one assembly plant (its pickup truck plant in Oshawa) and one transmission plant in Windsor during the crisis (although the transmission plant closure had already been announced some years earlier). Daimler permanently closed a heavy truck plant near London, while Navistar idled its heavy truck plant in Chatham. Other auto assembly facilities experienced major layoffs. Dozens of auto parts facilities were also closed, with many companies forced into bankruptcy protection during the crisis.

The automotive crisis reached its nadir in the spring of 2009, when General Motors and Chrysler Corp. both filed for bankruptcy protection in U.S. courts. The unprecedented downturn in North American sales had exhausted the financial reserves of both companies. A support package, financed jointly by the U.S. Treasury, the Government of Canada, and the Government of Ontario, facilitated the quick exit of both companies through an accelerated restructuring process. As a condition of Canadian government support for their restructuring (which totalled about $10 billion Cdn. for GM, and $4 billion Cdn. for Chrysler), both GM and Chrysler committed to the maintenance of proportional Canadian manufacturing "footprints." However, the governments in both countries also demanded reductions in labour costs at both companies as a condition of the bailout. This sparked a dramatic set of bargaining and political struggles as the union fought to defend previously achieved wages and pensions.

In the auto parts sector, meanwhile, job losses and bargaining pressure were even more catastrophic. From 2007 through July 2009 (the low point of the crisis), the parts industry shed some 30,000 positions, reaching a low of 57,000 jobs. In fact, the parts sector had already been shedding jobs for several years before the full crisis hit the industry (due to the rapidly appreciating Canadian dollar, among other factors). By mid-2009, therefore, auto parts employment was barely half of the peak levels attained early in the decade. In the parts sector, the union fought running battles against employer demands for concessions in dozens of different locations. When bankruptcies and closures occurred, in many cases the union also had to take dramatic actions (including plant occupations) to fight for legal and contractual severance benefits for the affected workers.

The CAW was founded in 1985, as the result of a split from its previous U.S. parent, the United Auto Workers. Through mergers and new organizing, the new Canadian union diversified substantially after its founding, so that by the time of the 2008-09 crisis, barely one-quarter of its total membership worked in auto assembly and parts (somewhat contrary to the union's name!).[1] Nevertheless, the auto industry still constitutes the organizational, political, and financial core of the CAW. Moreover, the union's identity has been shaped largely (although not solely) by many of the key epic battles fought in the auto industry over the years – resisting wage concessions and profit-sharing in the early 1980s (an ideological precursor to the subsequent split from the UAW), fighting to limit outsourcing during the 1990s, struggling to organize unorganized workers (especially in the auto parts industry, such as at Canadian parts giant Magna International), and lobbying hard for a new national automotive strategy after the World Trade Organization overruled the former Canada-U.S. Auto Pact in 2001.

How would the union respond to the unprecedented crisis which gripped the auto sector amidst the global financial turmoil? Its response would be important to the future course of the industry in Canada, and also to the course of the Canadian labour movement. As the global financial system seized up in the autumn of 2008, the union's National Executive Board met to discuss the escalating crisis, and passed a special statement (titled "We Will Fight This Crisis"), warning that "corporations and right-wing governments will try to shift the costs of financial chaos onto our backs," and making this commitment to pro-actively mobilizing in response to the meltdown:

> The CAW pledges to mobilize its members and activists, locally and nationally, to defend ourselves and

---

[1]   The other three-quarters of CAW members work in a wide range of other manufacturing, transportation, resource, and service sectors of the economy. About two-thirds of the union's total membership is in Ontario.

all working people against the effects of the financial crisis. We will take dramatic actions, if necessary, to protect our jobs and our workplaces; to keep working people in their homes; to fight for government help; and to demand accountability from the wealthy and powerful financiers who created this mess. The years ahead will be challenging for working people around the world. But just as occurred in the 1930s, adversity can be liberating, and can actually make us stronger – so long as we respond to adversity collectively, by fighting for our rights.[2]

How did the union try to concretely fulfil this ambitious pledge?[3]

This chapter will describe the impact of the crisis on the Canadian auto industry, and the union's response, in the following sections. First, we provide an overview of the North American and Canadian auto industry before the crisis, the clouds that were already gathering before the financial crisis hit, and the union's efforts to develop a broader alternative storyline about the industry's growing problems. Second, we review the specific conditions and the union's response in the auto parts sector, which was already experiencing acute labour relations conflict during the years leading up to the 2008-09 crisis. Indeed, the patterns established in the earlier restructuring of major auto parts companies (like Delphi, the former in-house parts division of GM) were replicated in the subsequent restructuring of the automakers themselves. Third, we then review the dramatic events involving the auto assemblers, including the bankruptcy filings of GM and Chrysler, the role of the U.S. and Canadian governments, the union's response, and the aftermath (including subsequent events at other automakers). The

---

2   Canadian Auto Workers, "We Will Fight This Crisis," Special NEB Statement on the Global Financial Crisis. http://www.caw.ca/assets/pdf/NEB_Statement_on_the_Financial_Crisis.pdf., 2008.

3   Making things more complicated, the union experienced a leadership transition just as the crisis was fully landing: Ken Lewenza was elected the new National President in September 2008, replacing Buzz Hargrove just days before the collapse of Lehman Brothers. The union's National Secretary-Treasurer and Quebec Director (completing the triumvirate of elected national officers) also retired and were replaced within the next year.

final section provides our conclusions and analysis, considering both the successes where the union was able to mobilize its members and supporters during the crisis and hence was left stronger as a result; and ways in which the union response to the crisis and its continuing impacts needs to be expanded and improved.

The Automotive Landscape Before the Crisis

The auto industry has long played a disproportionately important role in the economic development of Canada, and the corresponding evolution of the labour movement. For a sparsely populated country, Canada has benefited from an unusually large and (until the last decade, anyway) successful auto industry. This success is rooted largely in a unique "managed trade agreement" signed between Canada and the U.S. in 1965, known as the Auto Pact.[4] This agreement provided tariff-free access to the Canadian market for participating companies (for imports of both finished vehicles and parts), so long as they met specified threshold targets of vehicle production and value-added – defined relative to quantities of vehicles sold in Canada. Under the agreement, participating companies (including the major North American automakers, Volvo, and several heavy truck manufacturers) dramatically expanded their production in Canada, and the country soon became a net exporter of automotive products (rather than a net importer). Even though the Canadian UAW had originally opposed the Auto Pact (arguing instead for a more self-sufficient "Canadian car strategy"), the agreement's obvious positive impact on the Canadian sector led the union to quickly change its view. The Auto Pact became a defining example for the union of how managed trade (contrasted with free trade), and interventionist industrial strategies in general, could underwrite national economic development and progress for workers.

In the 1980s and 1990s, the momentum from the Auto Pact was reinforced by other factors including improvements in suppliers, logistics, and productivity; the then under-valued Canadian currency

---

4   See Dimitris Anastakis, *Auto Pact: Creating a Borderless North American Auto Industry, 1960-1971* (Toronto: University of Toronto Press, 2005), for a detailed history of the Auto Pact and its effects.

(which made Canadian production costs appear even lower[5]); and
the universal Canadian public health care system (which reduced
labour costs for the automakers by several dollars per hour relative
to U.S. costs for more expensive private health insurance coverage).
By 1999, at its peak, Canada ranked as the 4th largest auto assembler
in the world (producing over twice as many new vehicles as Canadians purchased – see Figure 1), enjoyed a massive automotive trade
surplus (totalling $15 billion), and benefited from the creation of
50,000 relatively high-wage jobs in the auto industry during the previous decade. For a country traditionally characterized by structural
underdevelopment and dependence on natural resource exports,
the success of Canada's auto sector was a very important but rare
instance of successful value-added industrialization.

Figure 1: Production-to-Sales Ratio, Canada

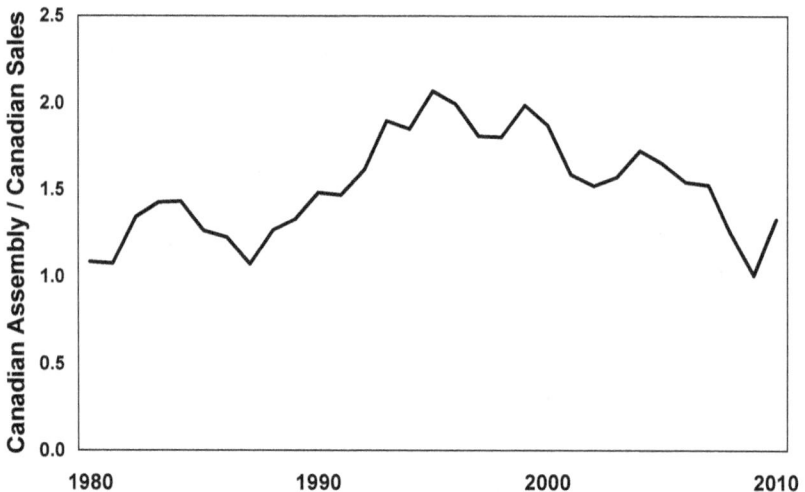

Source: Authors' calculations from Ward's Automotive data.

Production-to-Sales Ratio, Canada

---

5   According to OECD and IMF estimates, the "fair value" for the Canadian
     dollar based on purchasing power parity measures is in the low-80 cents U.S.
     range. When the Canadian currency trades below that level, Canadian prices
     and costs look artificially low; when the dollar trades above that level, the
     reverse is true. For most of the 1980s and 1990s, the Canadian currency was
     undervalued, reinforcing the appeal of Canada as a site for manufacturing
     investment; this relationship reversed with the dramatic appreciation of the
     Canadian dollar that began in 2002.

During this expansionary period, the CAW used its economic power to negotiate major improvements in wages, benefits, and job security provisions, at both the assemblers and the parts makers. The union's bargaining with the major auto assemblers where it is represented (GM, Ford, and Chrysler[6]) is conducted through a triennial process of "pattern" bargaining, whereby a master agreement covering core compensation and economic provisions is struck first with one target company, then replicated at the others. Simultaneous local agreements are also struck at each plant to regulate local work and operating conditions. The CAW's master agreements in 1996, 1999, and 2002 provided for significant wage gains (well above inflation), pension improvements, and other innovative benefits (like subsidized child care, tuition rebates, and others). Despite the expense associated with these gains, Canadian auto labour costs stayed well below U.S. levels, largely because of the undervalued Canadian currency as well as the rapid escalation of health expenses for U.S. autoworkers (especially retired workers, who at the time had their supplementary health benefits paid directly by the automakers on an unfunded, pay-as-you-go basis). So investment into Canadian facilities remained strong, further enhancing the union's bargaining position.

When the WTO overturned the Auto Pact (with an initial ruling in 1999, confirmed on appeal in 2001), the union warned in submissions to government that the future security of the industry's prosperity would be jeopardized – even though at the time Auto Pact producers were far exceeding the minimum production thresholds required under the treaty.[7] Unfortunately, in retrospect, the union was right, although the subsequent downturn reflected the influence

---

6   Since the late 1980s Japanese-based Toyota and Honda have also operated important vehicle assembly plants in Canada, but so far have avoided unionization. The CAW also represents vehicle workers at the CAMI facility in Ingersoll, Ontario, which was formally merged with GM in 2011, and at several heavy truck manufacturing plants – many of which have closed.

7   It should be noted that most of the economic significance of the Auto Pact was eliminated when Canada entered free trade agreements with the U.S. and Mexico, eroding most of the value of the Auto Pact's tariff-free provisions. Now, any firm could import vehicles or parts tariff-free from within North America, whether it produced anything in Canada or not. Nevertheless, the Auto Pact retained some residual value by offering avoidance of tariffs on products imported from outside of North America. See "Getting Back in Gear: A New Policy Vision for Canada's Auto Industry," www.caw.ca/assets/pdf/auto_policy.pdf, for more detail on the union's response to the WTO decision.

of many factors, not just trade policy. Beginning in 2002, world commodity prices began to rise dramatically, and this contributed to a dramatic appreciation of the Canadian currency – from a low of just 62 cents (U.S.) in 2002 to meeting and then exceeding par with the U.S. dollar by 2007. This 65% increase in relative costs converted Canada overnight from being relatively appealing on cost grounds to being relatively expensive (at least with respect to currency-sensitive inputs, like hourly labour costs).[8] At the same time, the geography of automotive investment, production, and employment within North America was being fundamentally altered by a southward migration,[9] destined in particular to the non-union right-to-work states of the U.S. southeast (Alabama, Mississippi, and South Carolina), and further still toward Mexico. New North American investments by offshore European and Asian manufacturers (many of them anxious to establish a production foothold in America as political "insurance" against potential future protectionism by the U.S. government) served as the front line of this southward migration (especially since the established North American producers were making few greenfield investments during this time). Mexico's auto industry, meanwhile, has developed both quantitatively and qualitatively (measured by the quality and reliability of output and logistics) since joining NAFTA in 1994. It surpassed Canada in terms of total auto assembly in 2009, yet its labour costs are still a small fraction (as low as one tenth) of those in the U.S. and Canada, in part because of official and unofficial suppression of independent union activity.

It wasn't just the changing geography of the auto industry within North America, however, that was threatening the traditional unionized industry of Canada and the northern U.S. The industry was also experiencing the effects of the more intense globalization of auto production and trade. The spectacular development of the export-oriented Korean auto industry, continuing one-way inflows

---

[8]   Against the benchmark of purchasing power parity, the dollar was undervalued by as much as one quarter during the late 1990s and early 2002 – but it is overvalued by a similar ratio when it trades at par with the U.S. dollar. At par, in other words, Canadian production costs look 25% "too" high relative to actual wage and price levels.

[9]   See Thomas Klier and James M. Rubenstein, "The Changing Geography of North American Motor Vehicle Production," *Cambridge Journal of Regions, Economy and Society* 3, no. 3 (2010): 335-347, for more on the shifting geography of the industry in North America.

of automotive products from Japan, and a rising automotive trade imbalance with Europe, all contributed to the loss of domestic market share by domestic producers, lost jobs, and a growing continental trade deficit. In the mid-1990s North America as a whole produced vehicles equivalent to over 90% of total continental sales. By 2008 that declined to barely 70%; net imports from offshore now consumed close to 30% of total continental sales. That is a far larger exposure to international imports than experienced in any other major auto-producing region in the world.

For Canada, the production-to-sales ratio plunged from over 2-to-1 in the later 1990s (when the industry peaked) to just 1-to-1 by 2009 (Figure 1). Canada's production relative to sales fell far below the minimum requirements of the Auto Pact.[10] The large automotive trade surplus of the 1990s melted quickly away into deficit by 2006, escalating rapidly to a record $15 billion hole by 2010 (Figure 2). The sudden and rapid contraction of automotive production and exports in the 2000s contributed significantly to the deindustrialization of the national economy during that decade, and reinforced the emerging reliance on production and exports of resource staples (especially energy).[11]

In an attempt to develop a counter-hegemonic storyline about the industry's decline (refuting the tendency in mainstream discourse to blame unions and high wages for all the problems), the CAW devoted considerable efforts to critiquing these impacts of neoliberal globalization on the Canadian auto sector. The union undertook considerable research and lobbying concerning the impact of free trade and globalization on the sector, and organized several grassroots education and activist campaigns in the 2000s to oppose further free trade agreements (such as with Korea) and support pro-active industrial strategies for the auto sector and

---

[10] The Auto Pact imposed two tests on member companies: they had to assemble at least one vehicle in Canada for each vehicle sold in Canada (and the test was applied separately to cars and trucks), and they had to produce value-added in Canada (including parts) equal to at least 65% of all value-added sold here. Because of the clever design of those tests (and the risk that companies would face large retroactive tariff penalties if they fell below the thresholds), they effectively required the maintenance of the sales-to-production ratio well above one.

[11] Jim Stanford, "Staples, Deindustrialization, and Foreign Investment: Canada's Economic Journey Back to the Future," *Studies in Political Economy* 82 (2008): 7-34.

other manufacturing.[12] The campaign against the proposed free
trade agreement with Korea was especially active, generating high
degrees of local membership participation and media coverage; it
played an important role (along with strong auto industry opposition) in forcing the then-minority Conservative government to
cease further negotiations with Korea in 2007.[13] Large numbers
of rank-and-file CAW members and other concerned Canadians
were engaged in this campaign in various initiatives, including
through a massive "Manufacturing Matters" demonstration that
attracted 40,000 protestors in Windsor in 2007.

Figure 2: Canada's Automotive Trade Balance

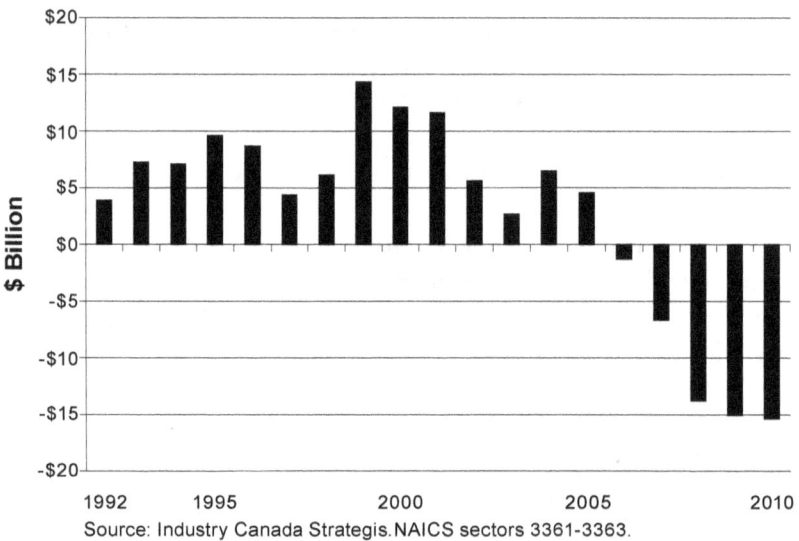

Source: Industry Canada Strategis.NAICS sectors 3361-3363.

We must also consider the specific factors affecting the North
American auto parts sector, which was already well into a decade
of upheaval and a fundamental restructuring of both its business

---

12   Daniel Poon and Jim Stanford, "Employment Implications of Trade
     Liberalization with East Asia," http://www.caw.ca/en/campaigns-issues-
     ongoing-campaigns-issues-employment-implications-of-trade-liberaliza-
     tion-with-east-asia-pdf.htm.
13   Under a majority Conservative government, however, the talks with Korea
     have again become active.

model, and its labour relations, long before the onset of the 2008-09 crisis. The shifting roles and responsibilities between auto assemblers and their major suppliers has been a defining feature of the transforming auto industry; this process was driven mostly by the assemblers. In terms of developments in labour relations, however, the obverse was true. The response of unions in both the United States and Canada to the financial crisis, and the shape of the eventual settlements over wages and working conditions for auto workers in the domestic assemblers after the bankruptcy and restructuring of General Motors and Chrysler, can be traced back several years to developments in the parts sector. In the story of modern labour relations in the auto industry, the parts sector is really "the tail that wagged the dog."

In the five years before 2008-09, the Canadian auto parts sector saw sales fall by $3 billion (or 10%), and parts exports declined by a similar proportion. As well, more than 10,000 Canadian auto parts jobs were already lost between 2002 and 2007 – well before the financial crisis, and in the midst of a North American new-vehicle market that was relatively buoyant.

Several factors lay behind this deterioration of the Canadian parts industry prior to the financial crisis, including the corrosive effect of unbalanced auto trade, a lack of meaningful industrial policy, and a rapidly rising currency. While these factors were central to the deterioration in conditions, what defined the landscape for auto parts workers in particular throughout the last decade was the ongoing restructuring of the industry's business model. At its heart, this restructuring involved a radical undoing of vertical integration that had defined the North American auto industry through its prosperous post-war period.

Major automakers ("original equipment makers," or OEMs) traditionally integrated and controlled all stages of production, from design and engineering, to comprehensive parts production, to final assembly and sales. But as the auto sector recovered from the recession of the early 1980s, domestic OEMs responded to falling market share in part by borrowing from the playbook of ascendant Japanese producers. They increasingly separated and retained core functions (usually centred on engineering, powertrain, and final assembly), while simultaneously expanding the role played by a network of primary, or "Tier 1", auto parts makers.

By emulating the just-in-time production methods pioneered by the much-vaunted Toyota Production System, this new division of responsibilities aimed to take advantage of technological advances in logistics, communications and supply-chain management. As well, of course, outsourcing major portions of the production process would help North American assemblers escape the wage- and work-rule confines created by a half-century of pattern bargaining and job-control unionism by the UAW and the CAW.

Central to this emerging business model was the outsourcing of major automotive components (e.g., seats, interiors, axles, frames and large stampings), alongside increasingly complex sub-assembly (e.g., completed dashboards) and sequencing work, all of which would be delivered just-in-time to feed into new "modular" methods of final assembly. These efforts to undo the vertical integration of the industry, and the resulting protracted battles over outsourcing, would largely define labour relations across the industry (at both the OEMs and their suppliers) throughout the 1990s.

This vast expansion of the role of auto parts companies through outsourcing led to consolidation of the parts sector and created a few giants (the size of which, in some cases, rivals the OEMs). In Canada it underlies the growth of home-grown powerhouse Magna International. Not only did the OEMs embrace direct outsourcing, but the drive to shed "non-core" operations also led to the spin-off of the massive in-house parts operations of Ford (in 1997 with the creation of Visteon), and of General Motors (with the creation of an independent Delphi in 1999, at the time the world's largest parts company). Developments at these companies would eventually set the pattern for labour relations in the entire U.S. auto industry, and are hence key to understanding the terrain for labour's overall response to the 2008-9 financial crisis.

Profits for the OEMs had been relatively strong during most of the 1990s, thanks in part to this outsourcing strategy – but also reflecting a surging new-vehicle market, low fuel prices, and the North American domination of new markets for high-profit SUVs, minivans and pick-up trucks. Profitability at the Detroit Three reached a record $18 billion (U.S.) in 1999 (a year which, not coincidentally, coincided with peak levels of auto production and employment in the Canadian sector). These profits did not reflect a strong structural position, however. Within a short time profits slid into sustained losses as competition ate into the Detroit Three's highest-profit segments, which were simultaneously declining in popularity. A sharp drop in market share across all segments (producing overcapacity and devastating price competition), surging imports from Japan (supported by the low yen at the time), and the boomerang effect of ill-advised subsidized leasing[14] all combined to create a withering drain on profitability. After several years of losses, the financial condition of all three OEMs was already very weak when the full effect of the financial crisis hit in 2008. And the OEMs responded to sustained losses by further tightening the pressure on their suppliers, demanding annual cost reductions in supplied parts while simultaneously passing along a larger share of expense and responsibility for engineering, design, and tooling. If anything, the financial condition in the parts sector was even more dire.

Thus the stage was set, in both the assembly and the parts sectors, for a fundamental and historical shake-out. When the financial crisis arrived, it ushered in a dramatic downturn in North American vehicle production and sales, and a resulting collapse in the financial viability of the domestic OEMs and many part suppliers alike.

Resisting the "Delphi Model"

As a result of the downward cost pressures imposed by the OEMs and accentuating competition (including from offshore), many major parts suppliers endured sustained losses through the 2000s. It was in that context that parts makers began to adopt a page from the playbook of the U.S. steel industry: the strategic use of Chapter 11 bankruptcy to seek protection from creditors, restructure balance sheets, and shed obligations to creditors, workers, and retirees.

The ability of employers in the U.S. to successfully and unilaterally override collective agreements and dump obligations while in bankruptcy has played a pivotal role in reshaping

---

14   Artificially attractive lease terms promoted more vehicle sales in the short-term, but eventually undermined both sales volumes and prices when leases expired and the used-car market was flooded with large numbers of used Detroit Three products.

labour relations outcomes in the auto parts sector.[15] Add in U.S. employers' relatively free access to the massive (although inadequate) U.S. Pension Benefit Guarantee Corporation, which picks up the pieces of defined benefit pension plans ejected through bankruptcy restructuring, and the ability of auto parts makers to dramatically re-shape labour relations was confirmed.

The strategic use of Chapter 11 bankruptcy restructuring, therefore, rather than signalling a death knell for a company, came to be increasingly seen as a viable business strategy. The auto parts sector pioneered this approach within the North American auto sector, but when the global financial crisis hit in 2008 it would be taken up by assemblers, too. Heading into Chapter 11 colloquially became known as "going for a rinse." And beginning in the early 2000s, a growing number of major Tier 1 auto suppliers did exactly that (see Table 1). Table 1 lists only the largest restructured companies; at least 35 auto parts companies in total filed for bankruptcy from the beginning of 2004 through the fall of 2005 alone.

Table 1: Major Tier 1 Auto Suppliers Entering U.S. Bankruptcy Protection	
2001	A.G. Simpson, Hayes Lemmerz
2002	Valeo, Exide
2003	Precision Tool and Die
2004	Oxford Automotive
2005	Tower, Collins & Aikman, Eagle Picher, Meridian, Delphi
2006	Dana
Source: Adapted from Timothy Sturgeon, Johannes Van Biesebroeck, and Gary Gereffi, "Value Chains, Networks and Clusters: Reframing the Global Automotive Industry," *Journal of Economic Geography* 8(3) 2010, pp. 297-321.	

---

[15]   A pioneering precedent in this regard was set by the case of *National Labor Relations Bd. v. Bildisco*, 465 U.S. 513 (1984), which allowed a debtor in court-protected restructuring to override a collective agreement without bargaining.

Because of separate incorporations in Canada, and a more limited legal scope under which to shed obligations to workers,[16] the auto parts industry in Canada witnessed fewer bankruptcies. However, the direction and impact of restructuring among many U.S.-based parent corporation did not stop at the border.

To many observers, the process of restructuring in the auto parts sector saw its defining moment when Delphi (at its formation the largest parts producer in the world) filed for bankruptcy protection in 2005. The decision to file followed immediately the rejection by UAW members in the fall of 2005 of company demands to cut the pay and benefits of its unionized U.S. work force by two-thirds. After a protracted two-year restructuring process, the company emerged from protection in the summer of 2007 with a new deal for its UAW-represented workforce. The deal comprised deep cuts to benefits, the implementation of a two-tier wage structure which reduced pay for new hires from $28 to $14 per hour, the elimination of the defined benefit pension for new hires, and dramatic reductions in health care benefits (especially for retirees, whose health benefits represented an unfunded "legacy cost").

Despite assertions from top UAW officials at the time that this new "Delphi model" would not set a precedent for the auto assemblers, just months later, in the fall of 2007, this approach, combined with an offloading of retiree health care obligations to union-administered trust funds, was adopted in new UAW agreements across the Detroit Three. The so-called Delphi model thus came to define the terrain of the industry and corresponding struggles for workers across the North American industry. The CAW's overall challenge in the parts sector, therefore, has been to try to turn back the Delphi model at the Canada-U.S. border – before, during and after the 2008-9 financial crisis.

Indeed, against a backdrop of deepening losses, the growing string of bankruptcies south of the border, a rapidly rising Canadian dollar, plant closures and thousands of job losses, the CAW faced a widening chorus of demands for deep concessions and the adoption of the Delphi model in Canadian plants. With more than

---

[16] In particular, there is no clear legal precedent in Canadian bankruptcy law, akin to the Bildisco case in the U.S., that would provide for the unilateral amendment of collective agreement terms by a company in bankruptcy protection.

100 separate collective agreements in the auto parts sector, operating under a generally decentralized bargaining structure, the union's local leadership faced a cacophony of employer demands for deep concessions, one workplace at a time. As pressure mounted across the industry, top leadership understood that they needed to develop a public, united response.

So at an emergency meeting in November 2005, more than 200 workplace representatives, leadership and staff from the auto parts section of the union debated and endorsed an Emergency No-Concessions Resolution, which stated that the union would not accept concessions in wages, pensions or benefits, or open collective agreements before their expiration, simply because employers wanted to bargain concessions. Additionally, the support of the entire union was pledged to those auto parts workplaces struggling to resist concessions, commitments were made to work with companies to enhance productivity and secure investments, and a call was made for meaningful government action on trade and industrial policy to strengthen the underlying economic condition of the whole sector (building on the union's earlier work against globalization).

Implicit in the policy is the recognition that during restructuring events that arise from well outside the control of the union, complete job security can never be won – no matter what workers agree to give back to the employer. Instead, it is vital during these periods to actively resist concession demands, thus enhancing the integrity of the union (the only institution through which workers can collectively protect and advance their economic and social conditions).

Over the history of the labour movement, of course, periods of progress often alternate with setbacks, when working conditions and wages deteriorate in the face of economic conditions and workers' limited bargaining and political power. However, accepting and acknowledging the limits to unions' ability to hold the line, when bargaining power is weak and investment and employment decisions are unilaterally determined by employers, is fundamentally different from accepting that labour costs and working conditions are somehow the root of the problem, and hence embracing concessions as a false "solution."

As the battle in auto parts shaped up, what employers wanted was clear: to cut wages, eliminate pensions, slash benefits, and impose a two-tier wage structure. Union leaders understood, however, that during a period of limited bargaining power, accepting wage cuts in one workplace would open the floodgates across the industry. They also knew that accepting a permanent second tier of workers would undermine the ability of the union to build solidarity within the work-place, and would eventually lead to a major historic deterioration in labour standards; the two-tier recipe had to be resisted at all costs.

The union's bargaining strategy in this context thus came to be characterized by a strategy of "picking battles:" holding on to what-ever was possible, taking less if inevitable in specified areas, but safeguarding core principles (in particular by resisting nominal wage cuts, protecting pensions, and refusing two-tier deals). A report on the union's bargaining outcomes was made to an auto parts leadership meeting in December 2007, highlighting key policy directions and guidance to negotiating committees. Bargaining during this period resulted in freezing most monetary compensation, adjusting work rules, adjusting some benefit programs and time off programs, while strongly resisting wage cuts, pension cuts, and the adoption of two-tier structures. As well, in those rare instances where work was secure and the company healthy, the union could continue to make modest gains. But in the context of the industry's brutal shake-out and employers' aggressive demands, resisting wage cuts, protecting pensions, and rejecting two-tier structures clearly constituted victories.

This overall strategy represented a careful and strategic balanc-ing act by the union. By picking its battles, rather than refusing to make any contract changes at all, the union could try to preserve some threatened plants and jobs (through work rule changes and other measures) where such measures might be effective. But by being willing and able to mobilize (including mobilizing pressure from other locals and the broader community to support strikes and other actions), the union showed employers its ability to resist the most offensive demands. It also showed its members their con-tinuing collective power to influence the course of events (if not to dictate them). The industry was locked in a brutal contraction that the union could not alter. But by showing that workers could attain better results through collective action and a careful bargaining strategy, compared to being "picked off" one plant at a time, the union proved its continuing worth.

The trend to lower wage gains and wage freezes across the auto parts sector is reflected in data on collective bargaining settlements (assembled by the Ontario government labour relations monitoring service). These data (see Figure 3) show a dramatic decline in negotiated wage settlements beginning after 2003, followed by the advent of near-universal wage freezes by 2008 and after (during which time the average wage settlement in auto parts fell close to zero). But in the context of an industry that was shedding half of its jobs, an escalating currency that added 65% to relative Canadian production costs, and employer demands for enormous wage cuts, most auto parts workers agreed that a wage freeze was a good outcome. CAW contract ratification votes in the parts sector remained strong in these years despite the modest settlements, in part because members saw the union fighting successfully and strategically to preserve core principles (no wage cuts, maintain pensions, and no two-tier). A review of 48 separate CAW contract settlements in the parts sector in 2006-7, covering a combined 8,600 members, reveals an average ratification vote of 87% – with more than two-thirds of settlements garnering positive votes greater than 80%. As illustrated in Figure 3, the trend to lower wage settlements was also experienced, although somewhat less dramatically, across Ontario's whole manufacturing sector, which was grappling with similar challenges.

Figure 3: Average Wage Settlements, Ontario

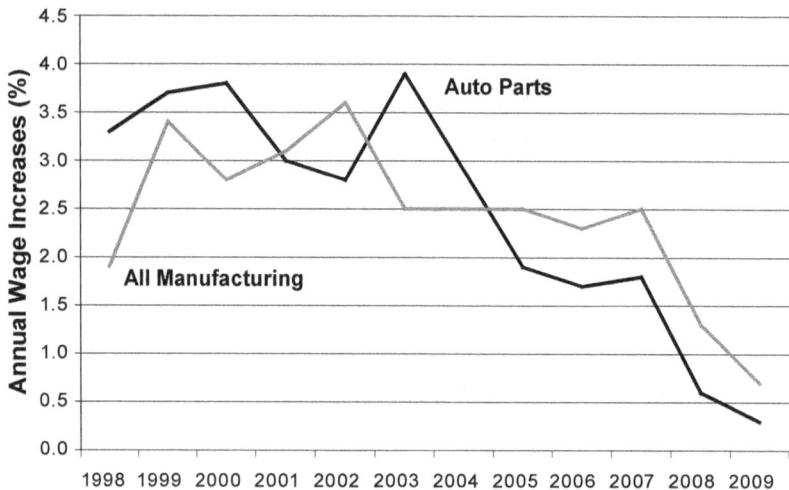

Source: Ontario Ministry of Labour, custom data.

Amidst this difficult environment, there were also several instances of the union's successful application of leverage with the OEMs to safeguard union-represented auto parts jobs at firms supplying the Detroit Three. For example, a Collins & Aikman plastic trim plant in Guelph that fed into a CAW-represented final assembly operation was under threat of closure in 2010, after the loss of its contract. By insisting that this was "our work," and that the 275 workers needed protection, the union convinced Chrysler to purchase the plant itself and then re-award it the contract. A similar application of influence at General Motors in 2010 resulted in guarantees that 70 workers for a small Ajax plant, Automodular, would move with their work (and their collective agreement) when that work was awarded to another supplier in the same region. The union's willingness to use its leverage with the OEMs (who are the final customers of the suppliers) to try to protect unionized parts jobs has been a major irritant with the OEMs (who would prefer to simply purchase the lowest-priced components available, and "pass the buck" for all labour issues and costs to the parts suppliers). This dimension of fightback, however, has been an important manifestation of the union's continuing capacity to wield its power and win incremental victories amidst the industrial carnage.

While struggling to defend contract provisions during bargaining, auto parts workers have also faced multiple "runaway" employers that shuttered plant gates on a moment's notice, attempting to dodge responsibilities for back-pay and severance. In response, the union embarked on at least six separate blockades and plant occupations over the course of two years (see Table 2). The tactic in many cases was to stop equipment removal and hence preserve a last bit of bargaining power with both the fleeing supplier, and their OEM customers. In one case the union even led support for a blockade by 2,400 auto parts workers at a *non-union* company (Progressive Moulded Products, which operated several plants in the Toronto area), which resulted in partial repayment of back pay and the establishment of a government-funded action and adjustment centre for the affected workers.

Occupying a workplace or blockading a plant – simply to ensure that workers receive basic entitlements they are legally and contractually promised in the event of job loss – may not sound like a victory in and of itself. However, within the context of the broader economic meltdown, and facing emboldened employers, these instances of militant action demonstrated to workers, and to employers, that the union was prepared to fight back to win a measure of justice. Absent these actions, the outcomes would undoubtedly have been far worse for these workers. Benefits were also attained by workers at other firms whose employers may have been dissuaded from taking similar actions by these acts of resistance.

Another union initiative in the auto parts sector, unveiled just as the clouds of the global financial crisis were beginning to gather, was an innovative effort to unionize workers at the non-union parts giant Magna under the terms of a new voluntary recognition agreement with the company. Under this so-called "Framework of Fairness," the union would be allowed unopposed access to Magna plants, and workers would vote by secret ballot on union membership. Members are covered by a Magna-wide master contract with several unusual features, including annual wage increases tied to the cost of living, and the reference of unresolved issues during triennial contract talks to final-offer arbitration. The implementation of this agreement was slowed during the crisis, as Magna closed several (non-union) facilities. Nevertheless, by time of writing workers at 4 Magna plants in Ontario had voted to join the new system, with one plant rejecting the deal.[17] The arrangement has thus provided a rare source of union membership growth amidst the crisis gripping the sector. Moreover, the wage improvements provided under the contract (which have averaged over 2 percent per year since the new framework was implemented in 2007) have been the best in the sector, and a welcome contrast to the wage freezes which prevailed in most other unionized auto parts workplaces.[18]

---

[17] Previously-organized workers at a Magna plant in Windsor continue to be represented under the traditional form of contract.

[18] For further description and discussion of labour relations at Magna and the CAW-Magna deal, see Wayne Lewchuk and Don Wells, "Transforming Worker Representation: The Magna Model in Canada and Mexico," *Labour/ Le Travail* 60 (2007): 109-138; Martin H. Malin, "The Canadian Auto Workers-Magna International, Inc. Framework of Fairness Agreement: A U.S. Perspective," *St. Louis University Law Journal* 54 (2010): 525-564; and David Doorey, "Neutrality Agreements: Bargaining Freedom of Association in the Shadow of the State," *Canadian Labour & Employment Law Journal* 13, no. 1(2007): 41-105. The CAW-Magna agreement itself is at www.caw.ca/ campaigns&issues/ongoingcampaigns/magna/pdf/FF_Agreement.pdf.

Table 2: CAW Auto Parts Plant Occupations and Blockades, 2007–9						
Year	Employer	Location	Workers	Issue	Union Action	Outcome
2007	Collins & Aikmans	Scarborough	200	Severance	Occupation, solidarity shutdown of two other plants	Daimler Chrysler guaranteed the severance
2008	SKD	Brampton	140	Equipment removal, closure agreement	Blockade	Closure agreement negotiated
2008	Ledco	Kitchener	70	Severance	Occupation	Detroit Three paid severance
2008	PMP	Toronto	2,400 at 11 plants (non-union)	Back-pay, severance, equipment removal	Blockades (CAW provided lead support)	Government funded, CAW sponsored action centre and retraining.
2009	BBI	Ajax	25	Severance	Blockade	GM, Chrysler, tier-one suppliers paid severance
2009	Aradco-Aramco	Windsor	80	Severance and termination pay	Occupation, disruption of equipment auction	Settlement over pay reached with employer

Source: CAW Research.

Even as the dust began to settle across the industry in early 2010, and production in Canada returned to higher levels, auto parts workers continued to be faced with demands for severe concessions. At a special two-day meeting of 250 auto parts workplace representatives in May 2010, speakers reported that there was no letting-up of employer demands, despite the supposed "recovery" from the worst of the crisis. They also reported that their members were growing frustrated and weary.

As an outcome of these meetings the CAW was determined to send another message to employers that after years of making sacrifices and job losses, with at least a partial economic recovery now underway and profitability improving, the union would once again take a strong and united stand against further cuts. As a first element of a broad "Auto Parts Workers United" campaign, the union adopted a renewed bargaining policy re-affirming its position against wage cuts, two-tier structures, and pension cuts. The union also highlighted its claim to an expanded right to "work ownership," whereby changes in sourcing decisions by OEMs should not be allowed to eliminate the employment or contract provisions of affected auto parts workers.

This broader campaign was buttressed with a mass day of action organized on October 27, 2010, with events sponsored at all CAW-represented auto parts workplaces. To mobilize a membership that may have been "beaten down" by the experience of the preceding years, renewed efforts were undertaken to engage with members in the workplace. An information booklet was prepared and delivered to each of the union's auto parts members, outlining current conditions in the industry, the union's bargaining policy, the aims of the campaign, and the need for collective action (including in the political arena). Parallel materials were distributed to the union's 25,000 remaining members at the Detroit Three OEMs (GM, Ford, and Chrysler), highlighting the aims of the auto parts campaign and readying the membership to offer support if needed to enhance the efforts of the parts workers. In his lead message to the membership, Ken Lewenza, CAW President declared that:

> Parts companies, auto executives and right-wing governments and business commentators continue to beat the drum about the need for workers to give up more. Yet parts workers didn't cause these problems, and there is no way that cutting our wages and pensions,

adopting two-tier wage structures and outsourcing our work will ever solve them.... Corporate decision makers must understand that we will fight for our jobs, and they must stop their demands for more and more takeaways.[19]

Coordinated outreach to unorganized parts workers was a further central element of the broader campaign. In the weeks preceding the day of action, teams of local union leadership and activists brought a message of solidarity and outreach to non-union auto parts workers, highlighting the union's campaign and explaining the union's position, through plant-gate leafleting of thousands of workers in dozens of non-union parts plant across Ontario.

On October 27, 2010, under the broad banner of "Enough is enough!," CAW members at more than 100 auto parts plants engaged in noon-hour rallies and protests to indicate to their employers and the OEMs that they had sacrificed enough. Workers declared that they would stand together to reject any further cuts. These actions garnered wide media attention. In the wake of the day of action, some local union leaders reported an easing of concession demands; in some instances, including producers Integram and Martinrea, demands for steep concessions actually were removed from the negotiation table in the aftermath of the event.[20] The campaign succeeded in broadcasting the union's renewed determination to move forward in the parts sector, including through organizing unorganized parts workers, and helped to maintain a sense of fightback among a membership that had survived a relentlessly painful decade of restructuring and restraint. Amidst the partial and still painful "recovery" in the auto parts industry since 2009, the union has continued its efforts to protect unionized parts workers from re-sourcing decisions by the OEMs (demanding job and contract protection for workers affected by re-sourcing), to resist concession demands, and to organize non-union parts workers.

---

19   Canadian Auto Workers, "Auto Parts Workers United," (October 2010): 2, www.caw.ca/assets/pdf/388-Auto_Parts_booklet_fin.pdf.
20   Howard Ryan, "Canadian Auto Parts Workers Say Enough is Enough," *Labour Notes* (October 29, 2011).

In sum, the CAW's response to the unprecedented downsizing and restructuring in the auto parts sector reflects an eclectic blend of militance and pragmatism. The union has engaged with auto parts employers and OEMs to try to preserve Canadian facilities where possible, despite the negative headwinds, through a range of measures including adjustments to work practices, and other incremental contract changes. Meanwhile, the union's determination to maintain core compensation (including wages and pensions), and to resist the two-tier system pioneered by Delphi, is unchanged and has been largely successful. And the union has shown it can back up that determination with collective action when needed – thus enhancing its bargaining power with both parts firms and OEMs, who recognize the threat of union action and adjust their own strategies accordingly. Meanwhile, creative measures have been taken (ranging from the application of leverage within the OEMs to protect union parts jobs, to the voluntary recognition agreement with Magna) to preserve a critical mass of unionization and prevent the free fall in union membership that has been experienced in the U.S. auto parts industry (where unionization is now less than 10%). Thus the union managed, amidst an industrial rout that reduced employment by about half, to hang onto both its principles and its organizational capacity, so that it can continue to fight on another day.

Indeed, symbolic fightback actions such as the occupation of runaway plants and the 2010 day of action are essential to demonstrate the union's continuing ability to mobilize a collective response not only though bargaining, but also through workplace actions. Each of these successful actions helped to shift the balance of power ever so slightly in favour of workers, if even for a day.

To the Brink and Back with the Detroit Three

The effects of industrial and labour relations restructuring were experienced earlier in the auto parts sector, but they would soon arrive with a bang at the auto assembly sector as well – ushered in by the financial crisis and resulting recession. As noted, the three North American OEMs began to experience large, sustained losses in the early 2000s – as their lucrative profit margins on sales of light trucks were eroded, offshore imports reached new highs, and gasoline and other commodities prices soared. These losses naturally affected contract bargaining with both the UAW and the CAW. For example, the CAW's triennial contract with the Detroit Three in 2005 contained much more modest improvements than the rich deals of 1999 and 2002. Then, in 2007, the UAW signed its landmark deals ushering in two-tier wages (following the Delphi model) and the spin-off of retiree health benefit costs to independent trust funds. All this fundamentally altered the cost comparisons that had traditionally underpinned the CAW's bargaining success. Where hourly labour costs in Canadian assembly were tradition-ally well below U.S. levels, by 2008 they rose to match and exceed U.S. levels – partly due to changes in the UAW contract, but more dramatically because of the run-up in the Canadian currency.

By 2008, with the global financial crisis gathering storm, the CAW's leadership took an unusual and pro-active step: it nego-tiated an early pattern contract with Ford in April, more than 4 months before the expiry of its existing deal. The deal was posi-tioned as "cost neutral," and reflected the union's fear – correct in retrospect – that by the normal time for bargaining that Septem-ber, economic conditions would have deteriorated substantially. It thus made sense to lock in whatever was possible in advance of the coming storm. That pattern deal was quickly replicated at General Motors and Chrysler.

However, no labour contract can stand in the way of economic catastrophe. As the financial crisis gathered force, economic con-ditions in the Canadian auto sector deteriorated dramatically. General Motors announced closure of a truck assembly plant in Oshawa (violating its brand new CAW contract, and sparking a 10-day blockade of GM's Canadian office headquarters by CAW members)[21]. The financial position of all three companies plunged deeper into the red. By the end of 2008, GM and Chrysler had sought bankruptcy protection in the U.S., and were surviving only with the joint assistance of the U.S., Canadian, and Ontario gov-ernments. The governments on both sides of the border made their support for the two firms contingent on many factors, including the renegotiation of labour contracts by both the UAW and the CAW.

---

[21]   This blockade culminated in GM seeking a court injunction to end the protest. The judge granted the injunction, but only after days of delay and with damning words regarding GM's absence of "clean hands" in the events leading up to the blockade. See Doorey, "Neutrality Agreements."

In the U.S., this demand was first expressed in a requirement (announced by former U.S. President Bush in December 2008) that UAW costs and work rules must be harmonized with those of "mature" non-union factories operated in the northern U.S. by companies like Toyota, Honda, and Nissan. These costs were then estimated at about $49 (U.S.) per hour worked, taking into account all labour-related costs (including wages, pensions, benefits, unemployment and restructuring benefits, and even government payroll taxes). In Canada originally the governments made a less specific demand, indicating merely that Canadian labour costs had to be reduced as a condition of the government aid. Later, however, the Canadian governments (both federal and Ontario) emulated the U.S. strategy, and demanded that all-in labour costs be reduced at GM and Chrysler plants in Canada to match the estimated level at Toyota's non-union Canadian plant – held at that time to approximately equal $57 Cdn. per hour worked.

These demands raised complex and controversial issues related to how to measure "all-in labour costs." The methodology of calculating all-in labour costs is very obscure: all labour-related costs of a firm are tallied, and then divided by the number of hours actually worked in the plants (excluding all downtime, layoffs, and paid time off). This methodology causes immense misunderstanding, including in the public – many of whom falsely believe that these all-in cost estimates actually constitute autoworkers' *wages*. The impact of "legacy cost" items (such as pension fund deficits or unfunded liabilities for the payment of health benefits to retirees) on all-in labour costs can be unpredictable and enormous, as can changes in the utilization of existing plants (which increase or decrease hours worked, which is the denominator of the fraction used to calculate all-in labour costs). Making matters worse, the so-called "benchmarks" for these comparisons – non-union plants operated in North America by Toyota and other offshore firms – do not publish their labour costs, and hence there is no transparency in the comparisons. The $49 and $57 benchmarks applied in Canada and the U.S. reflected very rough estimates by compensation consultants.[22]

---

[22]   For a full explanation and critique of the all-in labour cost methodology, see Jim Stanford, *How Much do Autoworkers Really Make?* (Toronto, Canada: CAW-Canada), http://www.caw.ca/assets/pdf/ Whats_YOUR_All-in_Hourly_Labour_Cost.pdf.

At an extraordinary meeting of workplace stewards from the auto assembly plants in February 2009, CAW officials initially agreed to engage with company and government in negotiations around a restructuring deal that would keep both companies operating in Canada. This meeting occurred several weeks before the government specified the $57 target. The union's agreement was made contingent on a number of conditions, including that the contract renegotiation must be accompanied by a commitment by the companies to maintain a proportional share of their production and employment in Canada, and a commitment by the federal government to the implementation of a new automotive policy (reflecting the union's effort to highlight what it saw as the true underlying problems of the Canadian industry's crisis: namely unregulated globalization). The union also made clear its determination to avoid any direct cuts in wages and pension benefits; this echoed the strategy of "picking battles" that the union followed during its restructuring negotiations in the auto parts sector.

Complicating the negotiations at GM was the fact that the company's pension fund was drastically underfunded at the time the crisis hit. General Motors had benefitted for years from a strange loophole in Ontario pension regulations, which allowed it to fund its pension fund to a lower standard (avoiding solvency funding requirements) than other private firms in Ontario. As a result, and due to the severe meltdown in financial markets (and corresponding changes in actuarial assumptions), the GM hourly pension fund in Canada faced an enormous $6 billion deficit at the time GM entered bankruptcy protection; on a wind-up basis, the fund was only 40% funded. This then posed a make-or-break financial burden on the company, but also posed an enormous threat to GM workers and retirees. Indeed, by 2009 there were over 4 GM Canada retirees for each active worker left in a GM plant. If GM had gone bankrupt and liquidated, those retirees could have faced cuts in their monthly company pensions of half or more.[23] The overarching need to protect pensions came to influence the union's whole approach to the negotiations.

---

[23]   In theory a minority portion of those pension losses would have been offset by payments from the Ontario government's Pension Benefits Guarantee Fund. However, that Fund had no resources to pay the enormous potential cost of lost GM pensions, and the Ontario government had publicly stated its intention not to inject more money into the Fund.

The union entered extraordinary contract negotiations with GM (in two separate rounds: one in March, and then again in May) and with Chrysler (in April), to reach agreements which shaved reported all-in hourly labour costs for active workers at each company by several dollars per hour through a combination of foregone time off, foregone bonuses, changes in some benefits, and changes in work rules (to attain greater productivity). Wages, core health benefits, and pensions were fully protected at both companies. In its bargaining, the union used the government-mandated methodology of all-in hourly labour costing to its advantage: more of the ground was covered by measures which increased hours worked per worker, increased productivity, or shifted compensation to other cost categories (such as the health care trusts for retirees, discussed below), rather than actual changes to true compensation. Nevertheless, the combined impact of foregone bonuses, foregone paid time off (including the loss of two weeks of paid leave, reducing maximum holiday time for a top-seniority employee from 8 weeks to 6), and higher co-pays for health benefits amounted to several dollars per hour in reduced compensation.

Throughout this bargaining, the union successfully fulfilled its commitment to avoid wage cuts, to fully protect pensions, and to avoid the U.S. two-tier system. The union also publicly and internally rejected the notion that high labour costs were the reason for GM's and Chrysler's bankruptcy; the contract renegotiation was essential to the survival of both companies only because the Canadian and U.S. governments (largely for "optics"-driven political purposes) had made it so. The union also continued to demand the implementation of Canadian job guarantees at both firms, which was realized in the form of production "footprint" agreements that were signed between the governments and the participating OEMs. These footprint agreements will cement production and investment plants for several years at GM and Chrysler. They are a key factor behind the surprising increase in Canada's share of total North American vehicle assembly since the crisis. In fact, by the end of 2010 Canada's share of total continental assembly reached almost 18% – its highest ever, a result all the more surprising given the continuing over-valuation of the Canadian currency.

A major aspect of the new contracts, explicitly required by the government funders, was the establishment of new independent trust funds to govern the payment of supplementary health benefits to retired workers (akin to similar structures recently created in the U.S.). The union accepted the principle that those benefits could be paid from an independent fund (in light of the financial difficulties posed by the existence of a large unfunded liability on the balance sheets of the companies). Unlike the U.S., however, the union demanded that those trust funds be endowed with enough money to meet the expected cost of future obligations, in light of assumptions regarding future inflation, investment returns, and other factors; moreover, in Canada the union required that the health trusts be funded with cash, not corporate equities. Agreement on the establishment of these trusts allowed for the transfer of several dollars of apparent hourly labour cost "off the books," even though the negotiated level of benefits would continue (assuming actuarial assumptions are validated). In this sense, too, the all-in labour cost methodology mandated by government was highly arbitrary, and the agreed reductions in those measured costs did not fully represent true reductions in compensation.

Throughout this turbulent period, the union sought to maintain readiness among its rank-and-file membership for collective action in support of the union's bargaining and policy demands. And the union had to fight a rearguard battle in the court of public opinion, where sentiment (from business and conservative commentators, but also expressed in call-in radio shows and letters to the editor) ran strongly against any government "bailout" of overpaid autoworkers. Public misperceptions of the workers' supposed "$70-per-hour" compensation (misinterpreting the all-in labour cost methodology) contributed to this nasty mood.

On several important occasions, the collective mobilization of CAW members (and retirees) at GM and Chrysler proved essential to the union's pursuit of its core bargaining goals. In April, then-Chrysler-CEO Tom LaSorda wrote a letter distributed to CAW members explicitly demanding major wage cuts and other core concessions from CAW members on threat of the outright closure of all of Chrysler's Canadian facilities. This threat was met with demonstrations at all of Chrysler's Canadian locations – including the highly photogenic mass burning of LaSorda's letter by CAW members at Chrysler's huge Windsor assembly plant. The union's strong rejection (from national leadership to rank-and-file membership) of LaSorda's demand eventually resulted in a deal with Chrysler that contained no cuts to wages, pensions, or core benefits.

Then, in subsequent talks with GM, provincial government officials (concerned with the huge cost of fixing GM's underfunded pension) demanded cuts in pension benefits for active workers at GM that would amount to approximately 30%. The union responded by restating its refusal to cut pension benefits. It organized a huge rally at Queen's Park, on April 23, 2009, that attracted some 15,000 members and retirees (including supporters from other CAW employers, and other unions). This was one of the largest mobilizations by the Ontario labour movement since the Days of Action protests against the Mike Harris government of the mid-1990s. The rally was supplemented by the occupation (again by members and retirees) of several provincial MPPs' offices in auto communities. The union pressured Ontario's Liberal government, arguing that the pension demand would cause a breakdown in the whole restructuring process. As a result, the demand for pension cuts was removed. The final restructuring deal with GM included the remarkable provision of public funds allowing indirectly for an extraordinary $3.28 billion contribution to the GM hourly pension fund, and the closing of the former GM funding "loophole" (so that in future GM will have to fund its Canadian pension plan to the same standard as other private companies). Thanks to this fightback, pensions for current and future retirees at GM Canada are more secure today than they were before the financial crisis.

The final agreements at both GM and Chrysler were ratified by strong majorities: by 87% across the Chrysler chain, and by 86% at GM. The union's demonstrated ability to fight actively to defend key principles through the restructuring process, combined with its willingness to engage with government and the companies in an overarching effort to maintain Canadian production and jobs, reinforced the confidence of members that this deal was the best possible under the circumstances. As in the numerous battles over concessions in the auto parts sector, protecting nominal wages and pensions, given the dramatic events of 2008-09, was widely interpreted as an important victory for the union.

With the new agreements in place, the accelerated bankruptcy restructuring process in the U.S. was completed for both GM and Chrysler within a few weeks, and the companies recommenced normal operations in the summer of 2009.[24] The CAW was committed through this process to retaining the "pattern" contract system, which had served it well in previous decades. So additional rounds of contract talks were then held for CAW members at CAMI Automotive (which until 2010 was a separate joint-venture company between GM and Suzuki) and at Ford Canada (which did not participate in the same restructuring process as GM and Chrysler). Those agreements were successfully negotiated and ratified with strong margins of support: two-thirds at CAMI and 83% at Ford.[25] Tying the contract changes to new investment commitments was essential to the successful bargaining at both firms. As part of GM's Canadian operations, the CAMI plant was covered by the same manufacturing footprint agreement negotiated with GM. At Ford, the union won the company's commitment to maintain at least 10% of North American manufacturing in Canada, and to continue to assemble (over the life of the new contract) at least one vehicle in Canada for each vehicle sold here (a reference back to the managed-trade principles of the former Canada-U.S. Auto Pact).

While production and employment have recovered partially in the Canadian assembly industry, with significant thanks due to the Canadian "footprint" agreements at GM (including CAMI) and Chrysler, the longer-run outlook for the sector remains uncertain. The continuing over-valuation of the Canadian currency, the take-off of Mexico's export-oriented industry, and continued pressure from offshore imports (including potential future imports from ultra-low-cost China) all threaten future Canadian investment and model allocation decisions by the OEMs. While the Canadian and Ontario governments intervened dramatically and powerfully to rescue the two companies during the financial crisis (and the footprint agreements constituted the most aggressive application of Canadian-content provisions in the industry since the Auto Pact was dismantled), the governments remain generally willing to accept the constraints of global market forces and the unilateral decision-making power of the OEMs. Indeed, even though

---

[24] Neither company entered bankruptcy protection in Canada, since their major liabilities in both cases (other than union-related liabilities) were held by the U.S. parent.

[25] In the U.S., in contrast, UAW members at Ford rejected a tentative agreement in 2009 that aimed to level the playing field with the other two OEMs.

the federal and provincial governments actually owned significant shares of both GM and Chrysler as a result of the restructuring, neither has been willing to actively leverage that ownership share in order to win Canadian investments – and both governments sold their Chrysler shares back to the company in 2011. The CAW has continued to argue that labour costs have not been important in either the crisis or the recovery of these companies,[26] and urged the federal and Ontario governments to wield their ownership shares actively (as do, for example, the governments of France, Japan, and Lower Saxony, Germany, through their equity shares of OEMs in those countries) in the interests of maximizing future Canadian investment. More fundamentally, the union continues to campaign against NAFTA-style trade agreements (such as the new proposed deal with the European Union), which will only reinforce the global constraints on the Canadian auto sector (and other Canadian value-added industries) in the years ahead.

Conclusion

After more than a decade of hard-fought industrial conflict, the CAW can certainly claim a partial victory in its long-run effort to protect unionization, labour standards, and compensation in Canada's humbled auto industry, despite the dramatic and painful effects of financial crisis and recession. Contract provisions that were negotiated in an earlier period of vibrant expansion and profitability (which lasted from the mid-1980s to the turn of the century) have been largely preserved, despite the Canadian sector's rapid and painful decline since then. The auto industry lost thousands of jobs (and the union thousands of its members), but nominal wages, most pensions, and most benefits were preserved. The union carefully picked its battles; its top priorities were the preservation of wages and pensions, and the rejection of full-fledged two-tier structures. It backed up those core demands with a continuing willingness and capacity to mobilize its members in flexible and creative forms – from traditional work stoppages, to plant occupations, the blockading of corporate headquarters, and mass political

---

[26] Jim Stanford, "Auto Labour Costs and Auto Recovery," Progressive Economics Forum, http://www.progressive-economics.ca/2011/08/12/auto-labour-costs-and-auto-industry-recovery/.

protests. At the same time, the union was willing to "deal" with both employers and governments on issues that were seen as less central to union principles and the union's future capacities; that willingness to engage was essential in reaching agreements (most notably the restructuring deals at GM and Chrysler) that kept jobs in Canada. That way, the union preserved both membership and credibility to "fight again another day." The trade-offs negotiated by the union have generally been strongly supported by CAW members, as represented in contract ratification votes, participation in mobilizations, and continuing strong local union activity.

The union's fightback at the level of individual firms, and across the industry, was framed in the context of its broader political-economic understanding of the crisis in Canadian manufacturing, and the historic U-turn in the country's economic development path. Indeed, the auto industry's decline both reflects, and reinforces, the broader deindustrialization which characterizes Canada's overall economic trajectory during this period. The union's critique of free trade agreements and globalization, combined with its continuing support for the principles of the former Auto Pact (which managed trade balances in the auto industry and hence backstopped Canadian employment and production levels), was central in its effort to shift "blame" for the industrial meltdown away from workers, their wages, and unions. The industry's crisis, it was argued, was rooted in shifting global trade and investment patterns, themselves a function of corporate greed and neoliberal policy. That effort to understand the immediate crisis through the lens of a critique of globalization, however, has its limits. While it helped members to articulate and express anger at the bigger economic and political forces causing the sector's downturn, and helped justify their resistance to the manifestations of that crisis, when workers face immediate bargaining and plant-closure challenges they must respond in "the here and now." Connecting the union's broader political-economic critique of globalization and deindustrialization to the micro-level fightbacks of specific groups of union members, remains a significant challenge.

Even worse, that broader analysis failed in most cases to gain much resonance in broader society. The union's concerns about lopsided globalization, surging automotive imports, and the lack of social responsibility on the part of automakers (whose investment decisions increasingly reflect cost-minimization criteria, rather than any responsibility to host communities) were usually written off as self-interested protectionism. The best example of the union's success in this regard was its effective campaign to stop free trade negotiations with Korea, in which it enlisted active support from politicians (of many stripes), local business leaders in automotive communities, and the automakers themselves to pressure the free-trade-oriented Harper government to shelve those talks. That success was an exception, however; in general, the union's campaign to pin the blame for the industrial crisis on globalization, and to resuscitate the core principle that trade and investment flows should be managed so as to guarantee a proportionate share of production and employment in strategic industries like auto to each jurisdiction, has not received widespread public support.

Another important weakness in the union's response to the crisis is rooted in its failure to unionize workers at the major non-union automakers. The union's innovative effort to organize employees at Magna (the huge parts maker) was discussed above. It has undertaken sporadic organizing efforts at the Canadian facilities of Toyota and Honda, dating back to the early 1990s. Those efforts, to date, have foundered in the face of sophisticated union avoidance tactics by the employers (including the unilateral paying of union-level wages, benefits, and pensions in order to reduce the apparent incentive for unionization), unfavourable changes in labour law (in particular the Ontario government's abolition of card-based certification in 1995, under Mike Harris), and the gradual anti-union shift in public attitudes and culture. Those challenges were amplified by the financial crisis and restructuring at the North American OEMs, which in popular discourse was widely blamed on the unions. In that setting, the association between union membership and potential job loss, in the eyes of many Toyota and Honda workers, was reinforced. The existence of a significant and growing non-union segment of the auto assembly industry undermined the union's bargaining power and political credibility during the financial crisis (as manifested most clearly by the government's use of the non-union compensation benchmark at Toyota Canada to leverage down labour costs at GM and Chrysler), and it will be a long-term drag on the union's economic and political power unless the CAW eventually succeeds in unionizing those plants.

The union's response to the continuing crisis in the sector will also be constrained by the growing divergence in both philosophy and contract terms between the CAW in Canada, and the UAW in the U.S. – and, more generally, by the differing labour market and labour policy conditions in both countries. Under free trade, and with the elimination of measures constraining corporate investment decisions (like the former Auto Pact), cost competitiveness comparisons become increasingly binding; the over-valued Canadian currency makes this problem worse. The UAW's decision to apply two-tier wages in the auto assembly sector, and to forego normal wage increases in the course of collective bargaining (in favour of lump sum bonuses of various kinds),[27] has incrementally tightened the competitive constraint on Canadian labour costs. However, the additional pressure on Canadian autoworkers resulting from two-tier wages in the U.S. should not be overestimated; because only a small share of the total U.S. workforce is paid those lower wages,[28] the impact on overall average labour costs is muted (in the near- and medium-term, anyway). This divergence in union strategy harkens back to the philosophical and strategic differences which contributed to the CAW's breakaway from the UAW in 1985, and indeed has ratified (in the eyes of CAW leaders and activists) the wisdom of that historic move. However, these negative developments in industrial relations in the U.S. auto industry will certainly not make it any easier for the CAW to defend Canadian standards, especially when amplified by an overvalued currency. In the auto parts sector, meanwhile, the challenge is even worse, due to deunionization in the U.S. parts industry, an all-out attack on legacy contracts, and aggressive labour market policy measures by U.S. state governments. For example, the new Republican Governor of Michigan introduced right-to-work legislation into

---

27 The UAW's 2011 contracts with the North American OEMs provided for no basic wage increases during their four-year term, and that follows several years of wage freezes and/or diversion of normal cost-of-living adjustments to health care and other benefits. By the expiration of the current contract in 2015, long-standing UAW members at those firms will have gone almost a decade without wage increases – while the wages for new hires, of course, have been cut dramatically under the two-tier system.

28 Because of the downsizing of U.S. employment at the Detroit Three OEMs, very little hiring has occurred, and hence the proportion of members earning second-tier compensation has remained very small so far.

that traditionally union-friendly border state, a move which will certainly have a chilling spillover impact on Canadian union activity in manufacturing.

Perhaps the greatest challenge to the union's capacity to defend jobs and labour standards stems from the continuing uncertain economic condition of the Canadian auto industry. After all, the historic ability of unions under capitalism to wrest economic improvements from employers has always been contingent on the existence of an underlying favourable dynamic of accumulation on the part of private business (supplemented, of course, by the willingness of unionists to fight for economic and social equality). GM and Chrysler were saved from destruction by the joint U.S.-Canadian rescue effort; the Canadian governments wrestled from them (with the union's support) a medium-term commitment to a sustained Canadian manufacturing footprint; and the subsequent recovery has produced a partial rebound in automotive employment. In Canada some 10,000 auto manufacturing jobs (more than half of those in assembly, the rest in parts) were won back in the two years following the June 2009 lowpoint of the crisis. But that represents only about one-sixth of the Canadian auto jobs lost between 2001 and 2009. And by other indicators, the Canadian industry remains fragile. Canada's automotive trade deficit has actually worsened since 2009 (in large part due to a growing imbalance with Mexico, reflecting the broader auto industry's accelerating migration to that low-cost NAFTA jurisdiction). The sluggish recovery in continental auto sales (especially in the hard-hit U.S. market), and the risk of another downturn (in the wake of the outbreak of the European debt crisis), continues to threaten the financial health of the three North American OEMs. Their determination to suppress labour costs, on pain of disinvestment, is more ruthless than ever. As the Canadian manufacturing footprint commitments at GM and Chrysler reach their expiration (around 2017), the union will face even heightened pressure to harmonize its costs and practices with U.S. levels, if not lower.

To respond to that historic challenge, the CAW will need to continue to draw on its past traditions of union education (providing a broader understanding amongst its leaders and activists about the nature and causes of this continuing industrial crisis), mobilization (in both the workplace and the political arena), and solidarity (including building stronger links with the UAW and other global automotive unions). One of the union's goals in negotiating the turbulent terrain of the past few years in automotive labour relations was simply to survive, in order to fight again another day. That day, no doubt, will arrive sooner, rather than later.

THE DECLINE OF THE LABOUR MOVEMENT: A SOCIALIST PERSPECTIVE

Murray E.G. Smith & Jonah Butovsky

Introduction

This chapter examines the gradual yet unmistakable decline of the Canadian labour movement over the past thirty years, arguing that its persistent malaise is due, above all, to the dominant influence of ideological perspectives that have long proven to be dead-ends for labour and obstacles to human progress.

Despite significant changes in the contours of global capitalism since the onset of the neoliberal era, Canada's labour officialdoms have maintained an essentially pro-capitalist and liberal-reformist outlook, one that has left organized labour severely handicapped in the face of an aggressive drive by the capitalist class to force working people to pay an ever-mounting bill to "save the system." Unfortunately, these leaderships – both within the unions and the New Democratic Party (NDP) – have been challenged altogether inadequately by the self-identified socialist left in Canada. At a time when capital is moving boldly to restructure class relations in response to the worst system-wide crisis of world capitalism since the 1930s, we argue that it is urgent for socialists to develop an orientation to organized labour that is based on a fully Marxist assessment of capitalism's manifest incapacity to chart a progressive path forward, and which builds on the major lessons of the international socialist and communist movements over the past century.

Capital's new class strategy, in response to the global slump precipitated by the financial crisis of 2007-08, has both national peculiarities and international dimensions. Almost everywhere, however, the capitalist class has chosen to redouble its commitment to a neoliberal policy of profit maximization, intensified exploitation, privatization, and cutbacks to popular social programs. Canada has been no exception in this respect. The failure of the labour movement to respond to capital's offensive in a resolute way has only emboldened the capitalist class to intensify its anti-labour offensive.

An effective labour counter-offensive, in our opinion, will require the emergence of significant political forces prepared to wage a determined fight for the fundamental programmatic positions of Marxist socialism. In light of the diverse meanings and confusions attached to the term "socialism" in contemporary political discourse, it is perhaps appropriate for us to begin with a clear statement of the specifically Marxist-socialist conception to which we adhere, one offered recently by Smith and Dumont:

> As a body of ideas and as a movement toward a society beyond capitalism, Marxist socialism stands for the dissolution of capitalist private property, collective ownership of the means of production and distribution, a democratically planned economy, and the replacement of antagonistic social relations of exploitation, competition and domination with relations of equality, cooperation and solidarity: a classless, communist society. From the Marxist perspective, socialism is not merely an ethical ideal: it is the only fully rational response to the intensifying contradictions of the capitalist world order.... Marx's most important contribution to socialist theory was his insight that the working class is the sole historical actor with the consistent objective interest, structural location and social power to replace capitalism with socialism, and that this class must organize itself as an *independent political force* to achieve that goal. [1]

We recognize of course that this programmatic vision, and the urgent need for a class-struggle workers' party to fight for it, are

---

[1]   Murray E.G. Smith and Joshua Dumont, "Socialist Strategy, Yesterday and Today: Notes on Classical Marxism and the Contemporary Radical Left," in *21st Century Socialism: Reinventing the Project*, ed. Henry Veltmeyer (Halifax: Fernwood Publishing, 2011), 120-121.

very remote from the day-to-day thinking of the great majority of working-class people in Canada. Socialist class consciousness has never been widespread in this country. What's more, thirty years of ascendant neoliberalism, the collapse of Soviet-bloc "socialism," the subsequent discrediting of the socialist idea in the eyes of millions, and the effective demobilization of the labour movement by leaderships increasingly committed to collaborating with rather than confronting capital – all of this has contributed to a significant *regression* in working-class consciousness. Nevertheless, the elementary responsibility of Marxist socialists remains to "speak the truth to the masses no matter how bitter it may be."[2] And the simple truth is that twenty-first century capitalism has nothing to offer working people but a menu of despair.

The Decline of Canadian Labour, 1975-2012

The Canadian labour movement reached the peak of its power and influence in the 1970s after two decades of struggles for a "better deal" for working people in a context of fairly robust economic growth. The cataclysm of World War II had created favorable conditions for high levels of profitability and capital accumulation in the post-war period. Meanwhile, the attraction exerted by the "actually existing socialisms" of the Soviet bloc placed considerable pressure on corporations and governments in the capitalist West to make significant concessions to their well-organized and powerful labour movements. The capitalist rulers were determined not only to cast Soviet-style Communism in the worst possible light, but also to convince working people in the West that real improvements in their living standards could be achieved within capitalism.

In Canada, the policy of the capitalist class in response to the Cold War and a perceived threat of a left-wing takeover of the unions involved an implied social contract to respect workers' collective bargaining rights so long as "moderate" labour leaders repudiated the more radical aims espoused by the labour movement's leftist militants. In exchange for its cooperation in purging the movement of such elements (a purge that was less thorough in Canada than

---

2   Leon Trotsky, *The Transitional Program*, ed. International Bolshevik Tendency (London: Bolshevik Publications, 1998), 68.

in the United States), the labour leadership was rewarded with a recognition by capital and the state that had previously eluded it. With this "capital-labour accord," the stage was set for a series of hard-fought battles – and real victories – by organized labour that nevertheless rarely transgressed the boundaries of legality or posed the question of working-class political power.[3]

Business Unionism, Stagflation and the Profitability Crisis of the 1970s.

The ideology and ethos of business unionism became thoroughly entrenched by the early 1950s. The "approved" role of the labour movement was to bargain for improvements in the terms and conditions of the sale of labour-power of wage-earners fortunate enough to be unionized, and to intervene in the political arena only in ways that reinforced the legitimacy of capitalist parliamentary democracy and its "rule of law." The unwavering message of the labour bureaucracy was that "bread and butter unionism" combined with a parliamentary struggle for limited social reforms (ideally through the CCF/NDP but also through pressure on the bourgeois Liberal and Conservative parties) would lead to the best of all possible worlds.

The stagflation and profitability crisis of the 1970s marked a crucial turning point in the fortunes of organized labour. In 1975, the rate of return on capital investment in Canada reached its lowest point of the post-war era. Faced with sluggish growth and soaring inflation, capital and the various branches of the capitalist state responded with an aggressive anti-labour offensive. The post-war capital-labour accord unraveled as strike-breaking legislation and wage controls were introduced.

Under pressure from a militant base that was influenced to an increasing degree by the left-wing radicalism of the period (above all in Québec and British Columbia), labour leaders tried to reassure the

---

[3]   A notable exception was the illegal postal strike of 1965, which not only resulted in the formation of the Canadian Union of Postal Workers and the Letter Carriers Union of Canada but also paved the way for serious unionization efforts throughout the public sector. See Bryan Palmer, *Canada's 1960s: The Ironies of Identity in a Rebellious Era* (Toronto: University of Toronto Press, 2009), chap. 7, for a discussion of the wildcat strikes and "unruly" class struggle that marked the 1960s.

ranks that these attacks would be held at bay. But no serious fight-back was ever organized – not against the draconian strikebreaking legislation of the British Columbia NDP government in October 1975, which initiated the capitalist state's onslaught against orga-nized labour by ordering back to work over 60,000 striking forest workers, supermarket employees, rail workers and truck drivers, and not against the Liberal federal government's wage-control policy announced less than a week later, which effectively repealed work-ers' rights to fight for wage increases outside the policy's guidelines. Even in Québec, where labour militancy had merged with a rising tide of Québécois nationalism to create a radicalized workers' move-ment highly receptive to socialist ideas, the militant struggles of the early 1970s – culminating in the near-insurrectionary mobilizations of 1972's Common Front – gave way to a period of bureaucratically enforced quiescence, abetted in some significant measure by workers' illusions in the *indépendantiste* Parti Québécois (PQ) government, elected for the first time in 1976. As capitalists and the state signaled their intention to make the working class pay for the economic crisis, the officials of the Canadian Labour Congress (CLC), the Québec Federation of Labour (FTQ), the Confederation of National Trade Unions (CSN, of Québec) and the major industrial and public-sector unions refused to lead or countenance any strikes that defied the federal government's "anti-inflation program." While a few protests were organized to allow rank and file militants to blow off steam, calls for a defensive general strike against the wage-control policy were rebuffed by the labour brass.

From that point on, the trade union leadership in Canada began to define a new role for itself: to not just promote the illusion that working people could prosper in a profit-driven, capitalist society, but to act more and more openly as the guardians of the capitalist order within the labour movement. The end of capitalism's post-war expansion and the intensifying contradictions of the system demanded that these "labour lieutenants of the capitalist class" assume a new duty on behalf of capital: to convince workers of the need for "restraint" and sometimes major concessions to capital, even as the capitalist state moved ever more decisively to curtail hard-won trade union freedoms.

After 1975, strike-breaking legislation became a routine matter for governments both federally and provincially, and the state expanded the roster of jobs defined as essential. At the same time, employers became much more likely to recruit replacement (scab) workers during strikes and lockouts. Actions to restrict or suspend workers' rights, originally used only in exceptional circumstances, become standard practice. And all of this was made possible by the labour bureaucracy's willingness to place respect for capitalist "law and order" – back-to-work legislation, bans on secondary boycotts, strike-breaking court injunctions, and so on – ahead of the principles and tactics that had built the labour movement: worker solidarity, impenetrable picket lines and militant defiance of the anti-labour machinations of capitalists, governments and courts.

Declining Living Standards

The upshot to this story is by now well known. Since the 1970s, real wages have stagnated or declined for most of the Canadian workforce. While unionized workers have made some real, episodic gains in wages and benefits, these have been offset by layoffs and downsizing – and, since the onset of the Great Recession in 2008, many past gains have been eroded or reversed. Meanwhile, non-unionized workers and the precariously employed have fared still worse, as minimum wage levels have failed to keep up with increases in the cost of living and the social safety net has become increasingly threadbare. Today, working-class households are contributing more labour to the economy than they did in the 1970s, while receiving less remuneration and enduring increased levels of taxation (via regressive sales taxes and government service fees). Cuts in education and health care spending have also contributed to a general decline in working-class living standards and quality of life.

The typical Canadian worker, faced with falling after-tax wages and a scaled-down "welfare state," has relied more and more on credit to plug the gap between wages and expenses. Average household debt doubled from about $20,000 in 2001 to over $40,000 in 2009. Furthermore, high unemployment and underemployment levels have become intractable, and an official unemployment rate of seven percent or more is now considered normal. Growing numbers of workers are consigned to dead-end, part-time employment, and forced to work two or even three jobs (often at minimum wage) in order to make ends meet.[4] While a "union advantage" remains in terms of higher wages and superior benefits, this advantage has diminished markedly with the recent gutting of pension plans and the introduction in several industries, most notably auto, of two-tier pay schemes that require new hires to accept drastically lower wage rates.

Union Density and the Decline of Labour Militancy

Despite the success of capital's anti-labour offensive in the second half of the 1970s, successful union organizing efforts continued into the 1980s. Union density – the percentage of the non-agricultural workforce that is unionized – peaked in the early 1980s at over 37%. Since then, however, there has been a gradual but steady decline to about 31% (in 2009) – and to just 17% in the private sector.[5] The drop has been precipitous in the manufacturing and extraction industries. Only a unionization rate of approximately 70% in the public sector prevented a much bigger decline in overall unionization levels.[6]

If strikes and lockouts are viewed as indicators of worker militancy (and of workers' resolve to defend themselves and effect positive change), then we can say that militancy peaked in the 1970s and went into steep decline after the early 1980s (see Chart 1). Waning militancy was caused by three interrelated factors: 1) the growth of unemployment during and after a series of severe recessions (those of 1981-82, 1990-92, and 2008-09) and the downsizing of unionized workforces in several key industries resulting from automation on the one hand and the relocation of production to lower-wage regions on the other; 2) the determined suppression of rank-and-file militancy by the trade union bureaucracy; and 3) the sustained assault on trade union rights by federal and provincial governments.

---

4   See Thom Workman, *If You're in My Way, I'm Walking: The Assault on Working People Since 1970* (Halifax: Fernwood Publishing, 2009) for a very useful historical survey.

5   HRSDC, Work – Unionization Rates (Ottawa: HRSDC, 2011).

6   Statistics Canada, "Perspectives on Labour and Income." Ottawa: Statistics Canada (2007).

Chart 1: Annual Average Hours Lost to Labour Disputes, Canada, 1976-2009 (per Employed Workers)

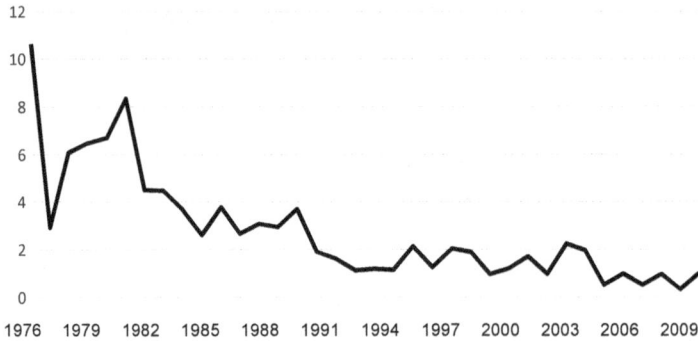

Source: http://www4.hrsdc.gc.ca/.3ndic.1t.4r@-eng.jsp?iid=14

Trade union leaders and their apologists insist that militant struggle by workers to resist the depredations of the past 35 years was impossible given the ability of firms to play the "global relocation" card as they bargained with an increasingly insecure workforce and the constraints imposed by ever-more restrictive labour legislation. While reflecting a profound and unwarranted defeatism, this argument contains an important element of truth insofar as it points to the need for the labour movement to develop *a political perspective* for implementing a "pro-labour agenda" rather than relying on militant skirmishes in what Marx once called the "guerrilla warfare" of unions against specific capital-ist enterprises. However, the labour bureaucrats' argument in no way recognizes the need for organized labour to adopt a class-against-class, socialist and internationalist perspective. Rather, it promotes the idea that the *sine qua non* for labour's advance must be the election of NDP (or even Liberal) governments that will resist the "excesses" of neoliberalism and counter the "corpo-rate agenda" (without challenging the capitalist system). For the labour reformists, only a change in the political complexion of the federal parliament, the provincial legislatures and the courts can "alter the relationship of forces" in such a way as to create a climate favorable to labour's forward march. And only a judicious division of labour between the movement's parliamentary/political and workplace/union wings can bring this about.[7]

This brings us to the question of the New Democratic Party – long touted as labour's "political arm" by the union bureaucracy and as the lodestar of "independent working class political action" by much of Canada's radical left.

Social Democracy and the NDP

The new party that emerged from the Cooperative Commonwealth Federation (CCF) in 1961 was formed to bring organized labour more centrally into what had been a predominantly petty-bourgeois social democratic formation, one with deep roots in British Fabianism, Christian socialism and prairie populism. In a general sense the NDP was modeled on the trade-union based British Labour Party. Individual unions and the English Canadian labour federations established well-defined organizational links with the party, providing the labour officialdom with formal representation and a distinct role in policy formation. In return, the party counted on the unions for massive financial support and other strategic resources (such as canvassers for election campaigns).

The central role played by unions in the formation of the NDP defined it as a "social-democratic labour party." It was, and remains, what Russian revolutionary leader Vladimir Lenin called a "bourgeois workers' party" – a party centrally based on the working class and its organizations but with an opportunist and fundamentally pro-capitalist program and leadership. In the 1960s and 1970s, under the leadership of T.C. Douglas, David Lewis and Ed Broadbent, the federal party accepted the "democratic socialist" label with some alacrity, although the "social-democratic"

---

7 The notion of a division of labour between the workers' party and the unions, with the former concentrating on "political" (that is to say, electoral and parliamentary) questions and the latter on the partial, day-to-day concerns of workers, has always been fundamental to the social democratic perspective. In the "classical period" of pre-1914 Social Democracy, it went hand in hand with a strategic orientation that divided the socialist program into a program of "minimal demands" achievable within capitalism and a "maximum program" that projected the abolition of capitalism and the socialist transformation of society. Between these two programs, as Trotsky later pointed out, there existed no meaningful "bridge" – and this led to an increasingly opportunist and reform-oriented practice for both wings of the modern labour movement.

designation came to be preferred over time. The NDP's association with the birth of Medicare, as well as the role of CCF and NDP governments in Saskatchewan, Manitoba and British Columbia in establishing non-profit, public auto insurance corporations, helped to define its distinctive profile as a party working for "the little guy" in opposition to "the status quo" and what Lewis called the "corporate welfare bums."

Initially, at least, some of the more left-wing New Democrats spoke vaguely of socialism as a long-term goal of the party (as did the party constitution), but policy platforms were always focused on the expansion of public health care and other social services, the reduction of poverty, and the extension of labour, women's and minority rights *within the capitalist framework*. As the mainstream political pendulum swung to the right, however, so did NDP policy. And as it registered successes in forming provincial governments in Western Canada, and ultimately in Ontario and Nova Scotia, the party displayed a growing appetite to demonstrate that it was ready and able to be a "business-friendly" steward of the capitalist economy and the public purse. As was the case with other social-democratic parties internationally, the differences between the NDP and what Douglas had called "the old line parties" progressively narrowed. Today's NDP leaders are now loath to refer to the plight of "workers" or the struggles of organized labour, preferring to profess solidarity with "families" and devotion to the interests of "Canadians."

Was this drift to the right inevitable? Those who argue that it wasn't sometimes cite the experience of the NDP's Waffle caucus in the early 1970s, a left-reformist formation whose 1969 manifesto called for an "independent socialist Canada" and whose leadership candidate, James Laxer, put up a strong challenge to David Lewis in the federal leadership race of 1971. But a serious examination of the Waffle reveals that its program and strategy were totally inadequate to reversing the rightward trajectory of the NDP.[8] Indeed, the left-nationalism that it pioneered morphed into an important mainstay of Canadian labour reformism as capitalism entered the neoliberal era.

As economic inequality and unemployment grew with the

---

[8]   See Murray E.G. Smith, "Political Economy and the Canadian Working Class: Marxism or Nationalist Reformism?," *Labour/Le Travail* 46 (2000) for an extended Marxist critique of the Waffle.

ascendance of monetarist and neoliberal policies, the labour reformists were determined to deflect the attention of their working-class base from the intensifying crisis tendencies of capitalism by emphasizing the need for "Canadians" to unite against a host of *external* threats: U.S.-based unions willing to sacrifice "Canadian jobs" as a deindustrialization process beset the American rust belt in the early 1980s; the 1988 Free Trade Agreement with the United States; and, above all, the North American Free Trade Agreement of 1994, which brought semi-colonial Mexico into the free-trade pact between Canada and the U.S. The free-trade agreements became especially convenient nationalist scapegoats for the dismal performance of the Canadian economy in the 1990s. As successive Conservative and Liberal governments pursued anti-labour austerity, the labour reformists blamed the economic malaise on the erosion of Canada's "sovereignty," thereby "absolving *capitalism* of the responsibility for the hardships that the [early 1990s] recession visited upon Canadian working people."[9]

Over time, the three pillars of the NDP's social-democratic reformism – overt class collaboration, economic nationalism and faith in the class neutrality of the "democratic" capitalist state – have become increasingly visible as its one-time pretenses to "democratic socialism" and to "independent working-class political action" have been discarded. More often than not, the political practice flowing from these "principles" has been in accord with the outlook of the trade union bureaucracy. But that practice has also led to occasional conflicts between the "parliamentary" and "workplace" wings of Canadian labour reformism.

The Bitter Fruit of Labour Reformism

NDP politicians and union bureaucrats never tire of lauding the historic accomplishments of organized labour. Yet most of those accomplishments – a trend toward rising real wages and improved benefits for unionized workers, Medicare, public auto-insurance programs and some other crown corporations in three Western provinces, pro-worker health and safety legislation – pre-date the watershed year of 1975. Against that relatively meager ledger, it's

---

9   Ibid., 361.

crucial to examine some of the labour leadership's major failures
and overt betrayals of working-class interests since then:

- As previously noted, in October 1975, the NDP government
  of British Columbia broke a strike wave involving 60,000
  workers, paving the way for Pierre Trudeau's introduction of country-wide wage controls a week later. The B.C.
  Federation of Labour refused to mount any serious opposition to the strike-breaking legislation and endorsed the
  NDP a couple of months later in a provincial election which
  the party ended up losing.

- In response to the federal Liberal government's anti-
  inflation (wage-control) program of 1975, the leaders of
  the union movement in English Canada and Québec alike
  limited their opposition to grumbling and non-disruptive
  protests. Calls for a limited general strike to break the wage
  controls, while popular in the ranks, were rebuffed by the
  top labour bureaucrats. (A one-day general strike, under
  the firm control of the labour centrals, was organized a year
  later, primarily in order to dissipate militancy and allow
  the ranks to blow off steam.)

- In the fall of 1975, the Québec Federation of Labour adopted
  a formal policy of "tactical support" for the bourgeois-
  nationalist Parti Québécois. Henceforth, the leaders of all
  three of the largest trade union bodies resisted calls for the
  creation of a labour party in Québec even as the PQ dropped
  its pro-labor pretenses. The socialist rhetoric of many of the
  union leaders in the early 1970s was abandoned in favour
  of a nationalist appeal to workers to make common cause
  with the PQ to achieve Québec independence. Labour leaders who went to jail in defiance of anti-union injunctions
  and railed against capitalism in the early 1970s became
  involved with a venture-capitalist Solidarity Fund in the
  1980s that enriched union coffers through investments in
  non-unionized enterprises.

- In response to rising sovereigntist sentiment in Québec,

the English Canadian trade unions and the NDP have frequently adapted themselves to anti-Québec chauvinism even while paying occasional lip service to the right of the Québécois to self-determination. A major consequence of the rise of nationalism in the English Canadian labour movement was resistance to the decentralization of the Canadian state and the promotion of the federal government as the primary vehicle for progressive social change. As leftists in English Canada and Québec identified themselves with the rising nationalist tides in their respective societies, they became unable to define a common program of struggle for the labour movement on a pan-Canadian scale. Such a program needed to recognize that neither the federal government nor Québec's provincial government, as key components of the Canadian capitalist state, could be relied upon to promote working-class interests.

- In British Columbia in 1983, Solidarity, a coalition of labour unions, leftists and community groups, mobilized against the Social Credit government in response to the latter's aggressive attacks on labour rights and social spending. Escalating, often illegal, strikes multiplied, accompanied by huge demonstrations in the streets, leading to growing sentiment in the labour movement for a general strike to oust the government. The thrust toward a general strike was ultimately thwarted by senior bureaucrats of the BC Federation of Labour, effectively derailing the most significant mass mobilization against the capitalist offensive of the 1980s.[10]

- In 1985, the Canadian division of the United Auto Workers (UAW) broke away from its U.S.-based parent to form the Canadian Auto Workers (CAW). Presenting themselves as a progressive alternative to the staid and ultra-bureaucratic UAW leadership, Bob White and his acolytes soon demonstrated that the CAW's major goal was to get a better deal for Canadian workers at the expense of their beleaguered

---

[10]   See Bryan Palmer, *Solidarity: The Rise and Fall of an Opposition in British Columbia* (New Star Press, 1986) for a compelling description of these events and an incisive Marxist critique of the role of the trade union bureaucracy.

(and largely African-American) counterparts in Michigan. Investment by the Big Three automakers poured into Ontario and Québec as they sought to lower labour costs by taking advantage of a weak Canadian dollar and Canada's publicly-financed health insurance system. The stage was set for a fragmentation of workers' struggles in the most internationally integrated industry in North America. Instead of campaigning for a program of international solidarity and class-struggle unionism throughout the North American auto industry (including Mexico), the "social unionists" of the CAW bureaucracy helped pave the way for the huge concessions to the auto bosses made by the CAW and the UAW alike following the financial crisis of 2008.

- In 1990, after several years of supporting a Liberal government in an informal legislative coalition, the NDP formed a government in Ontario for the first time. Under the leadership of Bob Rae, the NDP introduced public-housing and job-creations programs, allowed (non-migrant) agricultural workers to organize collectively (but not to strike!), and passed pay and employment equity legislation. But it also reneged on its popular campaign promise to bring public auto insurance to Ontario, claiming that, under the terms of the Free Trade Agreement, the province would risk reprisals from American-based insurance companies. In 1993 Rae introduced his so-called Social Contract as a means to reduce the provincial deficit in the wake of the severe recession of 1990-92. This *diktat* involved the unilateral re-opening of public-sector collective agreements to reduce wages and salaries – a fundamental assault on the principle of free collective bargaining. Thousands resigned from the party and many unions vowed to defeat the government in the next election. The wounded relationship between the NDP and organized labour in Ontario would take many years to heal.

- With little positive to show for its time in office, the Ontario NDP went down to severe defeat in 1995, having paved the way for a resurgent Conservative party led by the right-wing zealot Mike Harris. Harris's blend of neo-conservative and neoliberal policies encompassed cuts to healthcare, education and social programs, union-busting workfare schemes, layoffs to thousands of provincial employees, and the curtailing of union rights. Tax cuts to business and middle-income earners were paid for through vicious reductions in social assistance to single mothers on welfare and other victims of poverty. In reaction to Harris' right-wing offensive, an Ontario version of B.C.'s Solidarity movement emerged. The "Days of Action" were a series of one-day political strikes held between 1995 and 1998 to protest Harris's "Common Sense Revolution" and bring the Tory government to heel. Initiated mainly by the CAW and the public-sector unions and coordinated with a variety of community groups, the first two of these events were organized in London and Hamilton. Both succeeded in shutting down all but essential services. Much to the surprise of the union brass, more than one hundred thousand people demonstrated in Hamilton on February 23, 1996, suggesting the possibility that the movement could escape the control of the labour officialdom. With the obvious intention of winding the movement down, the labour tops selected two smaller centers, Kitchener and Peterborough, for what they hoped would be the last of the protests. But Harris was unyielding and offered the labour leaders precisely nothing in return for a cessation of the protests. Angry and insulted, the labour leaders decided to target Toronto for yet another demonstration of organized labour's might. The Toronto days of action shut down the city's transit system on Friday, October 25 and was followed up the next day by a march on the provincial legislature involving a quarter of a million protesters. Fueled by the militancy of Ontario public sector workers, popular sentiment and momentum were building toward a province-wide general strike. But instead of preparing such an offensive, the CAW and the public-sector union brass responded by calling for more city-wide shutdowns. In the end, the anti-Harris movement petered out as successively smaller days of action were organized in such lightly populated and/or relatively remote centers as St. Catharines, Kingston, North Bay and Thunder Bay. Thanks to the combined efforts of "social unionists" like Buzz Hargrove and "business unionists" like OFL chief Gord Wilson, the Ontario Days of Action – which had begun as one of the most promising fight-backs against neoliberalism anywhere in the world – ended with a whimper.

- Since the early 1970s, the NDP, with the full support of the trade union bureaucracy, has had a consistent record of openness to forming informal and even formal coalitions with Canada's major capitalist parties. In the early 1970s, David Lewis's NDP entered a parliamentary "corridor coalition" with the minority government of Trudeau's Liberal Party. In 2008, the federal NDP caucus entered into a formal agreement with the Liberals to defeat Harper's government and to form a coalition government with the backing of the Bloc Québécois. It has now been at least forty years since the NDP has presented itself as a clear pole of independent working-class political action in an election and just as long since it has distinguished itself from the parties of big business on any policy issue (either domestic or foreign) involving a clear, class-based principle.

- Between 1989 and 1991, the labour reformists joined hands with capitalist politicians in celebrating the restoration of capitalism in the Soviet bloc countries, "forgetting" that many of the gains made by the Western working classes in the post-war period had been won "in the shadow of actually existing socialism." With the disappearance of these bureaucratized workers' states, the ideological agents of capital stepped up their propaganda campaign to convince the working-class masses that "no alternative" to capitalism is possible – a campaign that was soon joined by mainstream social democrats in Canada as elsewhere.

- In the federal election campaigns of 2006, 2008 and 2011, the NDP, under the leadership of Jack Layton, ran on the most right-wing platforms in its history, embracing much of the neoliberal package ("no tax increases," "tough on crime") and with no mention of socialism or even social democracy. Even though the 2011 platform contained nothing about strengthening labour rights in Canada, the cohort of 103 NDP MPs elected in the May election included many activists from the CAW and the various provincial teachers' unions.

- Even as the NDP distances itself from the unions and downplays its nominally pro-labour platform under the new leadership of former Quebec Liberal Thomas Mulcair, an organic relationship with organized labour persists –but one perhaps that reveals less about the NDP than about the comatose state of the unions. The NDP continues its steady movement to the right – not in opposition to the trade union bureaucracy, but hand in hand with it.

Labour Reformism: A Marxist Critique

In the spring of 2011, as the confrontation between organized labour and Wisconsin's union-busting Republican governor Scott Walker captured public attention, CAW president Ken Lewenza contributed an opinion piece to the *Financial Post* explaining his vision of the indispensable role of unions in contemporary capitalist society:

> [Unions] push both employers and governments to act with a measure of fairness in the labour market, promoting equality, inclusion and hope. No society without free and vibrant unions is truly democratic. And no economy without widespread collective bargaining has ever attained truly mass prosperity.

> Imagine if the Scott Walkers of the world had their way, and unions were somehow banned altogether. The non-union workers at the local fast food outlet would still be making minimum wage, with no benefits, no security, and no pension. But a crucial, constructive channel through which their hopes and frustrations could be directed, has now have been closed off. Who

knows where and how the simmering fury of exploited, poor people would then bubble up?[11]

In this revealing appeal to the "business community," Lewenza spelled out clearly and unmistakably the *class-collaborationist* essence of the labour reformism espoused by the leaders of Canada's unions. Lewenza's message: *Unions contribute to the stability of capitalist society – without them all hell might break loose! Accordingly, capitalist employers and unions must work together to achieve a "truly democratic" society.* Who can believe that the Canadian labour movement can revive itself so long as it remains in the grip of such pro-capitalist ideas? Yet it would be foolishly naive to regard the bureaucratic conservatism of the labour officialdom as springing simply from mistaken ideas. The commitment of labour's misleaders to such views must be given a satisfactory *materialist* explanation.

In an article exploring the limits of the "social unionism" once espoused by the CAW leadership, we have previously outlined the principal material factors that contribute to the emergence of conservative union bureaucracies within the organized labour movement, along with some of the major consequences of that bureaucratization:

> At bottom, the bureaucratization of the labour movement is a product of three factors: the need for a functional division of labour and a cadre of full-time leaders and staff members within trade unions once these organizations have established themselves as on-going apparatuses commanding significant material resources; the ability of capital and the state to transform the full-time leaders of trade union organizations into "labour lieutenants" of the capitalist order, both through the cultivation of a labour aristocracy enjoying significant material privileges in relation to the mass of workers and through the institutionalization of a state-sanctioned collective-bargaining

---

[11]   Ken Lewenza, "Counterpoint: Fury of Poor Would Erupt Without Unions," *Financial Post*, April 8, 2011.

process which legally obliges union officials to contain workers' struggles within prescribed limits; and, finally, a "dialectic of partial conquests," which predisposes the labour movement as a whole to reject or retreat from more radical goals in order to avoid any confrontations with capital and the state that might jeopardize previously won gains.

Together these factors tend to continually reproduce conditions conducive to "bourgeois trade union consciousness" – an 'economistic' outlook which limits workers' struggles to an incremental improvement in the terms and conditions of the sale of labour-power within the framework of capitalism. The corollary to this in the parliamentary-electoral arena is an "independent working-class political practice" whose ostensible purpose is to exert pressure on the capitalist state apparatus to safeguard workers' rights and to implement pro-labour policies (without encroaching upon the fundamental prerogatives of capital).[12]

In reiterating this analysis and critiquing the bureaucratic leadership of Canada's labour movement, our intention is not to vilify or to impugn the commitment of the many well-meaning full-time and part-time union activists who occupy a variety of positions within the bureaucratic structures of organized labour. It is undoubtedly true that many of these activists have a more well-developed class consciousness than many rank and file union members. But it is also true that the militancy of the rank and file, at certain times and in particular situations, has often been constrained by the conservative impulses, routinism and reformist political conceptions that permeate those structures at virtually every level – and most of all at the top levels. To be sure, the spontaneous militancy of workers, in angry reaction to particularly egregious provocations by the bosses and the

---

[12]   Jonah Butovsky and Murray E.G. Smith, "Beyond Social Unionism: Farm Workers in Ontario and Some Lessons from Labour History," *Labour/Le Travail* 59 (2007): 72-73.

On "the dialectic of partial conquests," see Ernest Mandel, *Power and Money: A Marxist Theory of Bureaucracy* (London: Verso, 1992), 66-67.

state, can sometimes result in ill-conceived adventures with unfortunate consequences (although these have been exceptionally rare in recent years). Even so, such militancy can also engender opportunities for ordinary workers to acquire experiences that can lead to rapid leaps in class consciousness. For Marxists, the latter consideration decisively outweighs the former one – for only a qualitative growth in socialist class consciousness, impossible in the absence of significant social struggles, can safeguard the long-term interests of the working class and of humanity as a whole.

The point that bears emphasizing here is that the problem of bureaucratic conservatism can only be addressed through a determined *political* struggle, one informed by an adequate theoretical understanding of the class struggle under capitalism. Socialists need to criticize the bureaucratic leaderships of labour *primarily for their political and ideological commitments*, and not merely for their material privileges, their undemocratic practices, or their lack of commitment to workers' interests in particular times and places.

Pro-Capitalist Ideology versus Marxism

The basic premise of mainstream trade unionism and labour reformism in general is that capitalism is an essentially rational system in which, potentially at least, the interests of capital and labour can be reconciled. On this view, no good reason exists to think that the capitalist system should be unable to promote rising popular prosperity so long as labour productivity is improving. All that is needed to secure steadily improving living standards are sustained efforts to rein in corporate greed, protect the economic interests of the national community, and humanize capitalism through enlightened government regulation of the economy, the expansion of the public sector, the implementation of a progressive tax system and (perhaps, in some circumstances) the nationalization of specific industries. Unions contribute to such an outcome by defending the interests of particular sectors of the workforce through collective bargaining, supporting progressive-egalitarian and economic-nationalist policies in the political arena, and promoting the democratization of a state apparatus that is seen as "standing above" classes and as devoted, above all else, to a trans-class national interest.

These notions, which are deeply rooted in capitalist ideology and in Keynesian liberalism in particular, have been contradicted time and again by historical experience. Over the past two hundred years, the world capitalist economy has experienced some two dozen cyclical economic crises as well as numerous region-specific economic contractions that have inflicted untold hardships on billions of working people. Over the past century, the intensifying contradictions and crisis tendencies of world capitalism have yielded three serious global economic slumps, two devastating world wars, dozens of bloody regional conflicts, chronic underdevelopment across wide swaths of the Global South, severe and potentially catastrophic ecological crises, and the squandering of enormous economic resources on military expenditures, advertising and other wasteful activities. Over the past forty years, the living standards of the bottom 80 to 90 percent of wage and salary earners in even the most advanced capitalist countries have seen an appreciable decline, despite high and continuously rising levels of labour productivity. Over the same period, a rapidly expanding global "surplus population" – that now represents well over a third of the world's population – has been condemned to a remorseless cycle of dispossession, unemployment, underemployment and starvation.

Karl Marx, capitalism's most trenchant critic and the founder of modern scientific socialism, was quite willing to concede that capitalism had played an objectively progressive, indeed revolutionary, role in developing humanity's productive forces. Unlike the ideologues of capitalism, however, Marx predicted that these productive forces would become increasingly incompatible with the antagonistic social relations of capitalist society – that the capitalist imperative to subordinate economic life to private profit and to the "logic" of a competitive nation-state system would negate capitalism's progressive role. The accumulation of capital and the contradictions inherent to that process would entail a massive growth of poverty at one pole of an increasingly globalized class system and obscene wealth at the other. The rise in labour productivity brought about by on-going technical innovation would not, in any enduring way, secure a better life for the working class majority, but would, on the contrary, lead to recurrent economic crises and ultimately to the immiseration of that majority.

It is this ugly and grotesquely irrational side of capitalist development that is studiously ignored by even the most "left-liberal" defenders of the capitalist system, including the great majority of labour leaders who claim to speak on behalf of working people and against the "excesses" of the corporate elites. Little wonder, then, that the pro-capitalist labour bureaucracy chooses to reject or ignore Marx's critical analysis of the capitalist mode of production.

At the heart of that analysis is what Marx called the "law of the tendency of the rate of profit to fall" (LTRPF), a law which suggests a relationship between profitability, productivity and economic crisis that is, at first blush, strikingly non-obvious:

> The barriers to the capitalist mode of production shows themselves as follows: 1) in the way that the development of *labour productivity* involves a law, in the form of the falling rate of profit, that at a certain point confronts this development itself in a most hostile way and has constantly to be overcome *by way of crises*; 2) in the way that it is the appropriation of unpaid labour in general ... that determines the expansion and contraction of production, instead of the proportion between production and social needs, the needs of socially developed human beings.[13] [Emphasis added]

Capitalism is not fundamentally concerned with raising labour productivity in order to meet human needs or to reduce the burden of toil shouldered by workers. Rather it is about maximizing wealth in the class-antagonistic form of surplus-value (profit of enterprise, rent and interest). Surplus-value can only arise through the *exploitation* of wage-labour by capital – "the appropriation of unpaid labour." Thus, the system as a whole is decisively geared to perpetuating the domination and serving the interests of the capitalist class – a tiny fraction of the population that owns and controls the major means of production, distribution and exchange.[14]

The working-class majority of the population is employed, for

---

13   Karl Marx, *Capital Volume Three* (New York: Vintage Books, 1981).
14   For more detailed expositions of Marx's theories of surplus-value, capitalist exploitation and economic crisis, see Murray E.G. Smith, *Global Capitalism in Crisis: Karl Marx and the Decay of the Profit System* (Halifax: Fernwood Publishing, 2010).

the most part, to create or help realize the value that is embodied in marketed goods and services (commodities) and that finds expression in profits and wages. But economic growth is regulated by the average rate of profit, and this is defined by the relationship of capitalist income (surplus-value) to capitalist investment (the value of capital stock). Surplus-value, along with the new value embodied in the wages of productive workers, can only be created by living labour; and yet the antagonistic social relations of capitalism – the competition between capitalist firms and the conflict between capitalists and wage labourers – militate in favour of labour-displacing technological innovation at the level of individual enterprises. The result is a rise in "the organic composition of capital." The unintended consequence of this productivity-enhancing innovation is a relative, economy-wide decline in the role of living labour in production – which nevertheless remains the sole "input" with the capacity to create new value. As the pool of social surplus-value shrinks relative to the investment of the social capital as a whole, the average rate of profit falls.

The drive of individual capitalists to reduce costs and improve productivity (with the aims of maximizing profits and surviving the challenges of inter-capitalist competition) must lead to a long-term declining rate of return on capitalist investment – to a crisis of profitability for the capitalist class as a whole. To arrest this decline, capitalists resort to harsh measures aimed at ratcheting up the rate of exploitation of working people and by increasing productivity in ways that rely less on technical innovation and considerably more on intensifying the labour process, lowering real wages and cutting back on social services that form elements of what is sometimes called the social wage.

Numerous studies, including one by Smith and Taylor for Canada,[15] have confirmed that the performance of the advanced capitalist economies since World War II has conformed closely to Marx's theoretical expectations. Labour-displacing technological innovation has elevated the organic composition of capital and depressed the rate of profit. In response, the capitalist class has sought to raise national rates of profit by forcing workers to pay

---

[15] Murray E.G. Smith and K.W. Taylor, "Profitability Crisis and the Erosion of Popular Prosperity: The Canadian Economy, 1947-1991," *Studies in Political Economy* 49 (1996).

the medical bills of its ailing system, by promoting "financialization" and the proliferation of "fictitious capital," and by shifting
investment and some of the effects of the profitability crisis to other
countries or regions.[16]

A perspective informed by Marx's analysis could have afforded
the labour movement, in Canada and elsewhere, with the opportunity to take the offensive politically in the midst of the profitability
crisis of the 1970s – to argue that "the barrier to capital is capital
itself" and that the malaise of the system resulted from its own
inherent irrationality.[17] But the aversion of the labour leadership
to Marxist theory and politics, and its commitment to liberal-
Keynesian palliatives and nationalist economic policies, foreclosed
such a possibility. Today, in the midst of a global slump that has its
deepest roots in the persistent profitability problems of productive
capital, the struggle for the theoretical and programmatic heritage
of Marxist socialism within the organized labour movement has
become more urgent than ever.

Socialism and the Unions, Yesterday and Today

Historically, socialists have been divided in their view of unions and
their relationship to the struggle for a socialist society.[18] One of the
ways in which Marx and Engels distinguished their own scientific,
class-struggle socialism from other socialist currents (Owenite uto-
pian socialism, Proudhonist mutualism, etc.) was by insisting that

---

[16]   For the experience of the U.S. economy, see Murray E.G. Smith and Jonah
        Butovsky, "Profitability and the Roots of the Global Crisis: Marx's 'Law of
        the Tendency of the Rate of Profit to Fall' and the U.S. Economy, 1950-2007,"
        Historical Materialism 20, No. 4 (2012). See also Simon Mohun, "Aggregate
        Capital Productivity in the U.S. Economy, 1964-2001," *Cambridge Journal of
        Economics* 33 (2009).

[17]   See Smith, *Global Capitalism*.

[18]   Socialists have never been entirely united around the idea that they should
        support or work within the existing unions. Indeed anarcho-syndicalists, De
        Leon's Socialist Labor Party, the communist "ultra-left" of the 1920s, coun-
        cil communists and more recently the nominal Trotskyists who publish the
        World Socialist Web Site have all been hostile to the established unions and
        rejected working within them. Against such a stance, Lenin argued that revo-
        lutionary socialists who refuse to work in the unions consign themselves to a
        self-imposed isolation. And Trotsky added that such sectarianism should be
        seen as "opportunism standing in fear of itself." For Lenin and Trotsky, labour
        reformists and ultra-left sectarians make the symmetrical error of *identifying*
        the unions with the union officialdoms.

socialists had to support and involve themselves in workers' struggles for better wages and working conditions even when these struggles were led by trade unionists who opposed socialism. At the same time, they saw the trade unions as organizations in which socialists could educate the working class about its historic mission to end the rule of capital. It was precisely in an address on the Paris Commune to the International Workingmen's Association (which included many Liberal British trade unionists) that Marx defined the goal of the modern labour movement as the "smashing" of the capitalist state and the establishment of the "dictatorship of the proletariat" – a workers' state striving toward a global classless society.

In Germany, Marx's followers were directly involved in establishing some of the earliest trade unions. While always insisting that they should be open to all workers, regardless of their political commitments, the Marxists nevertheless sought the affiliation of as many unions as possible to the social-democratic workers' party. A "division of labour" was established between the unions and the party – but it was nevertheless taken for granted that socialists had a responsibility to educate the union ranks in the fundamental ideas of socialism.

In 1902, Lenin waged a famous struggle within the Russian Social Democratic Labour Party (RSDLP) against the so-called Economists who argued that socialists should confine their agitation among workers to simple trade union demands, while offering political support to bourgeois-liberal efforts to reform the absolutist state. Workers, it was assumed, could achieve a "social-democratic consciousness" as a spontaneous by-product of their trade union struggles. Against this, Lenin argued that the "history of all countries shows that the working class, exclusively by its own effort, is able to develop only trade union consciousness," while the "theory of socialism" had been developed by "the educated representatives of the propertied classes, the intellectuals." For Lenin, this didn't mean that workers were incapable of assimilating or adding to this theoretical legacy as they joined the ranks of the socialist movement; but it did mean that the struggle to fuse the ideas of Marxist socialism with the actually existing workers' organizations had to be an ongoing one. In the absence of such a struggle, the workers' movement would inevitably fall under the sway of bourgeois ideology.

As Lenin waged his battles with the labour-reformists within the RSDLP, the Polish-born Marxist Rosa Luxemburg was waging a parallel struggle for a revolutionary Marxist perspective within the German Social Democratic Party (SPD). Prior to 1914, she did so on two main fronts: by opposing the attempts of Eduard Bernstein and his fellow "revisionists" to win the party to a perspective that essentially repudiated socialism as its "final goal" and by challenging the well-established "division of labour" between the party and the unions which was leading the union leaderships to reject any "mass strike" tactic that could pose the question of workers' power. Luxemburg's insistence against Bernstein and the revisionist union leaders that the struggle for reform (the amelioration of the conditions of the working masses within capitalism) was merely the *means* of the socialist movement but that its *goal* had to remain *social revolution* anticipated her later break with the "minimum-maximum" programmatic dichotomy of the SPD – a break enunciated in 1919 in her speech to the founding convention of the Communist Party of Germany. There she insisted that the new party was "opposed to the separation of the immediate and so-called minimal demands formulated for the political and economic struggle, from the socialist goal regarded as the maximal program."[19]

World War I brought about the definitive split in the social-democratic Second International between the nationalist reformists and the revolutionary internationalists. By conducting an uncompromising struggle against "social patriotism" (the support extended to the war efforts of their "own" bourgeoisies by most of Europe's mass social-democratic parties) and subsequently leading the world's first successful workers' revolution in Russia in October 1917, Lenin was transformed from a revolutionary social democrat into the founder of the Communist International (CI).

The first four congresses of the CI elaborated a strategic and programmatic orientation that involved the transformation of the unions into organs of revolutionary struggle. A special wing of the movement – the Red International of Labour Unions (RILU) – was established to coordinate the trade union work of the CI's national sections. The second congress of the CI (held in 1920) stipulated that:

---

[19] Rosa Luxemburg, "Speech to the Founding Convention of the German Communist Party," in *Rosa Luxemburg Speaks*, ed. Mary Alice Waters (New York: Pathfinder Press, 1970), 413.

> Every party that desires to belong to the Communist
> International must carry on systematic and persistent
> communist work in the trade unions, in workers' and
> industrial councils, in the cooperative societies, and in
> other mass organizations. Within these organizations
> it is necessary to create communist groups, which by
> means of practical and stubborn work must win over
> the trade unions, etc., for the cause of communism.[20]

The third congress in 1921 spelled out the general programmatic content of the communists' work in the unions: "In place of
the minimum programme of the centrists and reformists, the Communist International offers a struggle for the concrete demands of
the proletariat which, in their totality, challenge the power of the
bourgeoisie, organize the proletariat and mark out the different
stages of the struggle for its dictatorship."[21] The fourth congress in
1922 passed a resolution declaring that the (not-yet-written) program of the Comintern should include "transitional demands." [22]

In North America, this perspective was implemented by the
Trade Union Education League (TUEL), an organization that
united communist trade union activists in the United States and
Canada. For a few years, the TUEL and other RILU affiliates in
Europe carried out exemplary work within the existing unions on
the basis of a nascent transitional program.[23] By the mid-1920s,
however, the Stalinist degeneration of the Soviet state and the CI
effectively brought an end to these promising initiatives. Henceforth, the national sections of the CI were subordinated to Stalin's

---

[20]   CI 1920 (Communist International), "Conditions of Admission to the
Communist International," in *International Communism in the Era of Lenin:
A Documentary History*, ed. H. Gruber (New York: Anchor Press), 244.

[21]   CI 1921 (Communist International), "On Tactics," in *Theses, Resolutions and
Manifestos of the First Four Congresses of the Third International* (London: Ink
Links, 1980), 286.

[22]   See International Bolshevik Tendency, "Transitional Demands: From the
Comintern to the Fourth International" in Trotsky, *The Transitional Program*,
209-10.

[23]   For somewhat differing assessments of this experience, see Chris Knox,
"Program for Power: Early Communist Work in the Trade Unions," in Trotsky,
The Transitional Program; Kim Moody, *The Rank and File Strategy: Building a
Socialist Movement in the U.S.* (Solidarity Pamphlet, 2000); and Bryan Palmer,
*James P. Cannon and the Origins of the American Revolutionary Left, 1890-
1928* (Champaign, IL: University of Illinois Press, 2007).

national-reformist policy of building "socialism in one country." The Communist parties were transformed into mere facilitators of this utterly anti-Marxist project, and their trade union practice reverted to the "minimum-maximum" approach of the classical social democracy.

However, the idea of a transitional program survived and was further developed by Leon Trotsky in the 1930s. One of the central leaders of Russia's October Revolution and of the CI in its early years, Trotsky had been expelled from the Communist Party of the Soviet Union in 1928 for his opposition to Stalin's policies and sent into exile a year later. For the next decade, until his assassination at the hand of a Stalinist agent in 1940, he carried out a tireless struggle against Stalin's bureaucratic oligarchy and its counter-revolutionary influence on the international communist movement.[24] In 1938, he launched the Fourth International (FI) as the legitimate successor to the first four (Bolshevik-Leninist) congresses of the Communist International. Although small and lacking much influence in the mass labour movements of their respective countries on the eve of World War II, the national sections of the FI were armed by Trotsky with a manifesto that, for the first time in the history of the Marxist movement, spelled out in some detail the content of a transitional socialist program for communist work in the trade unions. In an unfinished article on "Trade Unions in the Epoch of Imperialist Decay," he wrote:

> In the epoch of imperialist decay the trade unions can be really independent [of the bourgeoisie and the capitalist state] only to the extent that they are conscious of being, in action, the organs of proletarian revolution. In this sense, the program of transitional demands adopted at the last congress of the Fourth International is not only the program for the activity of the party but in its fundamental features it is the program for activity of the trade unions.[25]

---

24   On this history, see Murray E.G. Smith, "Revisiting Trotsky: Reflections on the Stalinist Debacle and Trotskyism as Alternative," *Rethinking Marxism* 9, no. 3 (1996-97).
25   Leon Trotsky, *On the Trade Unions* (New York: Pathfinder Press, 1969), 72.

With this statement, Trotsky reaffirmed what had been the common understanding of revolutionary socialists from the time of Marx and Engels: trade unions had to be seen as instruments in the struggle for a socialist society, and not ends in themselves. The primary task of socialists working within them is not to promote mindless, sectoral militancy but to carry out a determined *political struggle* for a program that anticipates the social and political content of a workers' state and the early phases of socialist construction – a program that intersects the defensive struggles of workers under capitalism but also projects solutions that involve confronting and dismantling the economic, political and military power of the capitalist class and its state.

To accomplish this important task today, revolutionary socialists must have the perspective of building class-struggle *caucuses* within the unions that are explicitly committed to popularizing a *system* of transitional demands. These demands would necessarily include a sliding scale of wages and hours (to fight inflation and unemployment), the expropriation of industry and the banks without compensation, workers' control of production, workers' defense guards, and, finally, a workers' government. The *exemplary* activity of such caucuses in carrying out both independent work as well as united-front work with leftward-moving forces around specific issues (such as organizing the unorganized, winning full citizenship rights for migrant workers, or organizing labour political strikes against imperialist wars[26]) is really the only way that a class-struggle socialist current can begin to challenge the pro-capitalist bureaucracy and eventually win the ranks of the broader labour movement to the theory and program of Marxist socialism.[27]

---

[26] On May Day 2008, following an initiative by socialist union activist Jack Heyman, the International Longshore and Warehouse Union shut down every port on the U.S. west coast to protest the wars in Iraq and Afghanistan. The one-day shutdown demonstrated the potential power of organized labour to seriously challenge the neocolonial adventures of U.S. imperialism – and indeed global capitalism itself.

[27] For an elaboration of this argument, see Smith and Dumont, "Socialist Strategy." as well as Chris Knox, "Revolutionary Work in the American Labor Movement: 1920s to 1950s," in Trotsky, *The Transitional Program*. See also Butovsky and Smith, "Beyond Social Unionism," and the interview with Trotskyist union activist Howard Keylor reprinted in Trotsky, *The Transitional Program*.

LABOUR'S RESPONSE TO THE CRISIS AND THE FUTURE OF WORKING-CLASS POLITICS[1]

David Camfield

The response of labour in Canada and Quebec to the economic crisis that first surfaced in the US financial sector in 2007 and became a global crisis in 2008 has been for the most part small-scale, low-key and timid.[2] By "labour" here I mean simply unions. Unions are by far the largest component of the working-class movement, which in Canada and Quebec also includes anti-poverty and injured workers' groups, workers' centres and groups fighting for the rights of unemployed workers and immigrants.[3] For many people critical of what capitalists and governments have done since the onset of the crisis and eager for alternatives, the weak union reaction has been disappointing. But simply deploring the labour response does not take us very far. Understanding *why* labour's response has been weak is more valuable; the way people who favour a different course of action explain the response so far will affect their proposals for change. This chapter opens with an overview of labour's response. It then offers an explanation of it that identifies the key forces as the impact of neoliberal restructuring on the working class, the weakness of the infrastructure of dissent, the state of unions before the crisis hit and the influence of political parties on the unions. It

[1]   Thanks to Sheila Wilmot, Tim Fowler and the two anonymous reviewers for comments on drafts of this chapter.

[2]   On the crisis, see David McNally, *Global Slump: The Economics and Politics of Crisis and Resistance* (Oakland: PM, 2011).

[3]   See my *Canadian Labour in Crisis: Reinventing the Workers' Movement* (Halifax and Winnipeg: Fernwood Publishing, 2011).

concludes by considering the implications of this analysis for the future of politics that treat the struggles of working-class people themselves as key to making progressive social change.

Labour's Response

With hindsight, we can see that in the spring of 2008 the crisis was still in its first phase. Attention was focused on US financial and housing markets.[4] The official unemployment rate in Canada was 6%, and the rate of participation in the paid workforce was at an all time high.[5] It was in this conjuncture that the top officials of the Canadian Auto Workers (CAW) made the surprise move of asking the "Detroit Three" (Ford, General Motors and Chrysler) to enter into early negotiations for the contracts covering assembly plant workers. The collective agreements negotiated in this round of "panic bargaining" contained notable concessions. These deals – and the way they were reopened in 2009 in response to the demands of the federal and Ontario governments for more concessions as a condition for guaranteeing loans to the companies – sent a very visible signal about how private sector unions would respond to the crisis.[6]

In May 2008, the Canadian Labour Congress's (CLC) triennial convention took place in Toronto. The economic policy paper, "Labour's Agenda for Good Jobs,"[7] stuck with CLC tradition by laying out a social democratic policy perspective with almost no discussion of how to get governments to implement it. The report was adopted with little debate. Aside from what was said from the floor by a few dissenting delegates, there was very little mention of problems such as those noted by one commentator later that year:

---

4   For example, Fletcher Baragar, "The Credit Crisis in Canada: The First Six Months," *The Bullet 92* (March 21, 2008), http://www.socialistproject.ca/bullet/bullet092.html.

5   "Labour Force Survey," (April 4, 2008), http://www.statcan.gc.ca/daily-quotidien/080404/dq080404a-eng.htm.

6   Sam Gindin, "The CAW and Panic Bargaining: Early Opening at the Big Three," *The Bullet* 105 (May 6, 2008), http://www.socialistproject.ca/bullet/bullet105.html; Herman Rosenfeld, "The North American Auto Industry in Crisis," *Monthly Review* (June 2009), http://www.monthlyreview.org/090608rosenfeld.php.

7   "Labour's Agenda for Good Jobs," http://www.canadianlabour.ca/sites/default/files/pdfs/LaboursAgendGoodobs.pdf.

Organizing – the hard work of bringing the benefits of unionization to unrepresented workers – has fallen off the map. Militancy is more often than not spoken of as ancient history. Partnership deals with employers are now regularly sold to members as the only solution. Too often, unions are now using concessions as the default position in their efforts to keep companies from closing workplaces entirely.[8]

Soon after the CLC convention, GM announced the closure of its Oshawa truck plant, despite having just extracted concessions from its workers. CAW Local 222's leaders organized a blockade of GM's Canadian headquarters, but the "largely symbolic" blockade and a 5000-strong rally were not used to try to build a campaign to stop the closing that involved a plant occupation.[9] More impressive was the blockade that non-unionized workers at Vaughan, ON's Progressive Molded Products (PMP), most of whom were racialized immigrants, organized after the company shut down despite owing over $30 million to workers. This bold direct action drew support from union activists in the region.[10] But the remarkably militant collective action of these workers was a very rare exception to how most wage-earners responded to lay-offs and shut-downs as the recession deepened: hunkering down and relying on their own family-based and individual efforts to get by.

Union activity during the campaign for the federal election of October 2008 was predictable. The top officials of the unions most supportive of the New Democratic Party (NDP) continued with their direct support to the party. Most of the leaders of CLC-affiliated unions promoted the CLC's Better Choice campaign, which is intended to promote discussion of priority issues and does not explicitly call for a vote for a specific party. A few unions, including the CAW, conducted their own "anybody but the Tories" campaigns designed to build support for Liberal and NDP candidates

---

8   John Peters, "Too Little, Too Late? The State of the Canadian Labour Movement Today," *The Bullet 159* (November 28, 2008), http://www.socialistproject.ca/bullet/bullet159.html.

9   Herman Rosenfeld, "The Oshawa Plant Closing," *The Bullet 128* (July 23, 2008), http://www.socialistproject.ca/bullet/bullet128.html.

10   Winnie Ng, "PMP Stands for '*Politicize, Mobilize and Power,*" *Labour/Le Travail* 64 (2009).

best-positioned to win their particular ridings. The CAW's Quebec wing and many Quebecois unions endorsed the Bloc Quebecois, as in previous elections.[11] More unusual was the official support given in December 2008 by the CLC and top officers of a number of other unions for the unsuccessful move to form a Liberal-NDP coalition government with BQ support, a government that would have been dominated by the Liberals and committed to "fiscal responsibility," including an end to budget deficits within four years.[12] This support for a coalition government took the form of the website makeparliamentwork.ca and mobilizing union members for rallies in a range of cities.

As the Great Recession deepened, employers moved more aggressively to extract concessions from unionized workers in collective bargaining. While some groups of workers struck to defend themselves (or found themselves locked out), fear and uncertainty increased while strike levels and workers' expectations declined. The number of strikes per year, which had averaged just over 328 between 1996 and 2005 before falling to 151 in 2006 and 206 the following year, dropped to 188 in 2008 and 157 in 2009. There were 174 strikes in 2010 and 148 in 2011. These were the lowest numbers of strikes recorded since the mid-1950s (when the workforce itself was much smaller). Time on strike as a percentage of time worked averaged 0.035% over the years 2008-2011. This represented the lowest level seen since the years 1938-1940.[13]

A few groups of workers who found themselves on the corporate chopping-block and fought back in these difficult circumstances deserve note. In March 2009, workers at the Aradco and Aramco auto parts plants in Windsor were told they were out of work because Chrysler was ending its contract with the firm that owned both plants. Presented with an offer worth less than one-eighth

---

[11]   Larry Savage, "Contemporary Party-Union Relations in Canada," *Labor Studies Journal* 35, no. 1 (2010): 12-13.

[12]   Canadian Labour Congress, "Why We Need a Coalition Government to Deal with the Economic Crisis," (n.d. [2008]); "A Policy Accord to Address the Present Economic Crisis" (December 1, 2008).

[13]   "Chronological Perspective on Work Stoppages," Labour Program (HRSDC), http://srv131.services.gc.ca/dimt-wid/pcat-cpws/recherche-search.aspx?lang=eng; "Number of Strikes and Lockouts, Employers and Workers Involved and Time Loss, Canada, 1901 to 1975" (Statistics Canada data). Early and mid-20th century strike-related data is less reliable than more recent data, but the trends are clear.

of the money owed to them, the workers rejected CAW officials' advice and voted it down. When Chrysler tried to remove materials from the Aradco factory, workers formed a blockade, defied a court injunction and occupied the plant. They demanded both the money they were owed and changes to legislation to improve access to unemployment insurance and protect workers whose employers go bankrupt. The occupation ended after CAW President Ken Lewenza, eager to put an end to this direct action, declared that a new deal had been won; this turned out to be worth less than one-quarter of what workers were owed.[14] Earlier, in January 2008, CAW members at Ledco in Kitchener occupied to win severance pay owing to them. February 2009 saw a blockade by CAW members at Bauer Industries in Waterloo to extract unpaid wages from their employer. In July, workers at CAW-organized BBI Enterprises in Ajax blockaded their plant for the same reason.[15] However, these militant responses were very much the exception.

On a larger scale, early 2009 also saw a round of union-organized protests. The largest of these, a multi-union demonstration in defence of pensions that drew approximately 15 000 people, was held at the Ontario legislature in April.[16] This was the biggest labour demonstration in the province since the Days of Action protests against the Conservative Mike Harris government in the second half of the 1990s. The Communications, Energy and Paperworkers Union (CEP) mobilized members for a "National Day of Protest" in Ottawa in June to focus on the plight of forest industry workers. In May, the Toronto and York Region Labour Council (TYRLC) held a Stewards' Assembly that drew around 1600 union officials and rank-and-file activists. Former CAW staffer Herman Rosenfeld noted that it was "the first such meeting in living memory" and "the result of an impressive organizing effort." Yet "rather than being an actual assembly, with open discussion, debate and space for the stewards to initiate points and ideas, it felt more like a

---

[14]   Jeff Shantz, "Factory Occupations in Ontario, Canada: Rebuilding Infrastructures of Resistance," *WorkingUSA: The Journal of Labour and Society* 13 (2010): 137-140.

[15]   Alan Sheldon, "Tools of the Trade: Resistance to the Crisis Around the World," *New Socialist* 66 (2009): 24; "Agreement at Bauer Industries Ends Blockade," *Canadian Auto Workers* (February 25, 2009), http://www.caw.ca/en/5590.htm.

[16]   "Activists Converge on Queen's Park for Massive Pension Rally," *Contact 39*, no. 17 (2009), http://www.caw.ca/en/7414.htm.

process of conveying information." There were "constant references to NDP politicians."[17] The evening ended with a speech by Toronto mayor David Miller.

The mayor's presence was especially significant because, at the time, two large CUPE locals representing City of Toronto workers were in contract negotiations and major demands for concessions were on the table. By the end of June, over 24 000 members of CUPE Locals 79 and 416 found themselves walking picket lines to fend off the Miller administration's demands for give-backs. Their strike overlapped with an even longer strike by Windsor's municipal workforce, which ended with a settlement that saw current workers give up post-retirement benefits for future hires.[18] The strike at the City of Toronto was especially significant.[19] Lasting over a month, it involved the largest union (CUPE), its largest local (Local 79), in Canada's largest city. Much as the CAW's deals with GM, Chrysler and Ford helped set the tone for how private sector unions would respond to demands for concessions during the economic crisis, the City of Toronto strike sent signals to workers and employers across the public sector and beyond. Most concessions were fended off but the leaders of Locals 79 and 416 signed contracts that give the employer some of the changes to sick leave provisions that were demanded, by giving up the existing plan for all future hires. However, the conduct and outcome of the Toronto strike were much worse than the settlement itself.

Union preparation for the strike was poor. Before the strike began officials did not clearly explain to members the issues on which they were refusing to give concessions.[20] There was almost no communication between the locals' leaders and striking workers during the strike. No membership meetings of any kind were held. Union members loyally walking the lines were left feeling isolated and in the dark. The locals' leaders organized no large marches,

---

[17]   Herman Rosenfeld, "Toronto Labour Council Organizes Stewards' Assembly," *Canadian Dimension* 43, no. 5 (2009): 37-38.

[18]   CBCNews.ca, "Windsor, Ont., Civic Strike Ends," http://cbc.ca/canada/toronto/ story/2009/07/24/windsor-strike-vote072409.html.

[19]   This discussion draws on *Canadian Labour in Crisis*, 23-29 and is indebted to an article by two members of CUPE 79: Julia Barnett and Carlo Fanelli, "Lessons Learned: Assessing the 2009 City of Toronto Strike and its Aftermath," *New Socialist* 66 (2009).

[20]   Julia Barnett to author, telephone communication, August 23, 2009.

rallies or other mass actions that could have bolstered strikers' morale and, if they had disrupted business as usual on the streets of Toronto, applied pressure on the employer to settle the dispute on favorable terms. Throughout the strike, the corporate media was filled with hostile coverage. The unions were portrayed as greedy and unrealistic for trying to defend paid sick day provisions in their contracts that were better than those of most workers. The fact that these provisions had been agreed to by their employer in exchange for monetary concessions by the unions in the past was almost never mentioned. The media coverage contributed to the "unusual... visceral level of hostility against the strikers" in the city.[21] Faced with this onslaught, the top officers of CUPE 79 and 416 did very little to rally members' resolve and counter hostile accusations. They did even less to make a case for why defending municipal public sector jobs was in the interest of all working people in Toronto, particularly women and racialized workers (a clear majority of the strikers were women and/or racialized people). For their part, most officials in other unions in Toronto did not treat the strike as the key struggle it was. The TYRLC president's ties with the mayor and his supporters on city council were one reason why the TYRLC leadership did not do everything possible to help the strike win. The outcome was a blow to labour in Toronto and beyond. The strike "was a political failure when it came to mobilizing sustained action and education, garnering public support as well as linking the defense of unionized jobs with fighting for workers in non-unionized jobs, the underemployed and the unemployed."[22] This made it easier for right-wing populist candidate Rob Ford to channel "concerns about particular public services against city workers, and the idea of the public sector as a whole" as part of his successful run to become the mayor of Toronto in 2010.[23]

As the official unemployment rate began to decline in mid-2009,

---

[21] Thomas Walkom, "Striking City Workers a Convenient Target," *TheStar,* June 27, 2009, http://www.thestar.com/Article/656836.

[22] Barnett and Fanelli, "Lessons Learned," 28-29.

[23] Parastou Saberi and Stefan Kipfer, "Rob Ford in Toronto: Why the Ascendancy of Hard-Right Populism in the 2010 Mayoral Election?," *New Socialist Webzine* (November 24, 2010), http://newsocialist.org/index.php?option=com_content&view=article&id=314:rob-ford-in-toronto-why-the-ascendancy-of-hardright- populism-in-the-2010-mayoral-election&carid=51:analysis&Itemid=98.

pensions became a higher priority issue for many union officials. This mainly took the form of efforts to motivate union members and other workers to support the CLC's "Retirement Security for Everyone!" lobbying campaign directed at the federal and provincial governments. The response from workers was significant, leading the CLC's 2010 Labour Day statement to claim that

> Over the past twelve months, working people did something they have not done for a very long time. They changed their government's mind... At a meeting in June, the country's finance ministers agreed that the best way to help Canadians save more for retirement was through the Canada Pension Plan. It was a sweet victory for working people.[24]

This celebratory optimism was soon dispelled by the reality of Conservative hostility to publically-administered programs: the finance minister proposed new private pooled pension plans instead of strengthening the CPP.

The largest social protests of 2010 took place around the summit of political leaders from the G-20 countries in Toronto in June. Initiative here was in the hands of community activists organizing through the Toronto Community Mobilization Network (TCMN), not unions. "In the end, the labour movement played a significant role in the anti-G20 mobilizations, but most of the collaboration between the TCMN and organized labour was invisible. This changed after state repression began in earnest."[25] Union efforts mobilized thousands of workers to take part in a large march on

---

[24] "Labour Day Message 2010," Canadian Labour Congress, (August 31, 2010), http://www.canadianlabour.ca/news-room/statements/labour-day-message-2010.

[25] Lesley Wood, "Bringing Together the Grassroots: A Strategy and a Story from Toronto's G20 Protests," *Upping the Anti* 11 (2010): 95-6. Herman Rosenfeld summarizes labour's response to the repression this way: "There were some union statements that condemned police actions and mass arrests in the wake of the demonstrations. A number of unions, including the CLC, denounced the repressive bail conditions handed some of those accused of conspiracy, but, with some exceptions, union officials have not gone out of their way to give much financial and political support for those still languishing in jail or mounting expensive legal defences." Herman Rosenfeld, e-mail message to author, December 21, 2010.

June 26. Top union officials immediately denounced the attacks on property that took place that day in a way that upset some left-wing labour activists.[26] A large, entirely union-organized protest that took place later in 2010 received much less media attention than the G-20 protests: the CAW's October 27 day of action for its members in auto parts manufacturing, a mostly non-unionized sector where employers have been aggressively demanding concessions, saw lunch-time rallies outside workplaces at over 100 locations across Ontario involving perhaps 15 000 workers.[27]

Early in 2011, a range of unions mobilized members to take part in a sizeable January 29 demonstration in solidarity with members of United Steelworkers (USW) Local 1005 in Hamilton locked-out by US Steel since November 2010.[28] Solidarity with these USW members was made easier by their Southern Ontario location and the efforts of an independent-minded mobilization-oriented local leadership (at odds with top USW officials) that consciously tried to make the dispute a political battle between the Canadian people and a US multinational company allied with a right-wing federal government.[29] In contrast, members of USW Local 6500 at Vale in Sudbury whose nearly year-long strike against concessions ended in defeat in July 2010 were not helped by their greater distance from

---

26 The CLC's press release ("Statement by Ken Georgetti, President of the Canadian Labour Congress on Vandalism Surrounding Toronto G20 Meeting," [June 26, 2010], http://www.canadianlabour.ca/national/news/ statement-ken-georgetti-president-canadian-labour-congress-vandalism-surrounding-toron) was responded to by an "Open Letter to Ken Georgetti and the Canadian Labour Congress" (e-mail in author's possession, n.d. [July 2010]) from over 200 union members that criticized it for being "shockingly silent about the violence perpetrated by the state and police, aimed at rendering the right of people to assemble, organize and resist obsolete, brutalizing our sisters, brothers and children" and argued that its "limited focus legitimizes the suspension of rights and liberties in this city, including the right to assembly and the right to political protest."

27 Howard Ryan, "Canadian Auto Parts Workers Say 'Enough is Enough!,'" *Labor Notes* (October 29, 2010), http://labornotes.org/2010/10/ canadian-auto-parts-workers-say-%E2%80%98enough-enough%E2%80%99.

28 Although a CUPE statement claimed that 9-10 000 demonstrators made this "the largest union protest in Ontario since the Days of Action in 1996 against the Mike Harris government" ("Big CUPE Contingent Joins Mass Rally Supporting Locked Out Hamilton Steelworkers," [January 31, 2011], http:// cupe.ca/pensions/contingent-joins-mass-rally-supporting), it was probably smaller than the April 2009 pension rally in Toronto mentioned earlier.

29 For a critique of the kind of left-nationalism seen in USW 1005's campaign, see Sebastian Lamb, "Challenging Canada," *New Socialist* 54 (2005-6).

big cities or a strategy based much more on outlasting the company
than on actively mobilizing strikers and supporters.[30] The largest
anti-austerity protest seen since the beginning of the crisis was the
demonstration of tens of thousands of people in Montreal on March
12, 2011 in advance of the release of the Quebec government's
budget; many union officials mobilized members for this event, in
contrast to the abstention of top officials from the previous year's
anti-budget protests.[31] In June, members of the Canadian Union of
Postal Workers (CUPW) carried out rotating strikes before being
locked out by Canada Post. In some places there was considerable support for postal workers, but when the federal government
moved to bring in an aggressively anti-worker back-to-work law no
solidarity action was forthcoming from other unionized workers.[32]
Faced with a lockout at the Electro-Motive Diesel factory in London
in January 2012, triggered by the highly-profitable employer's
demands for enormous concessions, the response of CAW officials
"had limited horizons and goals... refusing to accept the threatened
wage cuts, but planning for a plant closing that seemed inevitable."
The lockout ended with a closing that sent workers across Canada
and Quebec the message "that in the face of threats to cut wages in
half, you'd better not resist, or you'll lose your jobs."[33]

As this overview of the response of unions to the crisis and
some of its consequences suggests, labour's response has been, for
the most part, small-scale, low-key and timid. Militant resistance
to employer demands for concessions has been rare. When efforts
to beat back concessions have happened, they have mostly sought to
defend the past gains made by a specific group of unionized workers

---

30   John Peters, "Down in the Vale: Corporate Globalization, Unions on the
      Defensive, and the USW Local 6500 Strike in Sudbury, 2009-2010," *Labour/Le
      Travail* 66 (2010).
31   "Grande Manifestation pour un Budget Équitable pour Tous et Toutes,"
      http://www.nonauxhausses.org/2011/03/12/english-grande-manifestation-
      pour-un-budget-equitable-pour-tous-et-toutes/; David Mandel, "Fighting
      Austerity? The Public Sector and the Common Front in Quebec," *The Bullet*
      396 (July 25,2010), http://www.socialistproject.ca/bullet/396.php.
32   Dave Bleakney, "The Confines of Compromise," *Briarpatch Magazine* (November
      1,   2011),   http://briarpatchmagazine.com/articles/view/the-confines-of-com-
      promise. The Fredericton labour council did pass a resolution calling for a
      pan-Canadian day of action to support CUPW (copy in author's possession).
33   Herman Rosenfeld, "The Electro-Motive Lockout and Non-Occupation: What
      Did We Lose? What Can We Learn?," *The Bullet 615* (April 10, 2012), http://
      www.socialistproject.ca/bullet/615.php.

under attack without trying to make connections with what other workers, unionized and non-unionized, have been facing. Strikes have become rarer. There is no sign of workers changing how they organize strikes in order to make them more effective. Labour's political response has continued to rely on the well-worn methods of lobbying, advertizing and support for candidates at election time (in Canada, usually NDP but sometimes Liberal; in Quebec, usually BQ and PQ), backed up with occasional one-off demonstrations.[34] There have been a few partial exceptions to the general trend. These include the handful of workplace occupations noted, the US Steel struggle and the CAW's day of action for auto parts workers. The TYRLC leadership's work to build alliances between unions and community organizations and the rejuvenation of the Halifax-Dartmouth and District Labour Council must be noted too.[35] There have also been a few small educational initiatives designed to help unionists understand political economy.[36] However, these scattered partial exceptions have not had a significant impact on how the unionized minority of the working class has responded to the most severe crisis of capitalism since the 1930s.

It is useful to briefly compare this response with union responses to some earlier crises. In the early years of the Great Depression, "Most Canadian workers felt that ever-rising unemployment gave them little option but to accept whatever management threw at them, including plant closures, rationalization, deskilling, speed-up, intensified supervision, and wage cuts."[37] Time on strike as a per-centage of time worked in the years 1929-1931 was only slightly over 0.02%, even lower than the level in 2008-2011. Of the few strikes that did happen, many were by workers in unions affiliated to the radical Workers' Unity League, whose "most distinctive feature was a will-ingness to strike."[38] Closer to the present, the crisis of the mid-1970s that marked the end of the long post-war economic boom arrived at

---

[34]   See the CLC material for the 2011 federal election at http://betterchoice.ca.

[35]   On the TYRLC's efforts, see my *Canadian Labour in Crisis*, 32-33, 114-115, and on Halifax's labour council, 128.

[36]   On the education organized by the labour council in Vancouver, see Bill Saunders, "Workers Need Their Own Story Line," *Labour/Le Travail 64 (2009)*.

[37]   John Manley, "Canadian Communists, Revolutionary Unionism, and the 'Third Period': The Workers' Unity League, 1929-1935," *Journal of the Canadian Historical Association* 5, no. 1 (1994): 174.

[38]   Ibid., 176. Strike time calculated from "Number of strikes and lockouts."

a time when workers' militancy had been high for a decade. There were over 1000 strikes per year from 1974-1976, accounting for over 0.5% of time worked each of those years. In this context, demands for action pushed CLC officials to call a one-day general strike in October 1976 against the federal government's wage control policy in which approximately one million workers (mostly unionized) took part. However, taken as a whole the resistance led by labour officialdom was "fragmented and fairly inconsequential."[39] The CLC's response to the recession of the early 1980s was less militant than that of 1976: a 1981 demonstration in Ottawa of around 100 000 people.[40] There were over 1000 strikes per year from 1978-1981 as unionized workers tried to keep up with high inflation and resist concessionary demands. From 1976 to 1981, the number of wildcat strikes, in which workers defied the law (and usually union officials too) by striking during the term of a contract ranged from a low of 166 to a high of 242. Their significance is highlighted when contrasted with the number of such strikes in recent years: two in 2008, none in 2009, two in 2010 and one in 2011.[41] Even in the bleak recessionary years 1991-1993, the average annual number of strikes, 416 (of which an average of over 22 were wildcats), was over double that seen in recent years. The CLC also held another mass demonstration in Ottawa in May 1993 that drew as many as 100 000 people. Although its atmosphere was described by a London activist as "closer to that of a Labour Day picnic than to class struggle," recalling the very fact that it happened is a reminder that no pan-Canadian mass action of any kind by unionized workers has taken place to protest the effects of the current crisis.[42]

---

[39]   Bryan D. Palmer, *Working-Class Experience: Rethinking the History of Canadian Labour, 1800-1991* (Toronto: McClelland and Stewart Ltd., 1992), 344. The weak involvement of non-unionized workers in the 1976 "Day of Protest" is noted in Cy Gonick, "Where Do We Go From Here?," *Canadian Dimension* 11, no. 8 (1976). Strike data from "Chronological Perspective on Work Stoppages."

[40]   David McNally, "Mass Rally Shakes Ottawa," *Workers' Action* 72 (1981-82): 3.

[41]   Total strikes from "Chronological Perspective on Work Stoppages." Strikes during agreement from unpublished data provided by the Strategic Policy, Analysis and Workplace Information Directorate of Human Resources and Skills Development Canada.

[42]   Strike figures calculated from the same sources cited in the previous note. On the Ottawa demonstration, Gerry Rowe, letter in *Canadian Dimension*, September-October 1993, 3.

Explaining the Response

How do we explain why in Canada and Quebec the labour response to the current crisis of capitalism has taken the form we have seen to date? The most common line of explanation emphasizes how the crisis weakens unions. In the words of one academic:

> Far from representing an opportunity for labour, the financial crisis has so far dealt it a further blow by provoking massive layoffs in unionized industries like manufacturing and financial services throughout the world. Public sector workers, perhaps the unions' one remaining stronghold, are also being affected, because the need to cover public sector deficits caused by the rescue will lead to cuts in public spending and associated job losses.[43]

There is an important truth here: rising unemployment and workplace insecurity tends to intimidate workers. Fear of job loss is a powerful force that intimidates workers into accepting what their employers demand from them (it is important to remember that acceptance is not the same as active consent – for example, workers may give concessions to their employer simply because they feel that resistance will fail or make matters worse).

However, the economic impact of the current crisis is only a very partial explanation. There is much that it does not explain. For example, why have so few unionized workers facing the loss of their jobs responded by taking direct action? Why has the level of strikes since 2008 been significantly lower than during the recessions of the mid-1970s, early 1980s and early 1990s? The economic impact of the crisis does not explain why there has not even been a mass demonstration of the kind sponsored by the CLC in 1981 and 1993, let alone anything like the 1976 one-day general strike. Nor does it explain differences across countries in how labour has responded. In France, where unemployment is higher than in Canada, union-ized workers were at the forefront of massive protests against the

---

[43] Lucio Baccaro, "Does the Global Financial Crisis Mark a Turning Point for Labour?," *Socio-Economic Review* 8 (2010): 342. Financial service jobs in Canada are rarely unionized.

Sarkozy government's attack on pensions in the fall of 2010.[44] In short, economic crisis has an impact on unionized workers but does not by itself account for the nature of labour's response.

An alternative line of explanation points to the role of the union officialdom (the layer of elected and appointed officers and staff). For example, "time and time again, despite workers standing firm against employer attacks, union leaders have at best sat aside from the fight – leaving strikers literally for years – and at worst have sold their members terrible deals."[45] Or, in a more nuanced vein,

> Our unions and much of the leadership have lost faith in the capacity of workers to imagine and struggle for a different world. In doing so, they have too often been helping manage the decline of working-class living standards and freedoms, rather than leading in re-creating our union movement and helping forge a new socialist politics.[46]

This emphasis on what the union officialdom has (or has not) done since the onset of the crisis is important. The actions of top officials have had a definite influence on how labour has responded to the crisis. Managing decline is a good way of describing the stance of the officialdom has a whole. Some officials have indeed acted to dampen down opposition to employers' concessionary demands. At the same time, it is a mistake to imply, as does the first of the two sources quoted above, that in recent years workers have been determined to fight back while officials have not. This has been true in some cases, but there has not been a widespread push by workers to resist employers' attacks. It is also a problem to suggest that many officials have "lost faith" in workers' ability to fight for social change because belief in this has been almost

---

44 Jason Stanley, "The Fall Strike Wave in France: Battle over Public Pensions," *Against the Current* 151 (2011).

45 "From Hamilton to Cairo: Build the Resistance!," *Socialist Worker, Special Supplement,* (January 29, 2011) 1, http://socialist.ca/PDFs/SW_supplement_Hamilton.pdf.

46 Greg Albo and Bryan Evans, "Labour Day 2010: Austerity, Public Services and the Labour Movement," *The Bullet* 412 (September 6, 2010), http://www.socialistproject.ca/bullet/412.php.

nonexistent in the union officialdom for many decades.[47]

The union officialdom's actions have had a role in shaping labour's response to the crisis in Canada and Quebec. However, this and the economic impact of the crisis are not enough to explain the response. In my view, four interconnected forces have been key: the impact of three decades of capitalist restructuring on the working class, the weakness of the infrastructure of dissent, the condition unionism (including the officialdom) was in when the crisis arrived and political influences on unions.[48] I will discuss each in turn.

Capitalist Restructuring: Neoliberalism

Following the end of the long post-war economic boom in 1974-75, governments and capitalists scrambled to try to restore corporate profits and power. Eventually, "through a series of gyrations and chaotic experiments," they developed a way of attempting to reorganize capitalism to achieve their aims: neoliberalism.[49] There are many aspects of neoliberalism, but at its core is weakening or eliminating anything that acts as a barrier to capitalist profit-making. To implement the neoliberal reorganization of capitalism, employers and states stepped up the offensive against the working class that had begun in the mid-1970s.

Over the last three decades, millions of workers have lost their jobs as employers shut down or restructured their operations. Where it existed before, pattern bargaining, in which one bargaining deal is treated as the standard for settlements across an industry, has mostly been abandoned, leaving most unionized private sector workers to deal with each company separately. The loss of unionized jobs and the creation of many new jobs by non-unionized employers lowered union density in the private sector from 30%

---

47 Palmer, *Working-Class Experience.* Quebec during the 1960s and 1970s stands out as a time when a significant number of union officials were affected by radicalization taking place among workers, as can be observed in Sean Mills, *The Empire Within: Postcolonial Thought and Political Activism in Sixties Montreal* (Montreal: McGill-Queen's University Press, 2010),163-209.

48 What follows draws on *Canadian Labour in Crisis,* which discusses these issues in greater detail.

49 David Harvey, *A Brief History of Neoliberalism* (Oxford: Oxford University Press, 2005), 13. For an excellent analytical overview of neoliberalism, see McNally, *Global Slump*, 25-60.

in 1981 to 16% today.[50] Some work previously done by unionized workers has been outsourced to non-union firms. Employers have been able to make workers work harder and reorganize workplaces in ways that corrode the kinds of connections out of which solidarity is built. With average hourly real wages stagnant since the late 1970s,[51] many people have found themselves having to work longer hours to cover their costs. Many have also gone deeper into debt: the household debt to income ratio hit a record 150% in 2010, up from 93% in 1990.[52] Fewer wage-earners have full-time jobs without a fixed end-date; women and racialized workers are especially common among the ranks of the precariously employed. More people are working variable shifts, in the evening, overnight and on weekends. Access to unemployment insurance and social assistance has shrunk, along with benefit rates.[53]

In addition to these problems in the world of paid work, many in the working class are now faced with growing demands in other parts of their lives. Caregiving responsibilities have increased as elderly people live longer and health care cuts result in people being sent home sooner and sicker. This growing burden of care is borne disproportionately by women. Juggling different and often irregular paid work schedules along with child care; getting children to and from school and other activities; helping elderly parents – to name just some of the most common demands on the time of working-class people – has created a stressful time squeeze. Among other things, this harried way of living has "a way of suppressing

---

50 Remi Morissette, Grant Schellenberg, and Anick Johnson, "Diverging Trends in Unionization," *Perspectives on Labour and Income* 6, no. 4 (2005); Sharanjit Uppal, "Unionization 2010," *Perspectives on Labour and Income* 11, no. 10 (2010).

51 Ellen Russell and Mathieu Dufour, *Rising Profit Shared, Falling Wage Shares* (Toronto: Canadian Centre for Policy Alternatives, 2007).

52 "A Six Figure Family Day," Vanier Institute of the Family, (February 17, 2011), http://www.vifamily.ca/node/796.

53 Leah Vosko, "Precarious Employment: Towards an Improved Understanding of Labour Market Insecurity," in *Precarious Employment: Understanding Labour Market Insecurity in Canada,* ed. Leah F. Vosko (Montreal: McGill-Queen's University Press, 2006); Vivian Shalla, "Shifting Temporalities: Economic Restructuring and the Politics of Working Time," in *Work in Tumultuous Times: Critical Perspectives,* eds. Vivian Shalla and Wallace Clement (Montreal: McGill-Queen's University Press, 2007); Thom Workman, *If You're in My Way, I'm Walking: The Assault on Working People Since 1970* (Halifax: Fernwood Publishing, 2009), 99-120.

feelings and ideas that might challenge the status quo or the market culture" and "inhibits the individual from thinking about non-busybee issues" including "the state of the larger society."[54] Due to the weakening of unions and government-funded programs, more people are relying solely on individualistic or family-centred ways of coping with the growing demands they face.

With most of the working-class movement putting up at best weak resistance before the current crisis, and most of the union officialdom and the leaders of all the major political parties now accepting the neoliberal order, many working-class people have come to accept neoliberalism as "just the way things are." When people believe that the social conditions generated by capitalist restructuring are unchangeable, accept (consciously or not) that there is no alternative to neoliberalism and reject collective action, they become more "open to blaming others," such as immigrants and unions, for the problems in their lives, and to "supporting right-wing policies."[55] Ford's election as mayor of Toronto in 2010 is perhaps the starkest recent example of where this can lead.

All these effects of neoliberal restructuring have weakened the ability and the willingness of workers to organize collectively, to protest and resist. The current crisis has only intensified processes that have been underway for quite some time. This has powerfully influenced how unionized workers in Canada and Quebec have responded to the crisis.

A Very Weak Infrastructure of Dissent

The second key process shaping labour's response has been underway somewhat longer than neoliberal restructuring and is much less often recognized. Unions and other workers' organizations have always been fueled by people with critical understandings of the subordination of workers in capitalism. Equally important are the ways that workers have learned to organize collectively to try to improve their working and living conditions. A useful way of

---

54 Arlie Russell Hothschild, "Through the Crack of the Time Bind: From Market Management to Family Management," *Anthropology of Work Review* 28, no. 1 (2007): 6.

55 Meg Luxton and June Corman, *Getting By In Hard Times: Gendered Labour at Home and On the Job* (Toronto: University of Toronto Press, 2001), 256.

thinking about these critical sources of energy for working-class movements is the concept of the infrastructure of dissent: "the means of analysis, communication, organization and sustenance that nurture the capacity for collective action."[56] This involves both ways people interact and places where they do so. A thriving infrastructure of dissent produces worker activists with abilities to organize and analyze. People like this energize and sustain a movement. A weak infrastructure of dissent will lead to a movement that is weak at the grassroots, even if its formal organizations have many members and considerable financial resources.

From the mid-1800s to the mid-1900s, a significant number of people learned how to be activists through their participation in vibrant infrastructures of dissent. There were many elements to these infrastructures. Some union activists came together in formal or informal groups united by a common vision of what unions should be and do. The publications and educational efforts of radical left-wing political organizations rooted in the working class offered some workers at least a rudimentary analysis of history, capitalism and how to fight for a better world. Places that allowed people to cultivate bonds based in the shared hardships and pleasures of working-class life were another dimension of local infrastructures of dissent. These included halls, often set up by immigrants excluded from the dominant Anglo-Celtic culture of pre-1950 Canada, as well as particular bars and taverns. Certain neighbourhoods where many people were active in unions and other workers' organizations also sustained the capacity for collective action.

Working-class infrastructures of dissent crumbled during the second half of the twentieth century. Enormous damage was done by the right-wing political climate of the Cold War and the purges of supporters of the Communist Party and other "reds" from the working-class movement; the development of bureaucratic "responsible" unionism; changes to established working-class neighbourhoods during the economic boom in the decades after World War II in which new suburbs developed; and the widespread workplace shutdowns and dislocation since the mid-1970s.[57]

---

56   Alan Sears, "Creating and Sustaining Communities of Struggle: The Infrastructure of Dissent," *New Socialist* 52 (2005): 32.

57   Palmer, *Working-Class Experience;* Sears, "Creating and Sustaining."

The infrastructure of dissent in Canada and Quebec is now very weak. There are very few groupings of activists within unions who promote a different vision of unionism. The radical left is tiny and dispersed. It lacks roots among workers, being "very much centred in the university" with "a real disconnect from working people."[58] There are no institutions that develop workers' capacity for collective action on a significant scale, and fewer places where people from different workplaces, unions or other organizations can get to know each other face-to-face (although the Internet has created some new opportunities for communication). Few neighbourhoods cultivate workers' capacity for collective action. The kind of lively informal learning, discussion and networking that once took place in the working-class movement is now much less common. Lessons learned by previous generations of activists are rarely passed down.

With working-class "means of analysis, communication, organization and sustenance that nurture the capacity for collective action" so weak, most unionized workers have only had access to the ways of understanding the current crisis that have been on offer in the corporate media, which is dominated by neoliberal ideology. Almost all the explanations critical of neoliberalism that have had a hearing in the corporate media, such as those from economists associated with the Canadian Centre for Policy Alternatives, fail to appreciate that the crisis is a major crisis of capitalism; these are also the interpretations the union officialdom presents to members.[59] Similarly, very few unionized workers have encountered analysis that encourages strikes, occupations and other forms of mass direct action as part of a response to the crisis, let alone learned how to organize such collective action.[60] Horizontal communication that allows workers in different workplaces, sectors and unions to share experiences is extremely limited. There are very few rank-and-file networks that allow union activists to organize independently of the union officialdom. As a result, it has been very difficult for unionized workers to figure out for themselves what has been happening or to take independent initiatives. This has shaped labour's response.

---

[58] John Frieson (retired CUPW activist), November 19, 2008.
[59] For example, at the 2011 CLC convention session "What Derailed the Post-War Social Contract?" (http://www.canadianlabour.ca/convention/2011-convention/agenda/what-derailed-social-contract).
[60] See McNally, *Global Slump,* 87-88; Camfield, *Canadian Labour,* 117, 135-137.

Demobilized Bureaucratic "Responsible" Unionism[61]

Another key influence on how labour has responded has been the condition of union organization and the direction in which official leaderships have tried to steer the unions. Since the middle of the twentieth century, unionism in Canada and Quebec has, with a few exceptions, been contract unionism – a unionism focused on negotiating collective agreements with employers and enforcing contract rights through grievance and arbitration procedures rather than through direct action in the workplace. For the most part, it has also been a "responsible" unionism that accepts the legal ban on mid-contract strikes, sympathy strikes to support other workers and strikes for political objectives, treats parliamentary politics as the main or even the only legitimate kind of political action and endorses capitalism. Thanks to labour law, collective agreements and union constitutions, unionism is usually highly bureaucratic, meaning that it is structured by many formal rules that limit people's ability to determine what they do and how they do it. This is true for unions in which social unionism (which is concerned with both collective bargaining and social and political issues not directly connected to the workplace) is most influential as well as those in which business unionism (which is more conservative and narrowly focused on collective bargaining) is dominant.

Within the unions, there is an entrenched layer of officials (officers and staff) that has remained loyal to the legal framework of labour relations laid down in the 1940s. This officialdom, especially its top level, is preoccupied with preserving union institutions and its control within them as ends in themselves, regardless of what unions mean for members. Its usual approach is collaboration with the dominant class.[62]

---

[61]   This section draws on analysis developed in my *Canadian Labour*, which explores the relevant issues in more depth.

[62]   An example that highlights this was the response of the leadership of Amalgamated Transit Union Local 113 to the 2011 law that stripped Toronto public transit workers of the right to strike: an offer to renounce the option of a strike in the next bargaining round by sending unresolved issues to arbitration. See Bob Kinnear, "Presentation to the Standing Committee on General Government Regarding Bill 150," (March 9, 2011), http://wemovetoronto.ca/wp-content/uploads/2011/03/Bob-Kinnear-Presentation-on-Bill-150-March-9-2011.pdf.

From the early 1990s into the early years of the first decade of the new century, there were a number of important mobilizations and political debates that moved some unionized workers in a more activist and left-wing direction. These included the debate in Ontario labour about how to respond to the right turn by Bob Rae's NDP government, especially the 1993 Social Contract attack on public sector unions; the Days of Action and other resistance to the attacks of the Tory government that replaced Rae's; the 1996 pan-Canadian Women's March Against Poverty; a shift to the left by the CAW officialdom; the global justice movement of 1999-2002; mass anti-cuts protests and important public sector strikes in British Columbia between 2001 and 2005; and the 2003-2004 union fightback against Quebec's Liberal government.

The impact of these experiences was uneven across regions and unions. Their own specific limitations, the neoliberal offensive and the general rightward shift in the political climate that followed the terrorist attacks of September 11, 2001 helped put an end to them. As a result, when the Great Recession arrived the sections of the union movement that had for a time been more mobilized were no longer so. "The movement has turned more inward, so the lobbying becomes the actions" is how one insider described the situation.[63] Years before the crisis broke, most union officials who had previously favoured broader mobilizations had already returned to focusing on collective bargaining and lobbying politicians. A more inward-looking officialdom under pressure from employers and governments was more prone to disunity and destructive infighting.[64] In most unions, any debate that happens about politics is about whether workers should vote for the NDP across the board or instead vote either NDP or Liberal in order to defeat the Conservatives, not about the limits of the NDP and parliamentary politics for the working class. Most of the union officialdom was primed to respond to the crisis by accepting concessions, trying to defend their own particular union institution and moving to quell any rank-and-file efforts to fight back in ways that might challenge the

---

[63]   Anonymous, June 11, 2009.
[64]   For example, the conflict within UNITE HERE, discussed in detail in Steve Early, *The Civil Wars in US Labor: Birth of a New Workers' Movement or Death Throes of the Old?* (Chicago: Haymarket, 2011) and between the leaders of NUPGE and the CLC.

path of accommodation. The lack of space for discussing alternatives and the weakness of democratic membership control within unions are barriers to different responses by unionized workers to the austerity agenda. In understanding the low level of union activism, it is also worth noting that the officialdom is older, more male and whiter than the membership and has generally not made fighting racism and sexism or engaging younger workers a priority.

Political Influences on Unions

The last of the key forces shaping labour's response has been the influence of political parties within the unions, especially among officials and rank-and-file activists. Outside Quebec, the main political influence on the officialdom and activists comes from the NDP, although there is also significant Liberal influence in some unions. The NDP leadership is unquestioningly and exclusively committed to electoral politics. It opposes extra-parliamentary political action by unions, which it fears will hurt it at the ballot box. For example, provincial NDP leaders did not support the Ontario Days of Action (1995-1999) or the highly politicized, law-defying public sector strikes and "days of defiance" against the BC Liberal government of 2003-2005.[65] The NDP officialdom now accepts neoliberalism – witness the 2011 federal NDP election platform's pledges to keep the combined federal and provincial corporate tax rate below the rate in the US and cut small business taxes, and the record of the NDP in office since the early 1990s.[66] The Liberals are one of the two historic parties of the Canadian capitalist class. Under Jean Chretien, it was the Liberals who began the truly vigorous application of neoliberal policies at the federal level.[67] Within

---

65   David Camfield, "Assessing Resistance in Harris's Ontario, 1995-1999," in *Restructuring and Resistance: Canadian Public Policy in an Age of Global Capitalism,* eds. Mike Burke, Colin Mooers, and John Shields (Halifax: Fernwood Publishing, 2000); David Camfield, "Neoliberalism and Working-Class Resistance in British Columbia: The Hospital Employees' Union Struggle, 2002-2004," Labour/Le Travail 57 (2006); Jim Herring, *Labour, the NDP and Our Communities* (Vancouver: Solidarity Caucus, 2003).

66   Bryan Evans, "The New Democratic Party in the Era of Neoliberalism," in *Rethinking the Politics of Labour in Canada,* eds. Stephanie Ross and Larry Savage (Halifax: Fernwood Publishing, 2012).

67   Stephen McBride, *Paradigm Shift: Globalization and the Canadian State* (Halifax: Fernwood Publishing, 2001), 82-100.

Quebec, the main political influence within unions is that of the Parti Quebecois and Bloc Quebecois. These are neoliberal nationalist parties that cultivate both union and corporate support.[68]

However much the leaders of the NDP, Liberals and PQ/BQ compete with each other for votes at election time, they share a common belief that the only way to make political change is through the ballot box. To the extent that these party leaderships have influence within unions, they direct unionists' concerns about problems they cannot or have been unable to address into party activity. This has the effect of channeling energies away from efforts to mobilize workers, including extra-parliamentary political action against the effects of the economic crisis. With the NDP leadership now part of the neoliberal consensus that defines official politics in Canada and Quebec, it has not encouraged any criticism that digs deeper than Conservative or Liberal policies to question neoliberalism, not to mention capitalism itself. As for the radical left, it is now much too small to have any impact on labour's response.

The future of working-class politics

The term working-class politics as I use it here does not refer to any and all political actions by workers. A CAW document produced during the union's short-lived left turn described the central idea of working-class politics as being about:

> developing the working class into a political force: one that is independent of business, oppositional to the status quo, confident enough to counter the dominant ideas in society with an alternative common sense, and able to combine the defence of working people in their daily struggles with a longer term vision. Working class politics is, in short, about building a movement for social change.[69]

---

[68] Jacques B. Gélinas, "Comment le PQ a Bifurqué à Droite: Place Libre Pour une Véritable Gauche au Québec," in *L'Avenir est à Gauche: Douze Contributions Pour un Renouvellement de la Gauche au Québec,* ed. Pierre Mouterde (Montreal: Écosociété, 2008).

[69] Canadian Auto Workers, *Working-Class Politics in the 21st Century* (2000), http://caw.ca/crisis1/index.asp.

This is very different from the kind of politics that simply urges workers to vote for a party, such as the CLC's 2011 brochure that encouraged "working families" to think about voting for an MP and a party in the federal election as like "hiring someone to work for your family."[70] It is also very different from the NDP leadership's politics, which have never been about developing the working class into a force for social change. Today, the forces of working-class politics in Canada are, unfortunately, weaker than they have been for over one hundred years.[71] There is no significant political organization in Canada committed to working-class politics, only tiny radical left groups; in Quebec, a minority of the members of the small left-wing party Quebec Solidaire support some kind of working-class politics.[72]

Historically, there have been many different incarnations of working-class politics, including the most left-wing version of social democracy and various kinds of radical and revolutionary socialism (both Marxist and anarchist).[73] Its supporters have disagreed about many important questions concerning objectives, strategy, tactics, what kind of political party or organization should be built (if any) and how to relate to struggles against sexism, racism, heterosexism and other forms of oppression. Yet they have all agreed that the struggles of workers themselves are important for changing society. This has led them to advocate extra-parliamentary political action by workers.

The weakness of working-class politics in Canada and Quebec has been exposed by how unions, community organizations and the broad Left have responded to the economic crisis. Not only has the ruling class been able to make workers pay for the crisis through austerity policies, layoffs, wage and benefit cuts and other

---

70   http://www.canadianlabour.ca/sites/default/files/pdfs/leaflet-hiringcommit-tee.pdf (accessed April 12, 2011).
71   This has generally been ignored in recent discussions of union renewal. For example, it is not addressed in Pradeep Kumar and Christopher Schenk, eds., *Paths to Union Renewal: Canadian Experiences* (Peterborough: Broadview, 2006).
72   On the radical left in Canada, see *Canadian Labour*, 141 n51. For some observations about Quebec Solidaire, see Richard Fidler, "'Beyond Capitalism? Quebec Solidaire Launches Debate On Its Program for Social Transformation," *The Bullet 491* (April 12, 2011), http://www.socialistproject.ca/bullet/491.php.
73   Hal Draper's "The Two Souls of Socialism" (http://www.marxists.org/archive/draper/1966/twosouls/) offers insight into them, though its contrast of socialism from above with socialism from below cannot do justice to all dimensions of radical politics and it mistakenly excludes all anarchism (rather than many versions of anarchism) from the socialism from below tradition.

concessions, but they have not yet had to deal with much opposition or pay a high political price for forcing through their preferred measures. Although some people expected or hoped that the crisis would revive working-class politics, so far this has not happened.

On the radical left, some have argued that a key lesson of the current crisis is that a new anti-capitalist party or political organization committed to working-class politics must be built.[74] Such an organization would be active both within and outside unions; in the unions, its members would, among other things, push for democracy, militant action, active solidarity with unionized and non-unionized people under attack and popular education about the nature of capitalism and the need for a different kind of society.

A very strong case can be made that such a political organization is needed, provided that the primary commitment of its members is, as British socialist Sheila Cohen has put it, "building the movement" not "building the party itself."[75] However, arguing that this kind of organization is necessary is not the same as demonstrating that it is possible to create one in Canada or Quebec today. Most advocates of such an organization ignore the question of what conditions are required in order to create a viable political organization that many people who want radical social change will want to join or work with. Most also tend to ignore or skim over the history of previous attempts to build political groups committed to working-class politics in one form or another and what can be learned from these experiences. Since the early 1980s, when the main socialist groups built over the previous two decades collapsed, no radical political organization has managed to replicate even their modest achievements.[76]

---

[74] For example, Greg Albo, Sam Gindin, and Leo Panitch, *In and Out of Crisis: The Global Financial Meltdown and Left Alternatives* (Oakland: PM, 2010), 118-119.

[75] Sheila Cohen, "Starting All Over From Scratch? A Plea for 'Radical Reform' of Our Own Movement," http://thecommune.co.uk/2011/02/16/starting-all-over-from-scratch-a-plea-for-%E2%80%9Cradical-reform%E2%80%9D-of-our-own-movement/. A strong argument for political organization is made in David McNally, *Another World is Possible: Globalization and Anti-Capitalism*, 2nd ed. (Winnipeg: Arbeiter Ring, 2006), 386-391.

[76] Most of these organizations have suffered from the delusion that they were a party or the beginnings of one, as well as from dogmatism, a lack of democracy and the sectarian attitude that building the group is more important than advancing the working-class movement. Most have also had at least some illusions in the Stalinist bureaucratic dictatorships. For a few remarks and references about the largest of the groups, Quebec's Maoists, see Camfield, *Canadian Labour,* 88 n10.

A crucial reason for the failure of the "party-building" groups of the 1970s and later efforts has been the weakness of the infrastructure of dissent discussed earlier. This weakness and the global decline of the left that has taken place since the 1970s[77] have meant that, despite the neoliberal assault, few people have recognized the need for working-class politics and even fewer have had the skills needed to organize successfully to build support for them. Today, there are still supporters of working-class politics (most identify as feminists, anti-capitalists, socialists or anarchists rather than as "supporters of working-class politics"), most of whom are not affiliated to any radical left grouping. But currently there are not thousands of people ready to get involved with a new radical political organization, except perhaps in Quebec.[78]

Historical experience and developments in countries where support for working-class politics has grown in recent decades suggests that an upsurge of working-class struggle is a necessary (but not sufficient) condition for the arrival on the political scene of a new layer of people open to this kind of politics. "Without a rebirth of mass struggle, it is impossible to get much beyond the sphere of small radical groups, some of whom [sic] do good work, others of whom [sic] are more intent on squabbling."[79] Supporters of working-class politics should therefore make it their priority to do whatever they can to contribute to such a rebirth by working to change unions from below, build new workers' organizations and conduct radical political education.[80]

---

[77]   See my *Canadian Labour*, 81.

[78]   The remarkable 2012 Quebec student strike that at the time of writing had grown into a broader popular movement has undoubtedly radicalized many people, especially young people. However, the absence of political strike action by unionized workers, despite appeals for it from students and some support for it among union members, will likely make working-class politics not very compelling for many newly-radicalized people. The role of top union officers in negotiating the deal to end the student strike that was massively rejected by students in early May (see René Charest, "C'est le Temps de Faire du Syndicalisme Autrement!," *Presse-Toi à Gauche!* (May 15, 2012), http://www.pressegauche.org/spip.php?article10319) has not gone unnoticed by student radicals.

[79]   McNally, *Global Slump*, 178. The experience of France is instructive: support for working-class politics has increased since 1995, years in which many people have participated in movements against neoliberalism. See Stathis Kouvelakis, *La France en Révolte: Luttes Sociales et Cycles Politiques* (Paris: Textuel, 2007). In Quebec, social struggles stimulated working-class politics in the late 1960s and 1970s. See Mills, *Empire Within* and Pierre Beaudet, *On a Raison de se Revolter* (Montreal: Écosociété, 2008).

[80]   See my *Canadian Labour*, 118-127, 138.

NOTES ON CONTRIBUTORS

Jonah Butovsky is associate professor of sociology labour studies at Brock University. He has published articles on Canadian political values, migrant agricultural workers in the Niagara Region, and on the presentation of survey data in the press. He is involved in the labour movement, and is on the executive of the Niagara and District Labour Council.

David Camfield is an associate professor in labour studies at the University of Manitoba. His book, from Fernwood, is *Canadian Labour in Crisis: Reinventing the Workers' Movement.*

Akhter Faroque is associate professor of economics at Laurentian University, and has taught at Guelph, Brock, and the University of Toronto. He is strongly interested in the economic problems of developing countries, particularly Bangladesh, where he was born and educated to the M.A. level. Since receiving his Ph. D in economics from McMaster University, Dr. Faroque's research has focussed on applied macroeconomics. He has published in several scholarly journals including *Applied Economics* and *Empirical Economics.* Since the global recession of 2008-2009 he has been particularly concerned with financial regulation, income distribution, and other crisis-related issues.

Tim Fowler is a Ph.D. candidate in political science and political economy at Carleton University. His research focuses on the CAW's response to neoliberalism and globalization. He currently teaches political science, sociology, and labour studies at Brock University. He has previously published on Canadian labour's response to the Great Recession and the need for a working-class based socialist union renewal in Canada.

Brian K. MacLean is professor of economics at Laurentian University, where he has been chair of the department of economics. Dr. MacLean was born and raised in Charlottetown, Prince Edward Island, but speaks Japanese as a second language and has been a visiting professor at Hokkaido University and at Saitama University in Japan. His publications include the prescient edited volume *Out of Control? Canada in an Unstable Financial World* (Lorimer, 1999), and his recent research includes topics such as the implications for macroeconomics of the global financial crisis and recession. He has taught labour economics for many years, and has been a long-standing steering committee member of the Progressive Economics Forum.

Stephen McBride is the Canada Research Chair in Public Policy and Globalization and professor of political science at McMaster University. He is the author of *Not Working: State, Unemployment and Neo-conservatism in Canada* (1992) which won the 1994 Smiley prize, and *Paradigm Shift: Globalization and the Canadian State* (2001; 2nd edition 2005). He is the co-author of *Dismantling a Nation: Canada and the New World Order* (1993; 2nd edition 1997) and of *Private Affluence, Public Austerity: Economic Crisis and Democratic Malaise in Canada* (2011). His current research is focussed on the impact of globalization on the state, and the political economy of labour and the welfare state.

James Meades is a Ph.D. candidate in sociology at Carleton University. He is a co-president of CUPE local 4600, representing teaching assistants and contract instructors at Carleton.

Bill Murnighan is a National Representative in the Research Department of the CAW.

Mathew Nelson is a Ph.D. candidate in political science at Carleton University. He is a co-president of CUPE local 4600, representing teaching assistants and contract instructors at Carleton.

Murray E.G. Smith is professor of sociology and labour studies at Brock University. He has been active on the socialist left in Canada since the 1970s, participating in a variety of campaigns and progressive movements for social change. He is the author of *Invisible Leviathan: The Marxist Critique of Market Despotism beyond Postmodernism* (1994), the co-author of *Culture of Prejudice* (2003), and the editor of *Early Modern Social Theory: Selected Interpretive Readings* (1998). His articles on Marxism, political economy and social theory have appeared in such journals as *The Canadian Review of Sociology, Science & Society, Labour/Le Travail, Historical Materialism*, and *Review of Radical Political Economics*. His most recent book is *Global Capitalism in Crisis: Karl Marx & the Decay of the Profit System* (Fernwood 2010).

Jim Stanford is an economist in the research department of the Canadian Auto Workers, Canada's largest private-sector trade union. He received his Ph.D. in economics in 1995 from the New School for Social Research in New York. He also holds economics degrees from Cambridge University in the U.K. (1986) and the University of Calgary (1984). Jim is the author of *Paper Boom* (James Lorimer & Co., 1999), the co-author (with Tony Biddle) of *Economics for Everyone: A Short Guide to the Economics of Capitalism* (Fernwood, 2008) and co-editor (with Leah F. Vosko) of *Challenging the Market: The Struggle to Regulate Work and Income* (McGill-Queen's University Press, 2004).

Heather Whiteside is a Ph.D. candidate in the department of political science at Simon Fraser University. She is the co-author of *Private Affluence, Public Austerity: Economic Crisis and Democratic Malaise in Canada.*

www.ingramcontent.com/pod-product-compliance
Lightning Source LLC
Chambersburg PA
CBHW020350270326
41926CB00007B/376